# ULYSSES S. GRANT
# ON LEADERSHIP

# ULYSSES S. GRANT ON LEADERSHIP

*Executive Lessons from the Front Lines*

JOHN A. BARNES

**FORUM**
*An Imprint of Prima Publishing*

*To my wife, Mary,*
*for whose love I live*

FORUM
An Imprint of Prima Publishing
3000 Lava Ridge Court
Roseville, CA 95661

PRIMA PUBLISHING, FORUM, and colophons are either trademarks or registered trademarks of Prima Communications Inc., registered with the United States Patent and Trademark Office.

Barnes, John A.
Ulysses S. Grant on leadership : executive lessons from the front lines /
John A. Barnes.
p.  cm. — (On leadership series)
ISBN 0-7615-2662-5
1. Grant, Ulysses S. (Ulysses Simpson), 1822–1885—Military leadership.
2. Generals—United States—Biography. 3. Command of troops. 4. Leadership—Case studies. 5. Management—United States—Case studies. I. Title. II. Series.
E672.B35 2001
658.4'092—dc21                                                00-068197

01 02 03 04 HH 10 9 8 7 6 5 4 3 2 1
Printed in the United States of America

FORUM books are available at special discount for bulk purchases for educational, business, or sales promotion use.
For details, contact Special Sales
Prima Publishing
1-800-632-8676, ext. 4444

Visit us online at www.primaforum.com

# CONTENTS

# PREFACE

On December 19, 1990, Secretary of Defense Richard Cheney, accompanied by Joint Chiefs of Staff Chairman Colin Powell, arrived in Riyadh, Saudi Arabia. Four months earlier, Iraqi strongman Saddam Hussein had invaded and annexed the Persian Gulf sheikdom of Kuwait on Saudi Arabia's northeastern frontier, declaring it his country's "19th province." President George Bush had declared the invasion "will not stand" and had dispatched U.S. and allied forces to the vital region. Their mission had been changed in November from merely ensuring that Saddam did not continue his aggression into Saudi Arabia and its critical oil fields to ejecting the Iraqi forces from the land they had occupied.

The man in charge of this massive effort was U.S. Army Gen. H. Norman Schwarzkopf, a West Point graduate with more than thirty years in the army and two tours in Vietnam under his belt. Cheney and Powell wanted to hear from "Stormin' Norman"—the nickname the media instantly conferred upon the man of whom almost no one outside the army had heard just a few months earlier—exactly how he intended to accomplish this mission.

Unlike so many military officers, who liked to lay out a range of options from which their civilian superiors could choose, Schwarzkopf presented a single plan. It consisted of four stages: three in the air and one on the ground. It was the last that concerned Cheney, Powell, and the president the most. Political demonstrations were heating up back home and political opponents in Congress and the media were warning of "another Vietnam" in the making. Large-scale casualties, such as those that seemed certain to be incurred by any frontal assault on the formidable defenses Saddam was constructing along the Kuwaiti frontier with Saudi Arabia, would be a political catastrophe—even if they did ultimately result in the liberation of Kuwait.

Although ready for the worst—Schwarzkopf's top medical officer was prepared for 20,000 wounded and 7,000 killed—the commanding general had no intention of hitting Saddam exactly where the Iraqi strongman expected the blow would fall.

"Key portions of the grand campaign had been developed by a half dozen junior officers in their second year at the Army command and general staff college at Fort Leavenworth," writes author Bob Woodward in his book on the Gulf War, *The Commanders*. "These majors and lieutenant colonels, nicknamed the 'Jedi Knights,' had been sent to Saudi Arabia to apply the elements of advanced maneuver warfare—probing, flanking, surprise initiative, audacity—to the war plan."

Where did Schwarzkopf's "Jedi Knights" get these ideas?

Working in a small top-secret corner of Schwarzkopf's headquarters, they had applied the principles of the Army's unclassified 200-page operations manual. Chapters 6 and 7 on offensive operations were built around concepts established in General [Ulysses S.] Grant's 1863 Civil War campaign at Vicksburg. Instead of attacking directly into enemy fortifications, Grant sent troops in a wide maneuver around the Confederate front line, and then attacked from the side and rear. This indirect approach was deemed the best way to beat Saddam.

Indeed it proved to be, for the resemblances between the Vicksburg Campaign and Desert Storm are nothing short of uncanny. (Lt. Col. H. Parker Hills of the Mississippi National Guard has elaborated on the similarities in a presentation he makes to visitors at the Vicksburg National Military Park.) Like Grant, who used cavalry raids into Mississippi's interior to distract Vicksburg's Confederate defenders from the actual direction of his advance, Schwarzkopf used the threat of amphibious landings on the Kuwaiti coast to misdirect Saddam Hussein's attention away from the Allied buildup in the far west. Like Grant, Schwarzkopf intended to come at his objective via a lightly guarded "back door": the famous "left hook" through the Iraqi desert. (The CIA had told Schwarzkopf the route was impossible.) This movement caught Saddam as much by surprise as Grant's unexpected crossing of the river south of Vicksburg had bamboozled Vicksburg commander John C. Pemberton.

The two campaigns also had one other similarity: both won great prizes at quite a low cost. Grant took Vicksburg with fewer than 10,000 men dead, wounded, captured, and missing. Only 146 Americans died in Desert Storm, and just a few hundred were wounded. The specter of "another Vietnam," where nearly 60,000 Americans died, proved, thankfully, unfounded, thanks in part to the man Norman Schwarzkopf calls his personal hero, Ulysses S. Grant.

"Grant is worth knowing," said Mark Twain, who knew him well. We can be grateful that Norman Schwarzkopf agreed with the great novelist who published Grant's justly famed memoirs. But as Twain's comment implies, even Grant's contemporaries did not give the general his due, a shortfall that continues to this day. Robert E. Lee, whose elevation to near godlike stature began even before his death in 1870, continues to enjoy a cult following. On the surface, this is difficult to understand. Grant was far and away the best general in the Civil War on either side. For those who doubt this, consider these facts. Three enemy armies surrendered to Ulysses S. Grant: one each at Ft. Donelson, Vicksburg, and Appomattox. William T. Sherman had the next best record,

capturing one enemy army at the end of the war. Number of
Union armies that surrendered to Robert E. Lee: none.

Why, then, is Grant the Rodney Dangerfield of American
history, seemingly never getting any respect? The reasons lie
in Grant himself, his circumstances, and his times. Reserved
and modest by nature and reluctant to blow his own horn,
Grant thus allowed others to define him. While many assessed
him generously, others were not so kind. Grant's very successes caused jealous fellow Union army officers, both during
the war and afterward, to denigrate his abilities and smear his
reputation (his supposed fondness for drink being a favorite
topic). Grant's postwar entry into politics also embroiled him
in controversies that invited further criticism. Meanwhile, a
"Lost Cause" ideology was taking hold among Southern die-
hards who were eager to brand Grant a mindless "butcher"
who simply buried the Confederacy beneath overwhelming
numbers and resources. Grant's reputation was caught between these forces as if caught in a vise.

A fair-minded study of Grant, however, reveals a man
whose methods of management and leadership are well worth
examining by those who aspire to rise within any organization. As a general, Grant was anything but a plodder. Rather,
he learned to "think outside the box" and won the Civil War
by daring and unconventional strategies. In the Vicksburg
campaign of May to June 1863, he pioneered the style of warfare that, 80-odd years later, would be dubbed the blitzkrieg:
fast-moving troop columns unburdened by slow wagon trains
of supplies. He rejected the "on to Richmond" mentality so
prevalent among other Union generals and instead targeted
enemy armies rather than points on a map. Unlike George B.
McClellan, who whined incessantly for more troops and supplies and who insisted the responsibility would not be his if he
did not receive them and defeat resulted, Grant made do with
what he had and accepted responsibility for the outcome.

To implement his vision, Grant assembled an able team of lieutenants who were as innovative as he himself was: Gens. William T. Sherman, Philip H. Sheridan, James B. McPherson, James Wilson, and George Thomas and Adm. David Dixon Porter. He even managed to work well with (or at least work with) people he personally disliked, such as Gens. George G. Meade and Benjamin Butler. When he had to get rid of someone, such as the inordinately ambitious Gen. John McClernand, he bided his time until McClernand's own behavior made his removal uncontroversial.

He learned to deal with difficult superiors as well as subordinates. He managed to outlast (and eventually outrank) the insufferable Henry W. Halleck. He dealt diplomatically with a man sent to spy on him and eventually co-opted the spy. In his dealings with Abraham Lincoln, Grant never forgot who was boss.

Though he had a horror of public speaking, Grant was an effective communicator. His orders and directives to his subordinates are models of clarity and purpose. In making his plans, he consulted his subordinates freely and openly while reserving final decisions for himself. And while plans could be changed, the objective of the plan almost never was.

Above all, as military historian J. F. C. Fuller has pointed out, he possessed a tremendous reserve of common sense. "His common sense was such that he possessed the inestimable gift of being able to learn from his own mistakes, as well as from the mistakes of others," Fuller wrote. "He was never bound by traditions, he had a horror of formalities. His common sense was due to his reasoning nature, he always had a reason for what he did. Chance and luck he didn't believe in. . . . This is wisdom."

In these pages, I have not attempted an abbreviated biography of Grant or undertaken an original study. Rather, I have sifted the voluminous secondary literature in order to glean the lessons that can be learned from Grant's successes and his failures.

Many will question my judgments and conclusions or the entire validity of my approach. For example, many will say, to paraphrase T. Harry Williams in the preface of his master-piece, *Lincoln and His Generals*, that the book contains too much McClellan and not enough Lee. Early on, I decided to generally avoid explicit comparisons of Lee and Grant. This was because, first, many have been there before and done it far better than I feel qualified to do. Second, Robert E. Lee, despite his ultimate defeat, was undeniably a brilliant and ac-complished commander whose leadership style can be studied with profit. From the point of view of a manager, I believe there is far more to be learned by comparing the failure of George B. McClellan with the success of Ulysses S. Grant, since both men held the same position as general in chief of the Union armies at different points in the war.

In place of footnotes, I have sought to credit within the text those on whose scholarship I have drawn. In places, this might not have been possible, though I cite all sources in my bibliography. Of particular assistance has been the Ulysses S. Grant Home Page (www.mscomm.com/~ulysses), hosted by Candace Scott, which features a remarkable collection of of-ten little known writings by and about Grant, as well as an excellent message board that allowed me to bounce ideas and conclusions off of some real Grantophiles. Also of great as-sistance was the Web site of the Ulysses S. Grant Association (www.lib.siu.edu/projects/usgrant), which features a search-able copy of Grant's memoirs online.

No doubt errors have crept into the text, in spite of my own efforts and those of my editors. Needless to say, all errors are my responsibility alone.

# "NO TURNING BACK"

## The Wilderness of Virginia,
## May 4–7, 1864

———

AT 3:00 A.M. on the clear, starry morning of May 4, 1864, Colonel George Chapman led the dismounted troopers of his 3rd Indiana Cavalry down the slope that formed the north bank of the Rapidan River. Below them lay their objective, the crossing point known as Germanna Ford. Moving as quietly as possible, the men waded into the waist-deep stream and scrambled up the Confederate-held south bank. Primed for action, the Hoosiers were pleasantly surprised when their opponents, the pickets of the 1st North Carolina Cavalry, scattered into the darkness.

"We're stealing a march on old man Lee," said one Union veteran.

The rest of Chapman's command, the vanguard of Brigadier General James H. Wilson's 3rd Cavalry Division, made the crossing rapidly and began pushing inland. Behind it came engineers, whose horse-drawn wagons were laden with bridging equipment. An hour and a half later, two 220-foot-long wood and canvas pontoon bridges 50 feet apart were spanning the stream. The assembled mass of Major General Gouverneur K. Warren's V Corps of the Union's Army of the Potomac, snaking northward for miles along the roads leading from the ford, began crossing.

A few miles downstream, a similar scene was taking place at a spot called Ely's Ford, where cavalrymen under Brigadier General Alfred T. A. Torbert had cleared the way for Major General Winfield Scott Hancock's II Corps.

The Union's Army of the Potomac, at 118,000 strong the mightiest host ever assembled for battle in the Western Hemisphere, was on the move again.

It had seen this ground before, or at least those soldiers who were not raw recruits had. The Rapidan, a tributary of the longer Rappahannock, formed part of the river line that divided Union-held northern Virginia from the southern portion of the state still under Confederate control. Almost precisely one year earlier, Major General Joseph "Fighting Joe" Hooker had effected an almost precisely similar crossing and, initially, had achieved considerable success. But the effort met with disaster.

As with any defeat, there were numerous reasons. If only a Confederate cannonball hadn't struck the army's headquarters, knocking Fighting Joe unconscious on the front porch of the Chancellor House that gave the battle of Chancellorsville its name. If only someone in authority had taken seriously the reports of a daring Confederate movement around the Federal army's exposed right flank, thus preventing Confederate lieutenant general Thomas "Stonewall" Jackson from surprising and shattering the Union army's XI Corps. If only Hooker's newfangled telegraphic communications system had worked as advertised. If only the Union cavalry had cut the Confederate's railroad lifeline, as it was supposed to have done, and on and on.

Whatever the reason or reasons, the campaign had ended in what the troops called a "skedaddle" back across the river. It was a by-now-familiar posture for the Federal army. The same kind of retreat had been necessary six months before Chancellorsville, when another commander, Major General Ambrose E. Burnside, had pointlessly hurled wave after wave of unprotected troops against Confederate riflemen lined up six deep behind a stone wall at the town of Fredericksburg. It was the most lopsided major battle of the war, with the Union suffering thousands of casualties against a comparative handful for its Southern opponents. The primary legacy of the magnificently whiskered Burnside, it turned out, would be the word "sideburns."

Adding to the Federals' frustration was the fact that without exception they outnumbered their Rebel opponents by more than three to two and sometimes by as many as two to one. Materially, there was little comparison between the foes. The Army of the Potomac was vastly better equipped and fed than the army that was barring its way to the Southern capital of Richmond. Its artillery had, in most respects, always been superior to that of the Southern gunners. Even in cavalry, where the bluecoat troopers sat more and had better mounts than the graybacks, the latter, under the leadership of the dashing Major General J. E. B. Stuart, had literally run rings around the Union army.

"Leadership." In that word, many in the North had sensed for quite some time, lay the key to the problem. And President Abraham Lincoln was foremost among them.

He was well aware of the advantages the North enjoyed in numbers of men and matériel. For three years, he had vainly sought a commander who could take the Union army in hand and lead it to victory against the Confederacy, which had been formed when the Southern states that constituted it saw the control they had hitherto exercised over national politics slipping from their grasp. Victory would vindicate not merely the American form of government, Lincoln believed, but also the cause of democratic republicanism everywhere. Losers of elections would have to abide by the results and not be allowed to simply deal themselves out of the game.

And then there was slavery. At first, Lincoln sought to play down the extinction of this barbarous anachronism as one of the North's war goals because he was wary of alienating conservative opinion in the North. But as Southern obstinacy caused the war to drag on and the casualty lists to lengthen, the idea that the South could rebel and then, perhaps, one day even return to the Union without risk to its chattel property struck increasing numbers of Northerners as abhorrent. From a more practical standpoint, emancipation would give millions of Negroes, free as well as slave, hard reasons to back the Union cause and swell the depleted ranks of its army. At the same time, it would discourage the governments of Great Britain and France from intervening in support of a slaveholding government.

The abolition of slavery, therefore, was now a Union war goal. To be made fact, however, emancipation required final victory. But who would provide it?

Lincoln had certainly looked hard enough, and, in the Virginia theater at least, had come up empty. First came Irvin McDowell, a West Pointer of no particular distinction, who had provided the North's first defeat at Bull Run. He was replaced by the man who would create and name the Army of the Potomac, George Brinton ("Little Mac") McClellan.

Little Mac did indeed train and equip a magnificent army, but he seemed loath to actually use it. Excessively cautious, he found endless reasons for delay. Prodded by Lincoln, McClellan finally advanced on Richmond via the peninsula between the York and James Rivers, a move that ended with McClellan's army hunkered down under the protection of its gunboats at Harrison's Landing.

Instead of relieving the general of his command, Lincoln undertook the curious strategy of relieving the command of its general. The president brought in a high-handed, loud-talking Western general named John Pope, gave him most of McClellan's army, and then saw Pope and it promptly thrashed at Second Bull Run. With little choice, Lincoln gave the Army of the Potomac back to McClellan, who was able to check the first Confederate invasion of the North at Antietam Creek, near Sharpsburg, Maryland, in the bloodiest single day of the war. That was enough of a victory for Lincoln to issue his preliminary Emancipation Proclamation, but not enough to save McClellan's career. Lincoln sacked him in November 1862, saying he had a terminal case of "the slows."

But new commanders brought no relief. Burnside and Hooker failed the test. "My God! What will the country say?" the president had exclaimed after hearing of Hooker's decision to hightail it back across the Rappahannock following Chancellorsville. Later, when Hooker's successor, Major General George G. Meade, failed to follow up his brilliant defensive victory at Gettysburg with the destruction of Lee's army, Lincoln's patience snapped.

"There is bad faith somewhere," the president exclaimed to navy secretary Gideon Welles on July 14, 1863, as the two men crossed the White House lawn from the War Department after hearing the soul-crushing news that Meade had allowed the Army of Northern Virginia to successfully escape south across the Potomac. "What does it mean, Mr. Welles? Great God, what does it mean?" Robert Lincoln, the president's eldest son, who was visiting the White House from Harvard during this period, later recorded that this was the only day he ever saw his father cry.

The South, by contrast, seemed to possess leadership in abundance. True, Stonewall Jackson was now off the chessboard, dead after being accidentally shot by his own men at the climax of his great flank attack at Chancellorsville. But Stuart was still very much on the scene, as was James Longstreet, who commanded the army's other infantry corps. And then there was the man who towered above them all: General Robert Edward Lee.

The aristocratic Lee was already a legend. Refusing Lincoln's offer of command of the Federal armies at the war's start, he chose instead to offer his services to his native state of Virginia. After wasting Lee in staff jobs for more than a year, Confederate president Jefferson Davis named him to command on June 1, 1862, following the wounding of his predecessor, the retreat-minded General Joseph E. Johnston. In a mere twelve weeks, Lee carried the war from the gates of Richmond to the gates of Washington and beyond.

True, he had tasted defeat at Gettysburg, but few in the South held this against him. Indeed, he had worked miracles with the limited resources available to him, had taken chances that would have daunted a riverboat gambler, and—so far— had bought the Confederacy time. His men idolized "Marse Robert" almost beyond description. "I would charge Hell itself for that old man" was the typical comment of one of his veterans.

Lee's abilities had won him grudging respect in the North. "Are you not overcautious when you assume you can not do what the enemy is constantly doing?" was Lincoln's almost plaintive query in one of his last desperate efforts to goad McClellan into action. "Should you not claim to be at least his equal in prowess, and act upon the claim?"

But McClellan did not act and so was consigned to the ash heap of history. Lee had seemingly intimidated him, as he had intimidated all the other Union commanders. Up until now, anyway.

The army that moved south across the Rapidan at dawn on May 4 was technically still under the command of Meade.

But it was unquestionably under new management, in the person of Ulysses S. Grant.

A Westerner by both birth and reputation, Grant had been winning victories in the lower-profile Western theater of operations while Lee and his lieutenants were monopolizing the headlines in the East. Grant provided the North's only early victory, in February 1862, when he led a combined land and naval operation that resulted in the capture of two Confederate forts on the Tennessee and Cumberland Rivers. He almost became a cropper at Shiloh, however, where Confederates surprised Grant's men in their camps. By keeping his head and rallying his troops, though, he turned what looked like certain defeat into decisive victory.

Then there was Vicksburg, the Mississippi River fortress town that had prevented the Union from controlling the Father of Waters and cutting the Confederacy in two. It finally fell to Grant on July 4, 1863, after a single-minded campaign that stretched over many months. For an encore, he lifted the Rebel siege of Chattanooga in November of that year, setting the stage for the campaign against Atlanta by his ablest lieutenant, Major General William T. Sherman.

Grant's career, however, always seemed poised on a knife edge. After Shiloh, allegations of heavy drinking were leveled against Grant. These claims, lacking substantiation and usually originating among jealous fellow officers and their political sponsors, dog Grant's reputation to this day. At times, it seemed as though only President Lincoln stood between Grant and the abyss. "I rather like the man," Lincoln said to one of the many visitors who importuned him to fire the fast-rising commander in the West. "I think I'll try him a little longer." By the late winter of 1864, the commander in chief had tried him long enough. In March of that year, Lincoln promoted Grant to lieutenant general and commander of all the armies of the United States, the first man to hold such distinction since George Washington.

In fact, there were others besides Lincoln who believed in Grant, sometimes to be found in surprising places. Back in 1861, Confederate lieutenant general Richard Ewell, who would oppose Grant in the Wilderness, wrote, "There is one West Pointer, I think in Missouri, little known, and whom I hope the northern people will not find out. I mean Sam Grant. I knew him in the Academy and in Mexico. I should fear him more than any of their officers I have yet heard of."

Confederate lieutenant general James Longstreet, who had served as a groomsman at the Northern officer's wedding in 1848, was of like view. "That man," he said to an aide after hearing of Grant's elevation to supreme command, "will fight us every day of every hour until the end of this war."

Ewell and Longstreet had seen something that many of Grant's fellow officers in the North did not see or would not recognize if they did see it: the unshakable determination in the man. One of Grant's peculiarities was his refusal to retrace his steps. Even if he found he had come the wrong way on a city street, it was said, he would circle the block at the next corner rather than turn around the way he had come. During the seven years between the time he had resigned his army commission in 1854 and the outbreak of the war, he had refused to throw up his hands, despite his inability to find a stable civilian profession. He just kept plugging, in spite of everything.

He would need every ounce of that determination in the coming campaign. For whatever victories Grant might have won in the West and however high the regard in which some of his Southern opponents might hold him, the grizzled veterans of the Union's premier army remained to be convinced. The inferiority complex that had broken five previous commanders had filtered down through the ranks. Shortly after deciding to make his headquarters with the Army of the Potomac rather than in Washington, D.C., or with Sherman's

Army of the Tennessee, Grant dispatched his aides, most of whom he had brought with him from the West, to sound out opinion in the army that he would effectively be commanding. The results were virtually unanimous: "Well, let Grant try what he can accomplish with the Army of the Potomac. He cannot be worse than his predecessors; and, if he is a fighter, he can find all the fighting he wants. We have never complained that Lee's men would not fight."

And the fighting would begin in some of the least promising terrain to be found anywhere in North America. On the other side of Germanna and Ely's Ford lay a seventy-mile-long, thirty-mile-wide expanse of second-growth forest, tangled underbrush, stagnant water, and barren soil known locally simply as the Wilderness. In places, the tree canopy was so dense that the forest floor, even at high noon on a clear day, was bathed in a kind of twilight. Add in the smoke and confusion of battle, and men could easily become disoriented. A battle in this green hell would find the Union army vulnerable and could prove as fatal to Grant's career as it had been to Hooker's.

"Viewed as a battleground," said Lieutenant Colonel Francis P. Walker, the Wilderness "was simply infernal."

Controversy still clings to the intentions of the two commanders. The conventional interpretation is that Grant wanted to avoid battle in the Wilderness, while Lee sought it, the latter hoping to use the foliage to negate Grant's advantage in manpower and artillery. But few of Lee's orders survive from this battle (they were lost in the retreat from Richmond a year later), and those that do survive seem to show a commander far less certain of what his opponent was up to than has generally been believed. Grant, for his part, may not have sought a battle in the Wilderness, but he does not appear to have quailed before the prospect either. If Lee wanted to fight there, then the Northerner seemed prepared to accommodate him.

The one thing Grant was determined to avoid was allowing Lee a breathing spell after the first contact. The counterpuncher extraordinaire, Lee had won his previous victories by seizing the initiative and counterattacking after the Union commander had thrown his Sunday punch. No more would the Gray Fox be given such an opportunity. Indeed, the history of the rest of the war would show that, except for a few days in early June 1864, the Army of Northern Virginia and the Army of the Potomac would never again be out of contact.

The same principle would be applied to the Confederate forces as a whole. Grant's move would not be a one-act play. The commanding general had issued orders for simultaneous movements by Sherman's army against Confederate forces in Tennessee and northern Georgia, as well as advances by smaller Union forces along the Gulf of Mexico, in the Shenandoah Valley, and on the Virginia Peninsula. For the first time in the war, the pressure on the Confederacy was designed to be universal and relentless.

IN GRANT'S OWN headquarters, if not in the army at large, quiet confidence about the coming campaign prevailed. On the night of May 3, after issuing his last orders, Grant lit a cigar and relaxed with his staff. Then, uncharacteristically, the general leapt to his feet and stabbed with his finger at the map of Virginia on the wall. "When my troops are there," he said, pointing at the cities of Richmond and Petersburg, "Richmond is mine. Lee must retreat or surrender." It was plain Grant did not envision any retreat or surrender on his own part.

After first light the next day, Grant and his staff headed for Germanna Ford. There were scattered cheers from the troops as their new commander cantered past, but mostly there were just curious stares at this surprisingly small and modest-looking man. The normally undemonstrative Grant was also surprisingly well dressed. A sword swung from his left hip, and new yellow gloves held the reins of his horse Cincinnati. Three gold stars glittered in the sunlight from each shoulder.

Once across the river, Grant received a report from his advanced cavalry patrols that a large Rebel force was in motion. The Army of the Potomac had made good progress since sunup and could undoubtedly make more. But the army's slow-moving field train of 4,300 supply wagons and 450 ambulances was still crossing the river and could not be left exposed to attack. The decision was made to camp for the night while the sun remained high overhead.

Scattered skirmishing between cavalry units on the main roads stretching out of the Wilderness announced the beginning of fighting the next day. Meade, ever cautious, ordered a halt to the advance until Rebel intentions became clearer. Grant approved, but, unlike Meade, he wasn't going to hand Lee the initiative. "If an opportunity presents itself for pitching into a part of Lee's army," Grant wrote, "do so."

"Pitch in" the Union army did, though probably not even Grant was quite aware of just how large a "part" of Lee's army it was facing. Around 1:00 P.M., Warren's V Corps made its attack, and a rising crescendo of musket fire announced the start of the Battle of the Wilderness.

Over the next few hours, a confused, terrifying, and deadly ballet unfolded, one beyond the effective control of either commander. The 140th New York, one of the proudest units in the army, saw 238 of its 529 effectives shot down in the opening minutes of the fighting along the Orange Turnpike. "My God," cried their anguished commander, "I'm the first colonel I ever knew who couldn't tell where his regiment was!" A Maine soldier remembered that "a red volcano yawned before us, and vomited forth fire, and lead, and death." The woods became a science fiction–like world of smoke, fire, and noise so loud that soldiers could barely even distinguish the sound of their own rifle shots and could see only a few feet in front of them. One soldier said later that rifles were aimed by "earsight."

Back at headquarters, Grant sat on a tree stump whittling pieces of wood into formless shapes. The only other evidence of his nervousness was the endless succession of cigars he was smoking (twenty in all by the end of the day). He did find time, however, to issue orders that, except for one to carry the ambulances hauling the wounded back north, all the bridges over the fords in his rear were to be dismantled.

Farther south, along the Orange Plank Road, Hancock's II Corps was attacking Confederate lieutenant general A. P. Hill's corps. Hill's 7,500 men, badly outnumbered by Hancock's 25,000, barely managed to hang on in the face of repeated Union assaults. Only the coming of night brought a halt to the carnage.

That night would not be forgotten by those who lived to tell about it. "A woeful night," remembered a soldier of the 118th Pennsylvania. "The moans and wailings of the Wilderness battlefield stirred the stoutest heart, and yet they could not be relieved. . . . War's hard rules would not permit it. . . . There was no helping hand to succor, no yielding of the stern necessities of war."

Those necessities included leaving the wounded where they lay. Grant had directed that wounded soldiers were to be removed from the field, not by their comrades, as had happened in earlier battles, but only by designated stretcher-bearers. The reasons were bluntly mathematical. A wounded soldier assisted out of the action leaning on the shoulders of two of his comrades subtracted not one but three men from the firing line. Grant couldn't afford the reduction in firepower. Unfortunately, the stretcher-bearers often could not reach the wounded because the confused firing in the woods threatened their own safety. Thus, when the tinder tinder-dry woods caught fire, those too badly wounded to pull themselves to safety faced a terrifying fate.

It would be hard to find an optimist in the midst of such gloom, but Grant was an exception. "I feel pretty well satisfied with the results of the engagement," he told Meade around the campfire that night, "for it is evident that Lee attempted by a bold movement to strike this army in flank . . . but in this he failed." Grant was satisfied that he had prevented Lee from taking the initiative and was determined that the Southern commander should not take it on the morrow. He ordered Hancock to attack Hill again at 4:30 A.M., a start time that was later pushed back, at Meade's insistence, to 5:00 A.M.

One of the observers of the scene at Grant's headquarters was Henry Wing, a young correspondent for Horace Greeley's *New York Tribune*. Because Grant had cut all communications with Washington when he began his advance, newspaper reporters had no way of getting their stories back to readers in the North. Wing was chosen by his colleagues to make the desperate trip. Putting out of his mind for the moment the dark, deserted roads patrolled by Confederate bushwhackers that awaited him, he made his way over to where the commanding general was standing, reading dispatches by the flickering light of the campfire. He asked Grant if there was anything he wished to tell the country.

"Yes," said Grant between puffs on his cigar, not even looking up from the papers he held in his hands. "You may tell the people that things are going swimmingly down here."

His quote in hand, Wing turned and began walking away. He hadn't taken more than a few steps, however, when he felt a firm hand on his shoulder. Whipping around, Wing found himself face to face with Grant.

"You expect to get through to Washington?" Grant asked, out of earshot of everyone else in the camp. The young man nodded. Grant, guessing where Wing was likely to end up, leaned down and spoke to him in a low voice.

"If you see the president," Grant said, "tell him, from me, that, whatever happens, there will be no turning back."

Wing did as instructed. Against the odds, he managed to reach Washington. And, after insisting on being allowed to send a story to his paper, he met not only with Lincoln but also with the entire cabinet. When the meeting broke up, Wing lingered behind to have a private word with the chief executive. The president's reaction, when Wing conveyed Grant's special message, was summed up in the title of the reporter's postwar memoir, *When Lincoln Kissed Me.*

At first light the next day, May 6, Hancock struck hard at the exhausted remnants of A. P. Hill's corps and rocked the Rebels back on their heels. No longer able to take the punishment, the Confederates broke and ran for their lives. "Tell Meade we are driving them most beautifully!" declared Hancock, drawing out the last word for emphasis.

But Hancock's optimism was premature. His men needed reinforcement if they were to continue the drive; and Ambrose Burnside, the luckless former army commander who was now in charge of IX Corps and was supposed to be supporting Hancock, was eating a picnic lunch by the roadside. As fate would have it, however, James Longstreet and his corps, which had missed the first day's action because it had the farthest distance to travel from its winter camps, arrived in the midst of Hill's fugitives to shore up the crumbling Confederate position.

A local showed Longstreet a cut for an unfinished railway that ran right past Hancock's exposed left wing. Like Jackson's men the year before at Chancellorsville, Longstreet's broke from the woods howling the Rebel yell at the top of their voices, hitting Hancock's surprised men like a thunderclap. But this replay of Chancellorsville would exact an eerily similar price. Longstreet, like Jackson, was himself shot by one of his own men, though without fatal result. Longstreet's wounding took the steam out of the Confederate attack and gave Hancock's men time to construct earthworks in their rear. By the time the Confederates reorganized themselves and renewed the attack, the charge was as futile as George Pickett's had been at Gettysburg the year before. The Confederates fell back with heavy casualties. The effort to roll the Union army back to the Rapidan by turning its left had failed.

Over on the Union right, a remarkably similar scenario was playing out. Toward sunset, the Confederates struck Union VI Corps commander Major General John "Uncle John" Sedgwick in his flank. This attack produced something close to panic among the bluecoats. Messenger after messenger came galloping up to Grant's headquarters with tidings of doom. "I know Lee's methods well by past experience," gasped one excitable Union officer. "He will throw his whole army between us and the Rapidan, and cut us off completely from our communications."

Grant, who had no intention of returning to the Rapidan, maintained his unflappable exterior, calmly questioning each breathless messenger to determine the veracity of his information. But when the name of Robert E. Lee was finally mentioned one too many times, the Union commander's composure finally broke. "Oh I am heartily tired of hearing what *Lee* is going to do," he snapped. "Some of you always seem to think he is going to turn a double somersault and land in our rear and on both our flanks at the same time. Go back to your command and try to think what we are going to do ourselves, instead of what *Lee's* going to do."

Grant knew his commanders, and he had faith in "Uncle John" Sedgwick. That faith proved not to be misplaced, as Sedgwick was able to plug the gaps in his line and steady the Union right. But there was no question that Grant had been through far more than he was letting on. As his aide John Rawlins later wrote, "the general was confronted by the greatest crisis of his life." After the lines had been stabilized in the smoky, fiery woods on the night of May 6, Grant went into his tent and, depending on which account one believes, either slept or cried.

There was ample reason for the latter, for Grant's casualties beggared belief: 17,666 men killed, wounded, captured, and missing in two days of fighting. That was 400 more than Hooker had suffered at Chancellorsville. (Lee suffered losses of about 11,000.) There were other ways in which Grant came off worse than the hapless Hooker. The latter, after all, had suffered just one disastrous flank attack; Grant had sustained two. Instead of achieving surprise, Grant had himself been surprised by the strength of the Confederate forces he was facing. As Civil War historian Shelby Foote noted, "Lee had never beaten an adversary so soundly as he had beaten this one in the course of the past two days."

But the Wilderness wasn't a battle like the others, and Lee himself seemed to realize it, for he had not performed with his usual panache. The two flank attacks, instead of being coordinated, were made hours apart. Thus, while they unsteadied the Federals, Grant and his subordinates were able to contain the damage.

There was also evidence that Lee himself was emotionally rattled by this battle as by no other. At Antietam, when Hill's division arrived at the last possible moment and saved Lee's army from destruction, the Confederate commander had merely nodded. But when Longstreet appeared in the Wilderness on the morning of May 6, a similarly critical juncture, Lee allowed himself an almost unheard-of public display of emotion and relief, waving his hat and shouting, "Hurrah for Texas!" (Longstreet's lead brigade was from the Lone Star State.) He even moved to personally lead the Texans in their counterattack, a totally uncharacteristic display of reckless bravado that was thwarted only when the troops themselves insisted he go to the rear.

Grant had no way of knowing about Lee's apparent unnerving, of course. But how would Grant react to his situation? Hooker had skedaddled and had lost his command. As dawn came on May 7, the Union soldiers who had lived to see it perceived evidence that Grant was preparing to follow Hooker's lead. No attack orders had been issued, and the field ambulances began moving toward Ely's Ford to carry the wounded north to Washington. During the day, the artillery reserve was limbered up and sent in the same direction—to avoid clogging the roads that night, the soldiers told each other. Then, in late afternoon, came the expected orders to move.

Sedgwick's and Warren's exhausted survivors slung their packs, shouldered their muskets, and, covered by Hancock's men, fell in on the Brock Road, which was the main thoroughfare leading north-south in the area. But instead of heading north and west back toward Germanna Ford, the soldiers found themselves heading south and east. Of course, just beyond the Chancellor House, where Joe Hooker had been knocked senseless by a cannonball one year earlier, there was a road that led off to the left back to Ely's Ford. The fork to the right led south, toward a crossroads known as Spotsylvania Court House.

"Give way, give way to the right," a voice shouted sharply from the gathering darkness behind the line of marching men. A group of riders, silhouetted against the forest fires that were still burning in the woods beside the road, came jingling down the road. Grant was in the lead, looking almost too small for his powerful horse, followed just behind on his right by Meade. Cheering erupted, but Grant ordered it stopped, lest Rebel pickets scarcely half a mile away hear the movement.

Ahead lay the intersection. The sound started as a low buzz and then swelled to something like a loud murmur, moving backward from the column's front to its rear. The turn had been to the right, not the left. They were not returning to the river. The campaign would go on.

Two great leaders had met in the Wilderness. Grant came intent on forcing Lee into a showdown battle. He had failed. But Robert E. Lee had also failed, and his was the greater blunder. The Southern commander had had one chance, and only one, to establish his psychological supremacy over Ulysses S. Grant—to break him, as Lee had broken all of his predecessors. He had not done so. The quiet, undemonstrative, plebeian U. S. Grant had proved he had within him the sternness of character needed to accept momentary setbacks in order to move on to greater triumphs.

The soldiers' step quickened as it dawned on them that this small man sitting astride the big horse was different. The dead and wounded comrades they had left behind in the Wilderness, as on so many other fields over the past three years, were not sacrificed in vain. There would be hard fighting ahead, and many of them now marching down the Brock Road would not see the finish. *But there would be a finish.* None of them doubted that now—or doubted what shape that finish would take.

"The rank and file of the army wanted no more retreating," wrote a IX Corps artilleryman, "and from the moment . . . when we continued straight on towards Spotsylvania, I never had a doubt that General Grant would lead us on to final victory."

PART I

# THE ELEMENTS OF LEADERSHIP: LAYING THE FOUNDATION

# CHAPTER 1

# CHARACTER

## *McClellan Versus Grant—*
## *a Case Study*

———

*Character in many ways is everything in leadership.*
—DWIGHT D. EISENHOWER

*Grant is as good a leader as we can find. He has honesty,
simplicity of character, singleness of purpose, and no hope
to usurp civil power. His character, more than his genius,
will reconcile armies and attach the people.*
—WILLIAM T. SHERMAN

ON JUNE 25, 1862, Robert E. Lee, the newly appointed commander of the force he dubbed the Army of Northern Virginia, was preparing to strike Major General George B. McClellan's Union Army of the Potomac and drive it back from the gates of Richmond. As the campaign that would be known as the Seven Days was about to begin, McClellan began sending a remarkable series of telegrams back to Washington:

June 25, 6:15 P.M.

I incline to think that Jackson will attack my right and rear. The rebel force is stated at 200,000....

I regret my great inferiority of numbers, but feel that I am in no way responsible for it. . . . I will do all that a general can do with the splendid army I have the honor to command, and if it is destroyed by overwhelming numbers, can at least die with it and share its fate. But if the result of the action, which will probably occur to-morrow, or within a short time, is a disaster, the responsibility cannot be thrown on my shoulders; it must rest where it belongs.

The same day, 10:40 P.M.:

If I had another good division, I could laugh at Jackson.

June 26, noon:

I have just heard that our advanced cavalry pickets . . . are being driven in. It is probably Jackson's advance guard. . . . Do not believe reports of disaster, and do not be discouraged if you learn that my communications are cut off, and even Yorktown [fifty miles to McClellan's rear] in possession of the enemy.

The same day, 7:40 P.M.:

A very heavy engagement in progress just in front of me.

The same day, 9:00 P.M.:

The firing has nearly ceased. . . . Victory of today complete and against great odds.
I almost begin to think we are invincible.

June 27, 8:00 P.M.:

Have had a terrible contest. Attacked by greatly superior numbers. . . . Had I but 20,000 fresh and good troops we would be sure of a splendid victory tomorrow.

June 28, just past midnight:

I now know the full history of the day. On this side of the river [the right bank] we repulsed several very strong attacks. On the left bank, our men did all that men could do, all that soldiers could accomplish, but they were overwhelmed by vastly superior numbers, even after I brought my last reserves into action. The loss on both sides is terrible. I believe that it will prove to be the most desperate battle of the war.

. . . [H]ad I but 20,000 or even 10,000 fresh troops to use to-morrow, I could take Richmond. . . .

I again repeat that I am not responsible for this, and I say it with the earnestness of the general who feels in his heart the loss of every brave man who has been needlessly sacrificed today. . . .

I feel too earnestly to-night. I have seen too many dead and wounded comrades to feel otherwise than that the Government has not sustained this army. If you do not do so now the game is lost.

If I save this army now, I tell you plainly that I owe no thanks to you or to any other persons in Washington.

You have done your best to sacrifice this army.

Even today, nearly 140 years after they were written, these telegrams have not lost their capacity to shock. That any subordinate, let alone an army field commander, could address his superiors in such an insolent and accusatory fashion is beyond belief. The supervisor of army telegrams in the War Department couldn't believe his eyes either. He edited out the last two sentences of the final telegram before passing it on to Secretary of War Edwin M. Stanton and President Lincoln.

The telegrams reflect perfectly the mercurial, high-strung, contradictory character of George B. McClellan. (Military historian Joseph B. Mitchell provides one of the best analyses of them.)

In the first telegram, McClellan repeats his oft-made charge of being massively outnumbered, despairs of victory, and implicitly blames Lincoln. A few hours later, after melodramatically proclaiming his willingness to die with his army, he would be prepared to "laugh" at his opponents if he had but a single division. The next day, while predicting disaster, he insists there is no cause for alarm. By the evening, he is declaring his army almost invincible.

By the third day, however, his "invincible" army is under attack by vastly superior numbers, but then, in a non sequitur, the general expresses his confidence in a great victory the next day, if only he had 20,000 fresh troops (a full corps, by the way, not the mere one division he needed to "laugh" at Jackson). By midnight, all sense of perspective and self-control is gone. Despite having experienced what he calls an overwhelming attack by vastly superior enemy forces, the 20,000 troops that he needed earlier had been inexplicably cut in half.

He then gives full vent to his emotions, talking about dead and wounded comrades he could not possibly have seen much of, since McClellan stayed resolutely inside his headquarters throughout the battle. Repeating his denial of all responsibility, he then declares that the president and his aides have deliberately sacrificed the lives of American soldiers in a futile effort for their own nefarious purposes.

McClellan's communications were indeed cut shortly after the last telegram was sent. But the stream of near-hysterical messages resumed on June 30. McClellan reported trying to save his army by abandoning the expensive equipment and supplies he had so insistently demanded Lincoln provide him before he could even begin the campaign. On July 1, the 10,000 troops he needed to take Richmond on June 28 had ballooned to 50,000. On July 3, with his battered army huddled on the bank of the James River far from Richmond, he suddenly and without explanation revised that number further upward to 100,000 men.

The mind reels. How could such a man have been placed in command? The best that can be said is that it seemed like a good idea at the time.

More than a century after his death in 1885, controversy still rages around McClellan's short, tempestuous career on the national stage. "McClellan is the problem child of the Civil War," wrote T. Harry Williams in his classic study, *Lincoln and His Generals.* "His contemporaries revered or reviled him. Historians have defended or attacked him." "The McClellan-Go-Round" is how historian Joseph L. Harsh describes the endless imbroglio surrounding Little Mac's abilities. Was he mentally unstable, as historian Joseph E. Glatthaar argues? Or was he a misunderstood genius? Or was he, as some have suggested, secretly a Rebel sympathizer?

None of the above. McClellan's failure as a field commander in the Civil War is really not much of a mystery. As the telegrams from the Virginia Peninsula in June and July of 1862 make clear, McClellan—for all his undeniable talents as an administrator, organizer, and military showman—simply lacked the character to successfully lead a large organization, much less the army of a nation locked in civil war.

## WHAT IS CHARACTER?

"CHARACTER" IS A WORD that has been thrown around quite a bit lately, especially with regard to a recent president and the 2000 presidential election. T. Harry Williams, in an essay attributing McClellan's failure to his lack of character, defined it as "moral courage, or plain nerve." It is that, to be sure, but it is much else besides. Character is a quality difficult to define precisely, but a man of character can be described.

Edgar F. Puryear, Jr., interviewed many of the top American military commanders from World War II and asked them to talk about character. Their responses are applicable to leadership in any organization.

"Character," Dwight D. Eisenhower told Puryear, "is made up of many things, but I would say character is really integrity. When you delegate something to a subordinate, for example, it is absolutely your responsibility. . . . You as a leader must take complete responsibility for what that subordinate does."

A man of character doesn't abuse or take advantage of his subordinates.

"There are a lot of people who know the 'smart' way of getting things done," said General Mark W. Clark, "but they also run roughshod over people that they are supposed to be working with. I don't want that."

General William H. Simpson, an army commander in World War II, believed that "there are many qualities that go into a man of 'sterling character.' I don't know how to break it down. A man of high character has integrity, he is honest, he is reliable, he is straightforward in dealing with people. He is loyal to his family, his friends, his superiors." Omar Bradley, one of Eisenhower's lieutenants and one of the handful of American generals to wear five stars, agreed on the importance of character in a leader. He defined it as "dependability, integrity, the characteristic of never knowingly doing anything wrong, that you would never cheat anyone, that you would give everybody a fair deal. . . . If a man has character, everyone has confidence in him."

"An officer who stands up under fire, who has the courage to defend his convictions, not arrogantly, not stubbornly, but intelligently," said General Albert Wedemeyer, who designed the Allied plan for victory in World War II. "Someone who does not believe he knows all the answers, who will listen to others with different experiences, and different knowledge."

More recently, in a speech at Hillsdale College, H. Norman Schwarzkopf, commander of coalition forces in Operation Desert Storm said, "The main ingredient of good leadership is good character. This is because leadership involves conduct, and conduct is determined by values. You may call these values by many names. 'Ethics,' 'morality,' and 'integrity' come to mind. But this much is clear: Values are what make us who we are."

A man of character also thinks of how he can best do the job, not what the job can do for him. There was no advantage to Eisenhower in coming out of retirement in 1950 to become the first commander of the North Atlantic Treaty Organization (NATO), for example, and a good deal of personal and professional inconvenience. But he did it because his country—indeed, the entire Free World—needed him at that moment. It was much the same story when it came to the presidency, which he did not actively seek until he finally became convinced that all he had worked for in the postwar world might be at risk unless he ran himself.

Success alone is not a measure of a man's character. Men of poor character, such as Napoleon and Kaiser Wilhelm II, can achieve success for a time. Both these men, however, ended their lives as bitter exiles, abandoned by those who once fawned on them in better times.

Few of us will ever lead a large nation, an army, or even a corporation. But if one seeks lasting success in almost any field, the selflessness and stamina that character alone provides seem indispensable. George Washington lost more battles than he won. But his officers and men had faith in him, because Washington had character. Indeed, Washington was Eisenhower's role model: "The qualities that excited my admiration were Washington's stamina and patience in adversity, first, and then his indomitable courage, daring, and capacity for self-sacrifice."

Rudyard Kipling's famed poem "If" is one of the greatest descriptions of character ever written:

*If you can keep your head when all about you*
*Are losing theirs and blaming it on you;*
*If you can trust yourself when all men doubt you,*
*But make allowance for their doubting too;*
*If you can wait and not be tired by waiting,*
*Or, being lied about, don't deal in lies,*
*Or, being hated, don't give way to hating,*
*And yet don't look too good, nor talk too wise;*
*If you can dream—and not make dreams your master;*
*If you can think—and not make thoughts your aim;*
*If you can meet with triumph and disaster*
*And treat those two imposters just the same;*
*If you can bear to hear the truth you've spoken*
*Twisted by knaves to make a trap for fools,*
*Or watch the things you gave your life to broken,*
*And stoop and build 'em up with wornout tools;*
*If you can make one heap of all your winnings*
*And risk it on one turn of pitch-and-toss,*
*And lose, and start again at your beginnings*
*And never breathe a word about your loss;*
*If you can force your heart and nerve and sinew*
*To serve your turn long after they are gone,*
*And so hold on when there is nothing in you*
*Except the Will which says to them: "Hold on";*
*If you can talk with crowds and keep your virtue,*
*Or walk with kings—nor lose the common touch;*
*If neither foes nor loving friends can hurt you;*
*If all men count with you, but none too much;*
*If you can fill the unforgiving minute*
*With sixty seconds' worth of distance run—*
*Yours is the Earth and everything that's in it,*
*And—which is more—you'll be a Man my son!*

Ulysses S. Grant could have been Kipling's subject. George B. McClellan could not. Unfortunately for the country, it had to find out the hard way.

## MCCLELLAN'S LIFE AND FLAWED CHARACTER

GEORGE BRINTON MCCLELLAN was a man who expected to succeed, for success had come easily to him from an early age. The scion of a family that moved in Philadelphia society, the young McClellan proved a prodigy at languages and mathematics. Deciding on an army career at age ten, he spent two years prepping at the University of Pennsylvania before winning special permission to enter West Point in 1842 at age fifteen. After an initial period of homesickness, he quickly mastered the academy's demanding curriculum, graduating second in his class of 1846 and winning for himself a commission in the elite Army Corps of Engineers.

In the Mexican War that followed almost immediately after graduation, McClellan won a prestigious posting on the staff of General Winfield Scott and was promoted twice for gallantry. A scholar of military theory, he read the Swiss Baron Jomini's accounts of Napoleon's campaigns in the original French. That he appeared marked for higher things in the army was evident when Secretary of War Jefferson Davis named him as one of three officers sent in 1856 to observe European armies in action during the Crimean War. His report on that war was widely and favorably read. In his spare time, he designed a new saddle for the army, the McClellan saddle, which would be used for as long as the army had horse soldiers in the field. He also taught himself Russian and translated a 300-page Russian military manual. Nevertheless, promotion was slow in the peacetime army, even for stars like McClellan, and his restless mind was growing bored with army routine. In 1857, he resigned his captain's commission to enter civilian life as a railroad executive.

In the few years of peace that remained, McClellan enjoyed his success and lived life in his Cincinnati, Ohio, home as a virtual American aristocrat. When war loomed, he was a hot commodity, and New York, Pennsylvania, and Ohio competed for his services. He accepted Ohio's offer of a major generalcy and was soon placed in command of all Union troops west of the Allegheny Mountains.

Although only five feet eight inches in height, Little Mac, as his soldiers would call him, looked every inch a general. "Muscularly formed, with broad shoulders and a well-poised head," one observer noted. McClellan's hair was dark auburn, and he wore a short, thick mustache of reddish hue. When a series of small victories over Confederate forces in the mountains of western Virginia in the spring and early summer of 1861 were attributed to his leadership, a desperate President Abraham Lincoln, reeling from the disaster of the Battle of Bull Run, sent for McClellan.

He arrived in the nation's capital on July 27, 1861, six days after the battle and with the bloodied remnants of the Union army still staggering in from the field at Bull Run. McClellan soon found virtually all of official Washington—from Lincoln on down—lying at his feet. He was invited to meet with the president and his cabinet, as well as congressional leaders. Invitations to parties were pressed on him. Newspapers sang his praises, and someone dubbed him "the Young Napoleon." He had "an indefinable air of success about him and something of a 'man of destiny,'" said one who met him.

Sudden fame can be a heady narcotic for anyone, much less someone only thirty-four years old. And once McClellan inhaled the fumes, he was never able to get them out of his nostrils. "I find myself in a new & strange position here," he wrote in a much-quoted letter to his wife, Nelly. "Presdt, Cabinet, Genl Scott & all deferring to me—by some strange operation of magic I seem to have become the power of the land. I almost think that were I to win some small success now I could become Dictator or anything else that might please me—but nothing of that kind would please me—therefore I won't be Dictator. Admirable self denial!"

Far from practicing modesty or self-denial, McClellan showed every sign of believing his own press clippings. In his letters, he told his wife that nothing less than the fate of the nation depended upon him. It is not at all clear that being a dictator would have displeased him. The flaws in McClellan's character would not be widely revealed for some months, but for those who cared to look, they had been apparent for a long time.

There was McClellan's role in the western Virginia victories that had won him acclaim in the first place, for example. McClellan was scribbling orders at his own dining room table in Cincinnati, hundreds of miles from the action, when a small Union force under Brigadier General T. A. Morris nearly bloodlessly drove a small Confederate force from the field at the so-called Battle of Philippi on June 3, 1861. At Rich Mountain on July 11, McClellan was closer—just two miles away—but it was Brigadier General William S. Rosecrans's troops who overran the Confederate position while a befuddled McClellan and his force sat immobile. At Corrick's Ford on July 13, the skirmish that ended the campaign, it was Morris again who won the day. McClellan was twenty-six miles from the firing.

But McClellan had something no one else had: the telegraph. He had observed its use in a rudimentary form in the Crimea and was one of the first American officers to appreciate its possible military applications. He trailed a telegraph line after him wherever he went and lost little time getting the word of "his" victories on the wire.

"We have annihilated the enemy in Western Virginia," he declared in what was to become characteristic McClellanesque overstatement. "The troops defeated are the crack regiments of Eastern Virginia, aided by Georgians, Tennesseans, and Carolinians. Our success is complete. . . ."

McClellan's defenders have argued that he properly deserved the credit, since he was the general in overall command of the operation. That argument would have more force if he had looked after those who had helped him win distinction. But he did not. Rosecrans, instead of being brought to Washington for a major command in McClellan's new army, was instead left behind in the obscurity of western Virginia. That Rosecrans went on to emerge as a major commander in the Western, rather than the Eastern, theater of war was no thanks to McClellan.

Brigadier General Morris's case was sadder. Far from winning McClellan's praise, Morris was instead criticized by him for not pursuing the enemy more vigorously. When Morris's volunteer commission expired soon after Corrick's Ford, he fully expected to receive a Regular Army commission. But it did not come for well over a year, by which time Morris had concluded the Union had no use for his services. He took no further part in the war.

McClellan's relations with superiors were no better than those with subordinates. His fabled feud with President Lincoln and Secretary of War Edwin M. Stanton flowed from another of McClellan's character defects: his inability to relate to legitimate authority and accept responsibility for his actions. At the age of twelve, for example, he had a quarrel with his tutor for which, decades later, he felt compelled to insist he was blameless. At West Point, he thought he had been unfairly deprived of the topmost position in the graduating class. When he returned to West Point as an engineering officer after the Mexican War, he began a series of quarrels with the superintendent of the military academy that eventually reached the desks of the chief engineer of the army and the secretary of war. No mean feat for a mere second lieutenant. And needless to say, McClellan was not to blame.

Even friends were not immune from McClellan's peevish nature. Isaac Stevens, who had served with him in Mexico and had afterward become a territorial governor, asked McClellan's help in surveying possible routes for a transcontinental railroad in the Pacific Northwest. He and Stevens soon fell out, however, with McClellan, characteristically, disclaiming any responsibility in the matter: "The great consolation is that I was detailed in this service without either my knowledge or consent," he declared, completely untruthfully. (McClellan biographer Stephen W. Sears cites this statement as early evidence of McClellan's bent toward self-deception.) Even when selected for the plum job of the Crimea mission, McClellan still felt compelled to complain. The two officers assigned to accompany him were "d——d old fogies" who were little better than "corpses."

If these repeated scrapes with those in authority over him provoked any serious introspection on McClellan's part, there is no evidence of it. "I don't think I am of a quarrelsome disposition," he once said to his sister-in-law, "but I do have the luck of getting into more trouble than any dozen other officers."

Civilian life was more of the same. Within months of accepting appointment as chief engineer of the Illinois Central Railroad, he was clashing with the board of directors. In 1860, he left the Illinois Central to join the Ohio and Mississippi Railroad but was soon quarreling with his superiors there. His failed relationship with President Lincoln, therefore, was merely the latest in a long series.

McClellan, like most prewar army officers, was a Democrat and had supported Stephen A. Douglas for president in 1860. McClellan, however, never learned to see beyond his political differences with the president. Little Mac had known Lincoln briefly before the war in the future president's capacity as a railroad lawyer and was not impressed. Lincoln's election did nothing to change matters. McClellan thought Lincoln honest and well meaning, but fundamentally a country bumpkin far beneath the general's refined social standing. It wasn't long before disdain turned to contempt, and he began privately referring to the man who had elevated him to high command and shown him little but kindness as "the Original Gorilla."

Lincoln, for his part, was feeling his own way so early on in the conflict. Admittedly unschooled in the art of war, he was in no position to question McClellan's judgment and deferred to him at every opportunity. This probably only fed McClellan's scornful attitude toward his commander in chief. But the general was careful, at least for a time, to seem to respect Lincoln face to face.

War, McClellan believed, was a job best left to soldiers and not politicians. He viewed Lincoln's " drop-bys" at headquarters, with their questions and inquiries as to his plans for an early movement against the Rebels, as amusing at first, then annoying, and finally "interference" and "intolerable." That Lincoln was an elected leader, responsible to the public for the conduct of a war that was costing the taxpayers a million dollars every day, made no impression on the general.

Lincoln wasn't the only one to get this two-faced treatment from the Young Napoleon. His mentor, General in Chief Winfield Scott, was another. Scott, who had held a general's rank for more than a decade before McClellan was born, had come to respect the younger man's ability in Mexico. Scott himself had recommended McClellan to Lincoln.

He had attended McClellan's wedding to the beautiful Ellen "Nelly" Marcy in 1860. Yet no sooner had McClellan arrived in Washington than he began intriguing to displace the man to whom he owed almost everything.

In his dealings with Scott, McClellan flattered him by declaring "all I know of war I learned from you" and offering similar flowery encomiums. To influential senators and congressmen, however, Scott was "very slow & very old." In a letter to Nelly, he exploded, "I do not know if he is a dotard or a traitor! I can't tell which!" The old general, a hero of two wars and the man whose "Anaconda Plan" for strangling the Confederacy ultimately proved the successful strategy, was an "obstacle," an "incompetent," a "perfect imbecile," and many other negative things.

Scott's real sin, of course, was that he was virtually the only person in authority who could challenge McClellan, and he did not hesitate to do so. He scoffed at the young man's claim that a host of 100,000 Confederates was assembled in northern Virginia. Scott was right. The number of Rebels appears to have been around 50,000 at the outside. The 100,000 figure, which McClellan would continue to inflate, appears to have sprung from faulty intelligence estimates married to his own overheated imagination.

Scott, therefore, had to go. After a series of snubs and putdowns calculated to provoke the old man beyond endurance, McClellan finally got his wish on the last day of October 1861. Scott was packed off to retirement at West Point. Characteristically, McClellan gave the old man a hero's send-off at the train station and even shed tears on the occasion.

The younger man was now elevated to Scott's place as general in chief of all the armies of the United States. The man who, six months before reaching this exalted post, had never held an army rank higher than that of a captain now confidently declared, "I can do it all."

That he couldn't do it all, however, soon became apparent. It wasn't for want of effort; no one ever accused George Mc-Clellan of laziness. He worked seven days a week, sixteen to eighteen hours every day, organizing and drilling his new army. He became a familiar sight in the camps of the Army of the Potomac, riding up and down the lines, his staff trailing behind him at a respectful distance. He loved grand reviews and delivering frequent and stirring speeches to his assembled troops. He even had a portable printing press for churning out addresses and proclamations to them. Sensing that he identified with them, his soldiers idolized him. In those late summer and early fall months of 1861, McClellan brought order out of chaos and imparted to the new army a sense of confidence in itself.

But that achievement came at a high price. The overwork and lack of sleep left the commanding general with precious little time for contemplating how best to use this great machine he was building. As Lincoln and the politicians whom McClellan had cultivated over the past few months became impatient for action, McClellan became ever more firmly set in his refusal to discuss any plans for movement. This impasse further fed the general in chief's distrustful nature, which kept him from confiding in anyone but his beloved Nelly, not even his own staff. "I have no one on my staff to whom I can entrust the safety of affairs," he wrote his wife.

Ominous signs of McClellan's unfitness for high command continued to multiply. Most serious was the case of Brigadier General Charles P. Stone, a friend of McClellan's in the prewar army. No one had done more than Stone to help protect the capital in the early, anxious days of the war. On October 21, 1861, the three-month anniversary of Bull Run, McClellan ordered Stone to advance troops into Virginia from Maryland as part of a coordinated action to drive the Confederates out of Leesburg, Virginia.

McClellan, however, changed his mind and canceled the operation, but he neglected to inform Stone. The result was the disastrous Battle of Ball's Bluff, in which nearly 1,000 Union soldiers were killed or captured. One of the fatalities was a United States senator, Colonel Edward Baker, a close friend of the president's (Lincoln had named his second son after Baker). Although Baker, not Stone, was directly responsible for the fiasco, McClellan took no chances that he himself would be cast in the role of scapegoat. He ordered Stone's arrest. Though utterly guiltless, Stone languished in prison without charge or trial for 187 days. He was ultimately cleared, but his military career lay in ruins.

President Lincoln, for his part, displayed astonishing forbearance in his dealings with the Young Napoleon, telling friends who objected to McClellan's snubs and calculated indignities that he would hold the general's horse if it would bring victories. McClellan only rarely acknowledged the courtesy he was being shown by Lincoln.

Alienating himself from Lincoln was truly McClellan's greatest mistake. By so doing, he deprived himself, completely unnecessarily, of the counsel and support a superior can provide a subordinate with a difficult assignment. Lincoln was skeptical from the beginning that his commander could "do it all" and underlined that fact when he relieved Little Mac of his duties as general in chief in April 1862, leaving him in command only of the Army of the Potomac. At about the same time, onetime patrons such as War Secretary Stanton and Treasury Secretary Salmon P. Chase turned against him.

Instead of taking the hint and altering his behavior, McClellan sank ever deeper into the habits of mind that had landed him in difficulty. His superiors and critics, he raged to his wife and intimates, were incompetents and nincompoops. (Perversely, however, they were also devious and cunning conspirators.) He had not asked for this high post. (But he had accepted it.) God must have chosen him for some indefinable purpose. (So if the Almighty was unclear in his purposes, how could McClellan be held responsible?) And on and on.

This simmering brew of resentment and self-pity came to a raging boil during the Peninsula Campaign of April–July 1862. Unable to defer action any longer, McClellan devised a complex plan for taking Richmond by landing an army on the Peninsula between the York and James Rivers, thus bypassing the Confederate fortifications in northern Virginia. Lincoln was leery from the start. He thought the plan simply transferred the problem of a Rebel army to a different place on the map and did nothing to solve it. Dismissing the president's concerns, McClellan insisted on his plan. Anxious as he was for action of some kind, Lincoln chose not to veto the idea. But as a condition of approval, he demanded that McClellan leave behind enough troops to guarantee the safety of Washington.

This McClellan flagrantly refused to do. Lincoln did not discover this fact, however, until after McClellan had sailed for the Peninsula. Enraged, the president ordered that an army corps slated for duty on the Peninsula be held back to cover Washington. McClellan was beside himself when he found out and used this "withholding" of troops as an excuse whenever his plan looked like as if it was running into trouble—as it quickly did.

The Peninsula Campaign might still have succeeded had McClellan, after landing his army, marched it hell-for-leather to Richmond before the Confederates could shift their forces to meet it. But celerity was not one of McClellan's virtues. He moved his troops toward the Confederate capital with glacial slowness, giving its defenders time to construct fortifications and concentrate troops. Finally, so close to the city they could hear its church bells tolling, the Union soldiers were struck with a Confederate counterattack at Seven Pines on May 31 and driven back. They would not come so close again for three years.

The actual clash of arms that began at Seven Pines and continued through late June and early July in what became known as the Seven Days Battles seem to have completely unhinged the Young Napoleon, as evidenced by the stream of telegrams quoted at the beginning of this chapter. For the first time in his life, he was in the midst of a situation he could not control and went utterly to pieces. It was not physical courage that was lacking; the young McClellan had demonstrated in Mexico that he had plenty of that commodity. It was his character, his moral courage, in T. Harry Williams's phrase, that deserted him at this crucial time.

Nothing demonstrated the problem more starkly than his behavior just before the Battle of Glendale on June 30, 1862. McClellan boarded the steamer *Galena* (named, ironically, after Ulysses S. Grant's prewar hometown) and simply sailed away, leaving no orders, appointing no one to command in his place, and abandoning his commanders and beloved soldiers to their fate. That night, the man who five days earlier had talked bravely of dying at the head of his troops dined aboard ship, far from the fighting.

"Never did I see a man more cut down than Gen'l McClellan was," wrote Brigadier General Andrew A. Humphreys, a member of McClellan's staff, of the morning after Glendale. "He was unable to do anything or say anything." This paralysis persisted as the Battle of Malvern Hill got underway on the same day of Humphreys' observation. McClellan went ashore to inspect his lines and then, incredibly, reboarded the *Galena*, cast off, and sailed down the James River a second time. By some miracle, and at a high cost in casualties, the army eventually reached the relative safety of Harrison's Landing, twenty long miles from Richmond. The campaign was over.

The battlefield test for which George B. McClellan had been training himself since the age of ten had arrived, and he had failed it utterly. Obsessed with the avoidance of failure, he could not succeed. Any thought that the Young Napoleon might eventually have matured into a successful field commander melted before the harsh reality of his personal conduct on the Peninsula of Virginia.

Even so, Lincoln felt compelled to recall Little Mac to command for the September 1862 Antietam campaign. But McClellan failed there as well, even when victory was almost literally handed to him. By a stroke of luck that comes only once in a commander's lifetime, if then, a copy of Lee's orders fell into Union hands and revealed that the Confederate general's army was scattered and unprepared for battle. Instead of taking this gift from the gods and using it to chop up and destroy Lee's massively outnumbered army, the best McClellan could manage was a tactical draw. And that came at the cost of the bloodiest one-day battle of the war. During the fighting, McClellan never left his headquarters. Six weeks later, weary of McClellan's "slows," Lincoln relieved Little Mac of command.

## The Consequences of McClellan

While the decision to appoint McClellan to command in the first place was probably justifiable, given the desperate circumstances existing at the time, the consequences that flowed from that decision illustrate the danger of hiring someone on the basis of incomplete information. Lincoln appointed McClellan to high command before he had even met him or had an opportunity to assess his performance from afar over a long period of time. Little Mac's glittering résumé and high-placed references held no hint of the flawed character that lurked unseen within.

The cost of that mistake, for both the army he commanded and the country it served, was dire. Joseph B. Mitchell has observed that, long after he had left it, the Army of the Potomac remained Little Mac's "bodyguard" (in Lincoln's disdainful phrase). McClellan's character flaws—excessive caution, satisfaction with half-measures, extreme sensitivity to rank and privilege, a tendency to pass the buck and dodge responsibility—were to hobble the Army of the Potomac almost to the end of the conflict. The Eastern army seemed constantly to be missing opportunities because someone had been content to let the enemy get away, had stopped to rest or eat, or had decided to await orders rather than display initiative.

It would take the arrival of a different commander, one with a very different character, to even begin changing this state of affairs.

## GRANT'S LIFE AND CHARACTER

"WEIRD, WEARISOME AND WRATHFUL," was how Captain James G. Day of the 15th Iowa remembered the stormy night of April 6, 1862, at Pittsburg Landing, near Shiloh, Tennessee. He could have spoken for everyone in both the Union and Confederate armies, including his own commanding general, Ulysses S. "Sam" Grant. Bone weary after a day of combat, Grant was nevertheless kept awake by a painfully throbbing ankle, injured in a fall from his horse two days earlier. He tried with little success to sleep in the mud under an oak tree on the bluff overlooking Pittsburg Landing, where his army had entrenched after being pushed back in the fighting earlier in the day.

Around midnight, the insomniac general pulled himself up and hobbled into the log cabin that served as his headquarters. The building, however, had been commandeered by the surgeons, who were operating as fast as possible on men horribly mangled earlier in the day by minié balls fired from rifled muskets. Outside, their comrades awaited their turn in the rain. The commanding general did not stay long, recalling later in his memoirs, "The sight was more unendurable than encountering the enemy's fire, and I returned to my tree in the rain."

The immediate danger was past, but few could deny the battered state of the army Grant now led. A massive Confederate onslaught had torn through the surprised Federals at dawn that morning and pushed them back nearly two miles after a day of confused and ferocious combat. Many of Grant's subordinates, even his most trusted lieutenants, were firmly of the opinion that further retreat was unavoidable. Lieutenant Colonel James B. McPherson, the chief engineer of Grant's army and later a major general and one of his corps commanders, had encountered his chief earlier in the day and commented that things did not look promising. A third of the army was dead or wounded and the rest greatly demoralized.

"General Grant, under this condition of affairs, what do you propose to do, sir?" McPherson asked with some heat. "Shall I make preparations for retreat?"

Grant glared at his brazen young subordinate and shot back, "Retreat? No, I propose to attack at daylight and whip them!"

It was not false bravado. Early that morning, a steamer had brought Grant to Pittsburg Landing when he had first heard firing coming from the direction of his army's encampment. Throughout that long and terrible day, the small general atop the large horse had refused to panic. A battered slouch hat crowning his head, a rough private's coat with a general's stars pinned to the shoulders covering his back, he rode from one end of his line to the other. He offered encouragement to his commanders as well as his petrified soldiers, many of whom were so new to their trade that they did not even know how to load and fire their muskets. The picture of calm confidence, Grant scarcely noticed as the leaves in the trees above him rustled as if by the wind. Musket balls were flying overhead.

The first and most important problem that had to be solved was ammunition. Caught flatfooted, the Federals had to fight with what they already had in their cartridge cases. This supply was quickly exhausted. The South was short of ammunition too, and Grant knew the only way the Northern force could lose a firefight was if it mishandled its superior resources. He issued orders that ammunition resupply was to have the highest priority.

Bringing order out of confusion was Grant's next task. This was by no means simple. Early in the action, the colonel of the 53rd Ohio had simply declared that it was every man for himself and promptly vanished. The commander of the 6th Iowa was drunk and unable to give any orders. Thousands of fugitive soldiers, separated from their units, had sought the relative safety of Pittsburg Landing on the Tennessee River.

Reinforcements were on the way, Grant knew. But Major General Don Carlos Buell and his men were at least a half day's march distant. Long before Buell arrived, the entire Union Army of the Tennessee might be pushed into the river whose name it bore and forced to surrender. All Grant could do in the meantime was keep riding to and fro, offering encouragement, plugging the gaps, and hoping for the best.

Grant's lines held. The green troops in the Union center made a stand at a spot where the lead flew so thick and fast that the soldiers on both sides dubbed it "the Hornet's Nest." The Confederate commander, General Albert Sidney Johnston, could have chosen simply to bypass the Hornet's Nest, a move that likely would have doomed Grant's army. Instead, Johnston kept hammering the stubborn bluecoats for hours on end and eventually succeeded in overrunning them. But the delay afforded Grant an opportunity to get his artillery batteries organized. The final Confederate charge of the day thus dissolved in a blinding hail of double-shotted canister rounds. "Not beaten by a damn sight," Grant muttered through his beard as the graybacks fell back.

Hours later, back under his tree in the rain and the dark, Grant was approached by another of the fast-rising commanders, obscure until now, who would soon be known throughout the army as "Grant's men": William T. Sherman. The red-haired division commander had been in the heart of the firestorm all day. He had been shot in the hand, grazed by another bullet in the shoulder, had felt yet another go through his hat, and had seen several horses shot from under him for good measure. Holding the Union right, he had watched his command fall like wheat before the scythe around him under the pressure of relentless Confederate attacks. In his own memoirs, Sherman recalled that as he approached his friend and mentor, he firmly believed that the army was beaten and had best put the river between it and the Confederates as soon as possible.

But as he grew nearer, and saw the commanding general standing in the driving rain beneath the large oak tree, collar turned up around his ears, rain dripping from the brim of the hat pulled down over his eyes, and chewing on a cigar, Sherman found his attitude changing. Some "wise and sudden instinct" overcame him and caused him to banish from his mind all thought of retreat. Instead, he said to his fellow Ohioan, "Well Grant, we've had the devil's own day, haven't we?"

"Yes," said Grant, a puff of cigar smoke punctuating his words. "Yes. Lick 'em tomorrow, though."

And "lick 'em" he did, achieving one of the most remarkable turnabouts in American military history. Reinforced by the arrival of Buell's troops on the night of April 6–7, Grant attacked at 7:30 the next morning. The Confederates, exhausted by their efforts of the day before and demoralized by the death of Johnston late in the day, were pushed steadily backward, though not without what Grant would later call some of the hardest hand-to-hand fighting of the war. By late afternoon, the Rebels began withdrawing in the direction of Corinth, Mississippi.

The contrast with McClellan's behavior on the Peninsula could not be more stark, for Grant displayed Kiplingesque character of a truly high order at Shiloh. "Refusing to panic, he retained possession of himself and control over his army," wrote T. Harry Williams of Grant's performance that day. He saved his army because he was able to dominate a bad situation, rather than be dominated by it, as McClellan had been.

Shiloh remained a sore spot for Grant the rest of his life, however. The section on Shiloh is one of the few in his memoirs where he adopts an overtly defensive tone, arguing strenuously that he was not surprised there. In fact, it seems clear that he was. The important point to recall, however, is that Grant learned from this near-career-ending debacle: He was never again surprised on a battlefield.

Shiloh was the first really large battle of the Civil War. Grant's 13,700 casualties deeply shocked Northern public opinion. This was not the "picnic basket" war so many were expecting. Some of President Lincoln's closest political advisers importuned him to fire this incompetent Grant, who was also rumored to have been drunk at the battle. Lincoln listened closely to the advice. It is important to note, however, that just five days before Shiloh, George McClellan had left for the Peninsula. Lincoln was furious with Little Mac, for his months of inaction, for his ill-thought-out Peninsula scheme, and for his deception with regard to the number of troops left behind to safeguard Washington. It is within the context of McClellan's behavior that one must read the burdened president's famous reply to those who were demanding Grant's scalp: "I cannot spare this man. He fights."

Fight was what Grant had done for most of his life, not against armed enemies, but against adversity. Horatio Alger would have had a hard time making Grant's extraordinary rise believable. At the time of Fort Sumter in April 1861, Grant was on the brink of turning thirty-nine years old and unhappily employed under the supervision of his younger brother in their father's Galena, Illinois, leather goods store. In less than three years, however, he would become the first man since George Washington to hold the permanent rank of lieutenant general in the U.S. Army. Within eight, he would be inaugurated president.

Little had come easily to him, however—not even his name. Born Hiram Ulysses on April 27, 1822, in Point Pleasant, Ohio, near Cincinnati, he had little use for his given first name and was known instead by his middle name, which caused him to struggle against the nickname "Useless." Perhaps his love of horses and taking long rides far from home is what convinced Grant's father, a successful leather tanner, that his eldest son was more suited to the army than entrepreneurship. It was Jesse Root Grant's idea that Ulysses attend West Point, and his son's initial objections were quickly overcome.

Grant acquired the name we know him by thanks to an error by the congressman who appointed him, who dropped the cadet's given first name and gave him his mother's maiden name of Simpson as a middle name. Grant quickly gave up seeking to correct the error. Not only was army bureaucracy formidable, but being known as "U.S." Grant—United States, Uncle Sam, and, later, Unconditional Surrender—also beat being known as "H.U.G."

Critics have always made much of Grant's supposedly mediocre record at the military academy (twenty-first in a class of thirty-nine cadets in the class of 1843). Few note that the class started with seventy-seven members and that, academically, Grant did not do badly at all, excelling in mathematics and horsemanship. (He set a horse-jumping record at the academy that would stand for decades.) His lowered class standing was due to poor grades in French (the grim reaper of pre–Civil War West Point classes) and demerits he received for poor marching (he was tone deaf) and failing to observe military punctilio.

Unlike McClellan, Grant would not have been viewed by his contemporaries as "most likely to succeed." The same height as McClellan, he looked nowhere near as impressive as the Young Napoleon, suffering from a stoop-shouldered frame. He weighed about 135 pounds. His hair, which he later complemented with a short-trimmed beard, was chestnut brown. Unlike the always impeccably turned-out McClellan, Grant dressed simply and modestly (though he was never slovenly, as many unkind critics have claimed).

Grant did not aspire to be a leader among men any more than he aspired to be a soldier. His ambition upon leaving West Point was to eventually secure a position on the faculty as a mathematics professor. Had the Mexican War not intervened just three years after his graduation, Grant probably would have achieved his goal, with unknown consequences for the rest of his career.

Grant's later negative attitude toward the Mexican War is well known. At the time, however, he seems to have thought it very much the sort of romantic adventure that Kipling would subsequently make of the British army's exploits in India. Although assigned as a quartermaster in charge of supplies and stores (logistical training that later proved invaluable), Grant was determined to play an active part.

He fought in every major battle except Buena Vista. At Palo Alto, he saw his first man killed, "his brains and bones knocking down two or three others." But Grant discovered that, though the sight of blood revolted him, he was not unmanned. The very next day, he took over a company and led it in a charge against the enemy. At Monterrey, he volunteered for a dangerous solo mission to bring back badly needed ammunition. Finally, during the battle for Mexico City, he thought "outside the box" for the first time in battle. He hauled a piece of artillery into the steeple of a Mexican church and brought a Mexican unit under fire from this unlikely vantage point. Grant's commanding officer dispatched a messenger—Lieutenant John C. Pemberton, who would later surrender Vicksburg to Grant—to congratulate him. Grant was promoted for his quick thinking and gallantry.

Mexico was the true beginning of Grant's education as a soldier. He served under both great heroes of the war, Generals Winfield Scott and Zachary Taylor. While he respected both, it was the latter who made the strongest impression on the young lieutenant. Taylor dressed for comfort rather than show and scarcely looked the part of a general much of the time (unlike the resplendent Scott, who was—at least at that time—McClellan's hero). But in addition to his plain appearance, there were other aspects of Taylor's character that Grant noted carefully. "General Taylor was not an officer to trouble the administration much with his demands," Grant wrote later in his memoirs,

> but was inclined to do the best he could with the means given him. He felt his responsibility as going no further. If he had thought that he was sent to perform an impossibility with the means given him, he would probably have informed the authorities of his opinion and left them to determine what should be done. If the judgment was against him he would have gone on and done the best he could with the means at hand without parading his grievance before the public. No soldier could face either danger or responsibility more calmly than he. These are qualities more rarely found than genius or physical courage.

When he returned from the war, the woman to whom he had been engaged for four years, Julia Dent, was waiting for him; they were married in 1848. The realities of life in the peacetime army, however, were soon revealed in all their grimness. Not for Grant the relatively privileged life of an army engineer that McClellan enjoyed. Bleak, remote postings such as Sacket's Harbor, New York, and the newly won West Coast were the rule. The latter was particularly bad, since Julia could not accompany him on the dangerous journey. This was where Grant's fabled problems started.

Did he drink too much? The charge of drunkenness is one that, as William S. McFeely wrote, "is as fixed in American history as the idea that the Pilgrims ate turkey at Thanksgiving." Truly, people who could not tell you on what side Grant fought in the Civil War or that he was the eighteenth president of the United States somehow seem to "know" Grant was a drunk.

It is an odd charge to hurl at a nineteenth-century military officer, few of whom were noted abstainers. The evidence is extremely sketchy, but it appears that Grant drank when lonely or bored and that he didn't "hold" his liquor well. That is, a drink or two could cause him to become unsteady on his feet and start slurring his speech. Rumor has it that he resigned from the army in 1854 because he was threatened with court martial for drunkenness. There is no doubt, however, that he missed Julia and his children terribly on the West Coast and may have compensated by drinking. What is not in dispute, however, is that he was promoted to the rank of captain in the regular army shortly before he resigned. There were only fifty such men in the entire army at that time. That such an honor would be conferred on a man facing court martial seems unlikely.

Now began Grant's "wilderness years," in which he sought to make a living as a farmer. While the sedentary profession of farming would allow him to stay with his family, it proved an inauspicious choice for a man with an active mind and a taste for travel and adventure. In retrospect, it seems odd that he did not follow his heart and seek employment as a mathematics professor at one of the many new colleges that were springing up around the Midwest at that time.

Grant failed to make a go of farming, even as he sold firewood on the streets of nearby St. Louis as a sideline. The crash of the economy in 1857 forced Grant into his ill-starred ventures as a debt collector and real estate manager. And all the while, he was laboring under a $1,000 debt owed to the U.S. government for money stolen from the trunk of a brother officer in 1848—a theft for which Grant, as quartermaster, was held responsible.

All of this had to be profoundly humiliating for Grant. At a time when almost no Americans had a college education, much less one in a highly practical field such as engineering, his lack of success had to be galling. In his famed *Personal Memoirs,* Grant dealt with unpleasant memories mostly by simply refusing to mention them. The entire period between his resignation from the army in 1854 and the beginning of the Civil War covers barely eight pages, most concerned with the politics of the period rather than his own personal circumstances.

Yet, Grant persevered. The love and support of his wife during this period were of inestimable value. Julia told all and sundry, including her obnoxious, meddling father, that the man she married was destined for greater things. This period, Grant's dark night of the soul, prepared him well for the trials that were to come.

The Grant of the Civil War thus had little reason for boasting or bragging. "Modesty" is one of those words that clings closely to Grant, for the very good reason that it fits him well. "He was quiet in speech, although he had an impressively resonant voice," writes military historian John Keegan. "Undemonstrative in manner, indiscriminately courteous to all callers, and a listener rather than a talker. He would not tolerate gossip or backbiting, choked whisperers into silence, never swore, though he was surrounded by profaners, was careful not to chide a subordinate in public and in general tried to command by encouragement rather than reproof."

Perhaps the hurtful things that were said about him when he was down on his luck caused Grant to view his fellow men more generously. Grant's Indian aide, Brigadier General Ely S. Parker, commented on this aspect of Grant's character: "I have never heard Grant refer to any man in the way of sneer or detraction. He always sought to speak of the good in men rather than the evil, and if he had to speak of the bad qualities in a man he would close his remarks with the mention of his good points, or excuses why he did not have them. In his talk with others I have never heard him say or do anything which might embarrass or mortify them."

Grant was also generous with praise and credit. "He never tired of giving unstinting praise to his subordinates," wrote Grant's aide Horace Porter. "They felt that they would be left to the exercise of an intelligent judgement; that if they did their best, even if they did not succeed, they would never be made scapegoats; and if they gained victories they would be given the sole credit for whatever they accomplished. . . . His fidelity produced a reciprocal effect; and is one of the chief reasons they became so loyally attached to him."

Such was Grant's modesty that, for a long while during the war, he did without an orderly to look after his clothes and personal effects on campaign. (A runaway slave named Bill Barnes eventually attached himself to Grant for this purpose in 1864, in spite of the general's gentle efforts to discourage him.) Even so, Grant's needs in the field were simple to the point of being Spartan. His small tent contained a canvas bed, two folding chairs, and a wooden desk; his personal effects fit into a single trunk. Dining at Grant's headquarters bore no resemblance to McClellan's entertainments—the "champagne and oysters on the Potomac" about which Stanton grumbled. The fare was simple and Grant's was often simpler than that of his staff.

Unable to bear the sight of even animal blood, Grant ordered his meat cooked to the point of being burnt.

Grant was like McClellan in that he too could plead for more troops and supplies. Unlike McClellan, however, Grant was prepared to make do with what he had if his requests were turned down. "The more men we have, the shorter and less sanguinary will be the war," he wrote Lincoln on one occasion. "I give this entirely as my views and not in any spirit of dictation—always holding myself in readiness to use the material given me to the best advantage I know how."

Grant kept his superiors informed of his movements but did not consume their time with long, rambling discussions of the problems he faced. Lincoln appreciated this rare quality in Grant. "General Grant is a copious worker and fighter, but a very meager writer and telegrapher."

Ceremony and theater held no charms for Grant. When he arrived in Washington on March 8, 1864, to accept his commission from Lincoln as the first lieutenant general since Washington, he and his son Fred were unable to eat dinner in their hotel dining room because of the commotion his presence aroused. He fled the room before finishing his meal. The next day, he was very nearly crushed when a crowd of well-wishers at the White House suddenly mobbed him when he entered unannounced. Asked by Lincoln to make a speech upon receipt of his commission, a visibly uncomfortable Grant spoke just three sentences, in which he gave all the credit for his achievements to his men. He declined Lincoln's invitation to stay and attend a dinner in Grant's honor.

"Really, Mr. President, I have had enough of this show business," he declared. Besides, Grant added, displaying a concern for the value of time and money that was foreign to McClellan, "a dinner to me is a million dollars a day lost to the country."

And while Grant disliked politics and politicians ("I am not a politician, never was and hope never to be," he said), he recognized that he was working for politicians and must take their needs and priorities into account. Unlike McClellan, who wanted to make policy as well as carry it out and who eventually challenged Lincoln for reelection in 1864, Grant was content to let the war take its political course. While no abolitionist, Grant came to accept that the extinction of slavery would be one of the war's inevitable results, a conclusion that McClellan could never abide. When Sherman raged, McClellan-like, about political "interference" in military affairs, Grant cut him short. "In a popular war," he told his hot-tempered lieutenant, "we must consider political exigencies."

And while he loved his men and would not wantonly sacrifice their lives, he labored under no illusions about the nature of his business.

"I do not know any way to put down this rebellion and restore the authority of the Government except by fighting, and fighting means that men must be killed," he said during the Overland Campaign of the summer of 1864. "If the people of this country expect that the war can be conducted to a successful issue in any other way than by fighting, they must get somebody other than myself to command the army."

In short, Grant was possessed of that rarest of commodities: plain common sense. "And because he had this saving quality," wrote T. Harry Williams, "he was able to cope with all kinds of strange situations in this strange and modern war; situations that puzzled and even broke more traditional officers." Traditional officers like George McClellan.

From the beginning of the conflict, winning the war was Grant's only concern—not politics, not personalities, not ambition, and certainly not vanity. Except for the intense lobbying effort he undertook in the spring of 1861 to get back into the army, he did not put himself forward for high-ranking posts but waited to be noticed. "If I had sought the place or obtained it through personal or political influence," he said, "my belief is that I would have feared to undertake any plan of my own conception, and would probably have awaited direct orders from my distant superiors."

Indeed, Grant violated all the modern rules of corporate climbing. He did not "network"; he traveled with no printing press and issued no bombastic proclamations blowing his own horn; nor did he "dress for success," but allowed his record to speak for itself; he did not crave "face time" with important people but concentrated on the task at hand. He was driven by a passion to preserve the Union and set himself to that task the best way he knew how, come what may. A virtually non-existent ego made him all but selfless, a quality that endeared him to those around him. It is impossible to imagine Grant sacrificing someone such as Brigadier General Charles P. Stone to save his own skin.

"He was a success because he was a complete general and a complete character," concluded T. Harry Williams. That very completeness as an unpretentious man of character is what gave Grant the quality that historian Shelby Foote memorably described as "four o'clock in the morning courage."

Grant's aide Ely S. Parker described this trait:

> The most startling news in regard to the enemy requiring prompt action . . . would be brought to him. He would receive it without the change of a facial muscle, and give his orders immediately in the most matter of fact tones. In the most trying times he was the most self-possessed. At City Point [Grant's headquarters in the last year of the war], while he was sitting in his tent, 200 tons of powder exploded; men, mules and bodies were blown into the air, and everyone else was panic stricken. Grant sat imperturbable. He did not move from his seat or raise his hand, and only said, in his usual tone, "Babcock, go out and see what is the matter."

This was the quality that Lincoln liked best in Grant: the ability to accept responsibility with ease and even grace. In a private conversation, the president told his new general in chief that he, Lincoln, had "never professed to be a military man or to know how campaigns should be conducted, and never wanted to interfere in them." Throughout the conflict, the chief executive explained, he had simply sought someone who would "take the responsibility and act."

In Grant, he found his man. "Should my success be less than I desire and expect," Grant wrote his chief just as he embarked on the Overland Campaign against Lee in May 1864, "the least I can say is, the fault is not with you."

McClellan never wrote such a letter, because his character would not allow it. Grant's character demanded it. That fact goes a long way toward explaining why one man ended his career bitter and frustrated, while the other was hailed as "a Second Father of His Country."

---

## GRANT'S LESSONS

- Character and integrity are the building blocks of leadership. Your word must be good, and your actions must match your words.

- Loyalty runs down as well as up. Scapegoat your subordinates or "hang them out to dry" when the going gets rough, and you will find yourself without many subordinates.

- Most people are doing their best. Don't cast blame or hurl accusations without hard proof.

- Use common sense. Competitors are not ten feet tall. They have problems and difficulties just as you do. Delays and postponements help them as much as you. Waiting to move "until the time is 'just right'" might mean not moving at all.

CHAPTER 2

# VISION

*Know What You Want
and How You Are
Going to Get It*

———

*The art of war is simple enough. Find out where your enemy is.
Get at him as soon as you can. Strike him as hard as you can,
as often as you can, and keep moving on.*
—ULYSSES S. GRANT

THE STEEP HILLS and wide river that guard the approaches to Monterrey, Mexico, make it a town any general would rather defend than attack. In September 1846, a strong fortress manned by 7,000 well-armed and -provisioned Mexican troops backed by forty artillery pieces added to the difficulties faced by the outnumbered invading American army, one of whose junior officers was Lieutenant Ulysses S. Grant.

Grant was assigned as a quartermaster to the 4th Infantry regiment, a staff post that theoretically kept him out of combat but in fact did nothing of the kind. In a letter home to his future wife, Julia Dent, Grant disabused her of her father's assurances that Grant was out of danger. "Your Pa . . . pronounced me safe, for Qr. Mrs. did not have to go into battle," he wrote. "That is very true, but on the 21st of September, I voluntarily went along with the regiment and . . . continued through the fight."

The "fight" was indeed grim. After pushing the Mexicans away from the river, the hills, and the fort, the Americans found themselves engaged in fierce street combat around the town's main plaza. Eventually, commanding general Zachary Taylor was able to bluff his opponents into thinking he headed a much larger force than he actually did and so compelled their surrender.

The Mexicans received generous terms, being allowed to march out with their arms and equipment. They had fought with skill and determination. Still, Grant was struck by "how little interest the men before me had in the results of the war, and how little knowledge they had of 'what it was all about.'" Mexico, of course, was a dictatorship, whose people had little voice in how they were governed. And its dictator, Santa Anna, had no interest in those he commanded beyond using them as instruments to advance his own greed and ambition. That lack of vision was responsible, at least in part, for the ability of a small but highly motivated American army (with its belief in "manifest destiny") to defeat a much larger Mexican army fighting on its own soil.

Vision is thus an extremely powerful leadership tool. It has enabled small start-ups such as Bill Gates's Microsoft to ultimately challenge and even surpass behemoths such as IBM. Ronald Reagan had it: He wanted to end the Cold War and get the economy moving again. His successor, George Bush, did not. (The latter even made a flip reference to his lack of "the vision thing.") Reagan won reelection and was generally considered to have had a successful presidency. Bush was defeated.

Those aspiring to lead others must know where they are going and be able to communicate that fact to their subordinates. This does not mean that a leader has to put on dog-and-pony shows for his employees or invest in expensive training sessions. Such efforts are likely to prove counterproductive if undertaken in a vacuum of ideas.

One of Grant's keenest insights in the war—one that allowed him to eventually become master of the Civil War battlefield—was his early realization that the Civil War army was very different from the prewar regular army in which he had been trained and had served. Its soldiers could not be driven into battle, as Santa Anna's had been, but had to be led there. His encounter with his first Civil War command, the 21st Illinois, illustrates this:

> My regiment was composed in large part of young men of as good social position as any in their section of the State. It embraced the sons of farmers, lawyers, physicians, politicians, merchants, bankers and ministers, and some men of more mature years who had filled such positions themselves. There were also men in it who could be led astray; and the colonel, elected by the votes of the regiment, had proved to be fully capable of developing all there was in his men of recklessness. It was said that he even went so far at times as to take the guard from their posts and go with them to the village near by and make a night of it. When there came a prospect of battle the regiment wanted to have some one else to lead them. I found it very hard work for a few days to bring all the men into anything like subordination; but the great majority favored discipline, and by the application of a little regular army punishment all were reduced to as good discipline as one could ask.

In that passage, Grant showed a maturity and depth of perception that was to elude many of his fellow Union army generals. Grant himself summed up the blinkered attitude of many of these men in his assessment of the failure of Major General Don Carlos Buell to fulfill his early promise. "General Buell was a brave, intelligent officer," Grant wrote. But the man had a key failing:

He was a strict disciplinarian, and perhaps did not distinguish sufficiently between the volunteer who "enlisted for the war" and the soldier who serves in time of peace. One system embraced men who risked life for a principle, and often men of social standing, competence, or wealth and independence of character. The other includes, as a rule, only men who could not do as well in any other occupation.

Not that Grant was any softy when it came to discipline. He once knocked out a drunk with his fists and denied rations or tied to posts men who were late getting out of bed or who displayed a lack of discipline. But unlike Buell and others, Grant knew that simple punishment and displays of Napoleonic braggadocio would never get the best out of his men. They were fighting for a cause, and they had to know that their leader knew what it was and shared it—and that while he would not use their lives wantonly in its pursuit, he would nevertheless employ all the force necessary to achieve victory. Grant's vision succeeded on all these counts. It took two forms: his patriotic vision and his complementary strategic vision.

## GRANT'S PATRIOTIC VISION

AFTER CONFEDERATE FORCES fired on Fort Sumter, any chance of peacefully resolving the differences between North and South was gone. The United States Army, with its mix of Northern and Southern personnel, began falling apart as its officers chose their allegiances. George B. McClellan, second in the West Point class of 1846, had earlier left the army to become an executive of the Illinois Central Railroad, and his military services for the coming conflict were being avidly sought by several Northern states. Yet when his former

West Point roommate, A. P. Hill, announced his decision to "go South," McClellan was philosophical.

"I cannot blame you," the Northerner said to the Virginian. "I am an Ohioan, and I am standing by my state, too."

A few months earlier, a young Galena, Illinois, man with Southern sympathies burst into the leather goods store owned by Jesse Root Grant, where Jesse's eldest son, Ulysses, twenty-first out of thirty-nine cadets in the West Point Class of 1843, was unhappily employed. The visitor excitedly exclaimed that the convention of delegates from the states that had seceded from the Union, meeting at Montgomery, Alabama, had just elected Jefferson Davis president of the so-called Confederate States of America. When the young man repeated the news in a self-satisfied manner, Ulysses S. Grant, perched on a shelf ladder, glared down and displayed a rare flash of temper.

"Davis and the whole gang of them ought to be hung!" he snapped.

McClellan's mild, almost chivalric, reaction to Hill's decision and his approval of the primacy of local loyalties contrasts sharply with Grant's passionate outburst of loyalty to the Union. While it may be only a coincidence that McClellan's once brilliant military career ultimately ended in defeat and disappointment, while Grant's went from obscurity to triumph and acclaim, their very different outlook on the conflict that rent their nation suggests that it is not.

Grant's devotion to the Union and its cause is something that has earned surprisingly little attention from those who have studied his career. (Brooks D. Simpson is a notable exception.) It seems simply to be assumed. True, he was born in the free state of Ohio, and his father, the leather entrepreneur, was strongly antislavery. But Grant also had twenty-six cousins in Virginia and Kentucky, many of whom owned slaves, while he had only eleven cousins in Ohio. His West Point roommate, Frederick Dent, was from a well-to-do slaveholding family in Missouri, and Grant married Dent's sister Julia. (Although Frederick Dent remained loyal to the Union during the war, another brother, John Dent, was an open Rebel sympathizer and even went so far as to cross the lines and seek to travel through the Confederacy. The Confederates, not knowing what to make of him, imprisoned him.)

While Grant did not care for slavery, he knew that getting rid of it would be impractical. He thought abolitionists were troublemakers, lived in the slave state of Missouri for most of the time between leaving the army in 1854 and going to Galena in 1860, and even tolerated the "peculiar institution" under his own roof (Julia owned four slaves). Grant himself had briefly owned a slave before freeing him in 1859 (see chapter 12). He voted for the pro-slavery James Buchanan for president in 1856. Some of his closest friends at West Point and in the prewar army would go on to hold high positions in the newly forming Confederate army. In addition to James "Pete" Longstreet (a cousin of Julia's), these included Lafayette McClaws and Simon Bolivar Buckner.

Northerners with more tenuous ties to the South than these had decided to serve the Confederacy. Pennsylvania-born Confederate lieutenant general John C. Pemberton, who would lose Vicksburg to Grant in 1863, was married to a Virginia woman. And Major General Mansfield Lovell, who would lose New Orleans in April 1862, had served as deputy street commissioner in New York City under future Confederate major general Gustavus W. Smith. Grant, however, seems never to have entertained the notion of "going South." He was, above all else, a patriot. "With a soldier, the flag is paramount," he explained to a journalist late in life. Although he personally had doubts about the justice of the Mexican War, it never occurred to him to do anything less than his full duty. "I considered my supreme duty was to my flag."

By the time of Fort Sumter, changing political conditions and advances in technology were bringing to an end the era of purely local loyalties. The right of secession, if it existed at all, Grant believed, ended with the admission of new states to the Union. The passage of the Fugitive Slave Act and the Supreme Court's Dred Scott decision made Northerners, the great bulk of whom were not opposed to slavery in the South as long as they themselves had no part in it, complicit in the maintenance of the institution whether they liked it or not. The invention of the steamboat, railroad, and telegraph in the decades before the war had bound the regions more closely together than had previously been thought possible. The flourishing cotton trade between the lines during the war, in spite of Grant's efforts to stamp it out, demonstrated how close those ties had become.

McClellan, for his part, certainly considered himself a patriot. But as his parting words to Hill show, as well as his words and actions during the war, he was far too considerate of Southern sensibilities, very much including slavery, to fight the war to a decisive conclusion. He held fast to the idea that the South could be brought forcibly back into the Union with slavery intact, even as the lengthening conflict (and casualty lists) caused Lincoln, Grant, and most other Northerners to abandon the notion. The fact that McClellan's army did not mutiny when the Emancipation Proclamation was issued, as he thought it might, apparently did little to convince the Young Napoleon that Northern attitudes were swinging in the direction of making the abolition of slavery a Union war goal. Little Mac's vision of what constituted victory was thus cloudy and out of step with Northern opinion. Grant's was not. "One side or the other had to yield principles they deemed dearer than life before [the war] could be brought to an end," Grant wrote in the conclusion of his memoirs.

Some consider patriotism a simple, even simplistic, instinct. But Grant's patriotism, while deeply emotional, was not of an unthinking variety. He believed his nation's cause was just. He saw the United States as a strong, intelligent nation, populated by a peaceful, prosperous, self-governing citizenry—who were free to better their condition through industry and who had the right to retain the fruits of their labor. And this vision held no room for secession or what Grant believed was its ultimate cause, slavery.

Grant elaborated this position in his *Personal Memoirs:*

There was no time during the rebellion when I did not think, and often say, that the South was more to be benefited by its defeat than the North. The latter had the people, the institutions, and the territory to make a great and prosperous nation. The former was burdened with an institution abhorrent to all civilized people not brought up under it, and one which degraded labor, kept it in ignorance, and enervated the governing class. With the outside world at war with this institution, they could not have extended their territory. The labor of the country was not skilled, nor allowed to become so. The whites could not toil without becoming degraded, and those who did were denominated "poor white trash." The system of labor would have soon exhausted the soil and left the people poor. The non-slaveholders would have left the country, and the small slaveholder must have sold out to his more fortunate neighbor. Soon the slaves would have outnumbered the masters, and, not being in sympathy with them, would have risen in their might and exterminated them. The war was expensive to the South as well as to the North, both in blood and treasure, but it was worth all it cost.

Worth it because, with a Union victory, the South could be a part of a great, rich nation with its best days before it, rather than being a relatively poor independent nation of limited

potential. Grant also believed that the meddling by Great
Britain and France during the Civil War, especially the latter's
effort to establish a puppet empire in Mexico, was proof that a
divided country would inevitably tempt foreign powers to take
advantage of the situation:

> Seeing a nation that extended from ocean to ocean, embracing
> the better part of a continent, growing as we were growing in
> population, wealth and intelligence, the European nations
> thought it would be well to give us a check. We might, possibly,
> after a while threaten their peace, or, at least, the perpetuity of
> their institutions. Hence, England was constantly finding fault
> with the administration at Washington because we were not able
> to keep up an effective blockade. She also joined, at first, with
> France and Spain in setting up an Austrian prince [Maximilian]
> upon the throne in Mexico, totally disregarding any rights or
> claims that Mexico had of being treated as an independent
> power. It is true they trumped up grievances as a pretext, but
> they were only pretexts which can always be found when wanted.

Grant shared fully with his future chief, Abraham Lincoln,
the view of the United States as, in Lincoln's words, "the last
best hope of earth." While he could respect those who pas-
sionately believed in the cause of secession, including Robert
E. Lee, that did nothing to shake his belief in their cause as
"one of the worst for which a people ever fought, and one for
which there was the least excuse."

And that meant there was no room for any negotiated set-
tlement that would lead to separation. In an 1864 letter to his
political patron, Representative Elihu B. Washburne, that was
clearly intended for public consumption and that received
wide distribution at the time, Grant cogently summarized for
the Northern public, very much including his own soldiers,
what the South's terms were likely to be should the North's
"peace at any price" lobby prevail:

Our peace friends, if they expect peace from separation, are much mistaken. It would be but the beginning of war. . . . the South would demand the restoration of their slaves already freed. They would demand indemnity for losses already sustained, and they would demand a treaty which would make the North slave hunters for the South. They would demand pay or the restoration of every slave escaping to the North.

The ultimate proof of Grant's perception of the Civil War as being supremely a people's contest lay in his efforts during the 1864 presidential election to facilitate voting by soldiers in the field. The "soldier vote" went heavily for Lincoln—and, by extension, Grant—and against their former chief, Democratic nominee McClellan.

Grant's patriotism was the wellspring of his leadership. It gave him the inner strength he needed to retain hope in the eventual triumph of the Union's cause when many around him verged on despair. His love of country was stronger than his hatred of war, and Grant hated war very much. If it took a terrible war to preserve that country for future generations of Americans, then let it come. But a war without proper direction would be little more than a crime.

## GRANT'S STRATEGIC VISION

DENNIS HART MAHAN is best known as the father of Admiral Alfred Thayer Mahan, author of *The Influence of Sea Power upon History*. But the father had his own claim to fame as one of the leading instructors at West Point in the decades before the Civil War. A graduate of the famed French military engineering school at Metz, Mahan had never heard a shot fired in anger. But he was the intellectual monarch of

West Point, and he taught military engineering and what was termed "the science of war."

The raspy-voiced Mahan was a devotee of Napoleon Bonaparte and presided over the Napoleon Club, a discussion group devoted to the campaigns of the great Corsican, which only the most promising students were invited to join. Mc-Clellan was its star; Grant was shut out.

Mahan believed there were two things absolutely essential to success in military affairs. One was the need for "celerity," or rapidity of movement. The second was being unafraid to use one's own reason on the battlefield—despite what Napoleon might have done.

But, as military historian John Keegan has pointed out, Mahan added to his curriculum one further lesson that he could not have derived from Napoleon, who campaigned mostly in the densely populated lands of western Europe, with its good roads and historic towns. For a continent-sized nation such as the United States, with its few good roads and widely dispersed people, a different approach was needed. "Carrying the war into the heart of the assailant's country," he said in his lectures, "is the surest way of making him share its burdens and foiling his plans."

McClellan, despite his stature as Mahan's pet pupil, seems not to have absorbed these lessons from his mentor. Rather, he seems to have paid more attention to prevailing European interpretations of Napoleon's campaigns, which emphasized destroying the enemy's army in a single, showdown battle, seizing strategic points, and capturing the enemy's capital. Grant, who could not have cared much for Mahan's strict military discipline in the lecture hall and who studied Napoleon carefully without worshiping him, seems to have listened rather more closely.

Around Vicksburg and at Chattanooga, Grant moved with undoubted celerity. Nor did he ever become so wedded to a plan that he thought it couldn't be changed. Finally, Grant and his most trusted lieutenant, William T. Sherman, made pushing the war into an enemy's country and "making him share its burdens" into an art form when they marched through the heart of the Confederacy.

In his official report, written after the war, Grant used a country metaphor to describe the movements of the Union armies prior to his taking command. They were, he said, "without concert, like a balky team, no two ever pulling together." Grant was the first of Lincoln's generals to see the war as a whole, just as his chief had done from the outset. Here is how he described his strategy for winning the war in his memoirs:

> The Union armies were now divided into nineteen departments. . . . Before this time these various armies had acted separately and independently of each other, giving the enemy an opportunity often of depleting one command, not pressed, to reinforce another more actively engaged. I determined to stop this. To this end I regarded the Army of the Potomac as the center, and all west to Memphis along the line described as our position at the time, and north of it, the right wing; the Army of the James, under General [Benjamin] Butler, as the left wing, and all the troops south, as a force in rear of the enemy . . . concentration was the order of the day, and to have it accomplished in time to advance at the earliest moment the roads would permit was the problem. . . . My general plan now was to concentrate all the force possible against the Confederate armies in the field. There were but two such, as we have seen, east of the Mississippi River and facing north. The Army of Northern Virginia, General Robert E. Lee commanding, was on the south bank of the Rapidan, confronting the Army of the Potomac; the second, under General Joseph E. Johnston, was at Dalton, Georgia, opposed to Sherman who was still at Chattanooga. . . . Accordingly I

arranged for a simultaneous movement all along the line. Sherman was to move from Chattanooga, Johnston's army and Atlanta being his objective points.

As for Meade's Army of the Potomac in the east, the orders were similarly straightforward: "Lee's army will be your objective point," Grant wrote. "Wherever Lee goes, there you will go also."

Thus, no longer would strategic points on a map or the capture of the enemy's capital ("on to Richmond") be paramount. These would fall into Grant's hands as ripe fruit from a tree once the armies protecting them had been defeated. He would also stay on offense, giving the enemy no rest and thus discarding any McClellan-like quest for a single, pitched battle. If the enemy blocked his path, he would take advantage of his army's superior mobility and firepower to use a part of his force to "pin" the enemy in place while the remainder swung around to envelop the enemy.

Grant's soldiers caught on quickly, dubbing this "the jug handle movement." After the war, it would be adopted by the United States Army as its primary strategic doctrine. General Norman Schwarzkopf's famed "left hook" through the Iraqi desert, which struck the Iraqis hard in their right flank while other Allied forces pinned the Iraqis in place in Kuwait, was pure Ulysses S. Grant.

Like most brilliant insights, Grant's strategy was stunningly simple in its design. The execution would prove rather more difficult than probably even Grant anticipated. In spite of Grant's efforts at applying relentless pressure, Lee was still able to detach Lieutenant General Jubal Early on a diversionary raid toward Washington in 1864. And a relatively small Confederate force was able to keep the incompetent Ben Butler bottled up on the Virginia Peninsula.

Striking the Confederate armies in the field, however, was only a part of the plan. Those armies needed food, uniforms, weapons, and ammunition in order to fight. Their horses needed forage and shoes. Most of all, they needed men, trigger-pullers in the ranks. By the spring of 1864, virtually every able-bodied white Southern male of military age was already serving, as were a good many who were not of military age. Prisoners being taken now included smooth-faced young boys and gray-bearded old men. The South was "robbing the cradle and the grave alike," Grant said, in order to keep fighting.

To deprive the army of matériel, Grant dispatched the Union cavalry to the Shenandoah Valley. Lying between the Blue Ridge and Allegheny mountain chains, the great valley of Virginia had served for three years as a base of supply for Confederate armies in Virginia. The forces under Phil Sheridan, the Union commander, were to carry off grain, cattle, and horses and then burn and destroy what they could not carry. A crow flying over the Valley, Grant told his cavalry chief, should need to carry its own rations if it wanted to survive there. Elsewhere, Southern railroads were torn up, the ties burned, and the rails twisted to prevent their repair. Southern ports from which blockade runners operated were captured and turned to Union use.

Depriving the South of soldiers was more complicated. The most straightforward way was by killing them, though this method certainly was costly to Grant as well.

Fortunately for the Union infantry, there were other, less costly, ways of subtracting Southern numbers, and their chief was determined to exploit each of them. First, Confederate recruitment was dampened by the shortage of food and equipment within its armies in the last year of the war, as well as by the sight of Northern armies marching virtually unopposed through Georgia and the Carolinas. Second, Grant's abolition of the system of prisoner exchange (see chapter 12) played to the North's superior manpower pool and prevented captured Confederates from fighting again.

Third, the abolition of slavery and the recruitment of freed slaves into the Union army had the dual advantage of augmenting Grant's own ranks while encouraging enslaved blacks in the South to desert their plantations. The loss of slave labor thus forced plantation mistresses and small children into the fields to avert starvation, a situation that presented Southern husbands and fathers in gray with an agonizing choice between their military and family duties.

All of these factors combined caused substantial numbers of Southern men to opt out of the struggle. In the last winter of the war, Grant estimated the South was losing the equivalent of a regiment a day to desertion.

Grant and Sherman have often been accused, usually by latter-day Southern partisans, of waging "uncivilized" war against innocents in their quest for victory. Harsh it certainly was, which Sherman never denied. "Uncivilized," however, is a loaded term that can easily be flung back at those who hurl it.

Was the Confederacy's declaration that captured black Union soldiers would be treated, not as prisoners of war, but as slaves in rebellion (and so would be executed) an example of "civilized" warfare? Wounded and surrendered black Union troops were massacred at Fort Pillow, Tennessee, and Poison Springs, Arkansas, in 1864, and there were several similar incidents at other times and places. Free blacks who were unfortunate enough to fall into Confederate hands during the Gettysburg campaign were sent south into slavery.

And none of this is to mention the practice and defense of chattel slavery itself, which most of the civilized world had repudiated by 1861.

Grant never advocated or condoned the killing of un-
armed civilians. In fact, one of the interesting aspects of the
Civil War is not how *many* civilians were killed, but how *few*.
Only a single civilian, a teenaged girl named Jenny Wade, was
killed at Gettysburg, the bloodiest single battle of the war
(and she by a stray shot).

President Harry S. Truman braved the charges of being
"uncivilized" for ordering the atomic bombings of Hiroshima
and Nagasaki because he believed the most civilized thing he
could do was bring the war to as rapid a conclusion as possible. Grant's view of his own role in the Civil War was remarkably similar.

## The "Machine Thought"

In the end, Grant created a military machine such as the
world had never seen, not simply in terms of the number of
men or the amount of equipment, but also in terms of the
"machine thought." As he described it in his memoirs:

> European armies know very little what they are fighting for,
> and care less. . . . The armies of Europe are machines: the men
> are brave and the officers capable; but the majority of the sol-
> diers in most of the nations of Europe are taken from a class of
> people who are not very intelligent and who have very little in-
> terest in the contest in which they are called upon to take part.
> Our armies were composed of men who were able to read, men
> who knew what they were fighting for, and could not be in-
> duced to serve as soldiers, except in an emergency when the
> safety of the nation was involved, and so necessarily must have
> been more than equal to men who fought merely because they
> were brave and because they were thoroughly drilled and in-
> ured to hardships.

He might also have added the Mexican army that he had seen surrender at Monterrey nearly twenty years earlier. The lesson is clear: If you want the best out of your people, they must know what they are doing and why they are doing it. Vision provides the motivation; you must supply the vision.

## GRANT'S LESSONS

- Know what you are trying to achieve.

- Be able to communicate that fact to your subordinates in terms they can understand.

# CHAPTER 3

# PLANNING AND DECISION MAKING

*Think First, Then Act—*
*and Keep the Initiative*

———————————

*He would sit and think and listen to everything you said*
*and say nothing in reply.*
—GRANT'S NEIGHBOR ELIZA SHAW, ON MEETING THE
GENERAL DURING THE VICKSBURG CAMPAIGN

*Making decisions is of the essence in leadership.*
—DWIGHT D. EISENHOWER

ON SEPTEMBER 4, 1861, U. S. Grant, promoted to
the rank of brigadier general barely one month earlier, established his headquarters at Cairo, Illinois, the southernmost
major town that had remained loyal to the United States after
the secession of the Southern states. Cairo's strategic value
was obvious, situated as it is at the confluence of the Ohio
and Mississippi Rivers. Most other generals would have concentrated on fortifying and holding it, dismissing all other
concerns as being of secondary importance.

Barely twenty-four hours after arriving, however, Grant
demonstrated he was not just another general.

A Negro spy brought the newly arrived commander word that on September 3 Confederate forces had occupied Columbus, Kentucky, a town located barely twenty miles downriver from Cairo and whose bluffs commanded the mighty Mississippi. Grant knew that orders were strict to avoid violating the tenuous neutrality that Kentucky sought to maintain in the spreading civil war, for the side that first marched troops into the Bluegrass State would likely tip that divided state's loyalties into the other camp's column.

It would not be the last time in this war that Grant would rely on the word of a black man as the basis for a major change in his plans. (Vicksburg would be another.) Now that the South had moved first, Grant was determined not to lose a moment. Forty miles up the Ohio River from Cairo lay the Kentucky town of Paducah, which commanded the mouth of another of the South's great rivers, the Tennessee. Realizing that if he knew the value of Paducah, the Rebels likely would too, Grant immediately began organizing troops for the move upriver and commandeered local steamboats for transport.

Grant telegraphed his plans to his superior officer, Major General John C. Fremont. When Grant received no response by the evening of the 5th, however, he dispatched another telegram stating that if he received no orders to the contrary, he would sail immediately. Grant then cast off before he could receive any reply.

Arriving at Paducah at dawn on the 6th, Grant's men were disheartened by the sight of Confederate flags fluttering over the buildings. Had the Rebels beaten them after all? No, it turned out. The citizens were indeed expecting troops—but the ones who wore gray. Many were crestfallen at the sight of bluecoats marching up their streets instead. Later that day, for good measure, Grant sent troops farther up the river to seize the town of Smithland, at the mouth of the mighty Cumberland River.

Quick thinking and fast action of the kind Grant displayed in grabbing the two towns was highly unusual at this early stage of the war. (It would remain unusual, on the Union side, in any case, almost to the end.) Why did he do it? Simple: He learned from experience.

A few months earlier, while still in command of the 21st Illinois, Grant moved toward Florida, Missouri, which was believed to be the camp of a Confederate colonel named Thomas Harris and his command.

> As we approached the brow of the hill from which it was expected we could see Harris' camp, and possibly find his men ready formed to meet us, my heart kept getting higher and higher until it felt to me as though it was in my throat. I would have given anything then to have been back in Illinois, but I had not the moral courage to halt . . . I kept right on. When we reached a point from which the valley below was in full view I halted. The place where Harris had been encamped a few days before was still there and the marks of a recent encampment were plainly visible, but the troops were gone. . . . It occurred to me at once that Harris had been as much afraid of me as I had been of him. This was a view of the question I had never taken before; but it was one I never forgot afterwards. From that event to the close of the war, I never experienced trepidation upon confronting an enemy, though I always felt more or less anxiety. I never forgot that he had as much reason to fear my forces as I had his. The lesson was valuable.

Thus, without even coming under fire, Grant had learned the lesson that would eventually serve as the foundation for his entire approach to leadership. Opponents are not Supermen. They have problems just as you have problems. They feel fear as you feel fear. Delay helps them as much as it helps you. Thereafter, Grant chose to concentrate on what he was going to do to them, rather than worrying about what they were going to do to him. In other words, he would keep the initiative.

That proved easier said than done, at least for the moment. Unfortunately for Grant, the Confederates weren't the only ones frightened by his daring. So were his own superiors. Grant's pleas to be allowed to advance on Columbus, Kentucky, before the Confederates fortified it too strongly received no reply. Nevertheless, the occupation of Paducah had laid the groundwork for the riverine operations that would become Grant's signature. Almost by accident, the newly minted brigadier general had invented the concept of "combined operations" between the army and navy. It was one he would refine further and eventually master. Temporarily stymied after Paducah, Grant returned to his desk in Cairo, lit his pipe (cigars would come later), unfolded his maps, and began to ponder.

Paducah was captured more or less on the fly, with minimal planning involved. But with the Federal war effort as disorganized as the Confederate at this point, that scarcely mattered. As the war went on, however, and operations became larger and more complex, Grant discovered that his actions had to be preceded by careful, detailed planning. His mastery of this art had much to do with his success.

## GRANT'S PLANNING PROCESS

"WAR IS ESSENTIALLY CHAOS," states Lieutenant General Charles "Chuck" Horner in his memoir of the Gulf War, *Every Man a Tiger* (written with Tom Clancy). "The line between control and sickening confusion is paper-thin. If one takes care, the violence applied can be focused with precision. Yet even when care is taken, it can easily degenerate into wild and formless mayhem. . . . It is no surprise that commanders devote much of their best effort to reducing chaos. One of the major means to that end is 'The Plan.'"

Chaos and mayhem are the very antithesis of organization. Planning is designed to reduce (it can never eliminate) the likelihood of either occurring. Planning—and decision making based on the plan—is where vision meets reality. Since the scope of human action is almost unlimited, the planning process involves winnowing down all the many possible courses of action to those that fit both the time and resources available. If your budget is $100,000 and you have three months, don't put a plan on your CEO's desk that will cost $2 million and take a year to implement.

This was the aspect of planning that McClellan could never grasp. His desire to dominate others inhibited the free-ranging discussion that an effective planning process requires. Grant's success as a planner, in contrast, was due to the fact that he was a *listener* as well as a *thinker*. He summarized his approach when he explained why he wasn't big on business meetings:

> I never held a council of war in my life. [Not true. He held one early in the war, but found it unproductive and did not repeat it.] I never heard of Sherman or Sheridan doing so. Of course I heard all that everyone had to say, and in headquarters there is an interesting and constant stream of talk. But I always made up my mind to act, and the first that even my staff knew of any movement was when I wrote it out in rough and gave it to be copied off. It is always safe in war to keep your own counsel. No man living ever knew what my plan and campaigns would be until they were matured. My orders were generally written in my own handwriting. I was always walking and conferring with generals, and hearing what one would say and another. But the decision was always my own.

"Taciturn" is a word often associated with Grant. He could indeed be a man of few words. Many have mistaken Grant's long silences for a lack of intellectual drive. Nothing could have been further from the truth. Grant could be a lively, amusing conversationalist. But unless he had something useful to contribute, he did not open his mouth simply for the sake of doing so. Rather, he listened to those talking around him in an effort to help him make up his mind.

Sherman's proposed March to the Sea from Atlanta through Georgia in late 1864, for example, was one of the most contentious issues with which Grant had to grapple as general in chief. The decision-making process is well described by Horace Porter, Grant's aide in the last year of the war.

"Many evenings were occupied in discussing the pros and cons of the contemplated movement," wrote Porter. "The staff had in fact resolved itself into an animated debating society. The general-in-chief would sit quietly by, listening to the arguments, and sometimes allowed himself greatly amused by the vehemence of the debaters. One night the discussion waxed, particularly warm, and was kept up for some time after the general had gone to bed. About one o'clock, he poked his head out of his tent . . . 'Oh do go to bed all of you! You are keeping the whole camp awake!'"

Note that Grant merely sat and listened to the discussion between the two contending camps. Arguing in the negative was John Rawlins, Grant's chief of staff, who thought that Sherman's idea for cutting loose from his supply base and living off the Georgia countryside would lead to disaster. In the affirmative was Porter, who had visited Sherman in Georgia at Grant's behest and had been convinced by the fiery general that the March to the Sea would work. Grant used the resulting discussion to hear the pros and cons of each point of view and weigh them in his own mind. Encouraging this sort of intellectual sparring on one's staff can help a manager in any organization do the same.

The informal give-and-take that took place around Grant's headquarters was greatly to be preferred to formal, sit-down meetings, he believed. "Councils of war don't fight" was an adage Grant believed in wholeheartedly. Such gatherings tended to dilute the sense of individual responsibility. Furthermore, some people participating in a formal meeting would undoubtedly be in opposition to the course ultimately decided upon. Thus they might be persuaded, even subconsciously, to give less than their best effort, believing that success might reflect badly on their own judgment. Better to allow people to express themselves informally; that way, if the decision goes against them, they will not have been publicly humiliated by having their views discounted.

Concentrated listening, however, does not preclude the asking of questions. Grant's brother-in-law, Frederick Dent, who served on his staff, noted this aspect of his chief's modus operandi. "He was constantly questioning his officers on various points in a very modest way, and never saying much himself. In this way he formed his opinions of the men he had to deal with, and knew who could do certain work best."

So simple was this talking through of options that members of the staff caught on and began using it in order to get their ideas in front of the general. Adam Badeau, who served with Grant in the field and later wrote a history of Grant's campaigns, described how this worked to his roommate, Henry Adams after the war: "For stretches at a time, his mind seemed torpid. Rawlins and others would systematically talk their ideas into it, not directly, but by discussions among themselves, in his presence. In the end, he would announce the idea as his own, without seeming conscious of the discussion; and would give the orders to carry it out with all the energy that belonged to his nature."

This process was successful not merely with his immediate staff but with high-ranking subordinate field commanders as well. Shortly before the grand offensive of May 1864, Grant made a special trip to Fort Monroe, Virginia, headquarters of the prickly, militarily incompetent—but politically power-ful—Major General Benjamin Butler. "This was the first time I had ever met him," Grant wrote. "Before giving him any or-der as to the part he was to play in the approaching campaign I invited his views. They were very much such as I intended to direct, and as I did direct, in writing before leaving."

Thus, although Grant was ultimately compelled to fire Butler, his solicitous attitude at this first meeting got a poten-tially rocky relationship off on the right foot.

A manager should also never lose sight of the fact that many subordinates are intimidated by authority and are reluc-tant to volunteer their views. One wouldn't expect that the hot-tempered Major General Phil Sheridan would fall into the latter category, but on at least one occasion near the end of the war, Grant felt compelled to draw him out. The commanding general had heard through intermediaries that Sheridan had ideas for attacking the Confederates around Petersburg but was reluctant to offer his chief unsolicited advice. Grant im-mediately sent for Sheridan and asked for his thoughts. The re-sult was the successful Battle of Five Forks on April 1, 1865, the clash that ultimately unhinged the Confederacy.

But woe to a subordinate who thought he could get away with a lack of details or fuzzy answers. "Grant, I think," as Sherman once told John Russell Young, "knew every tin can in the army." He was a slow, careful reader who went over every page as if studying it, putting his finger on the passage when interrupted so as to be sure to find the place. He rarely forgot what he read—indeed, his memory might well have been pho-tographic. He never generalized over facts or merely gave one an impression of things. "What he knew he knew," Young wrote. "You could not forget a figure or misplace a phrase in his presence. It was not safe to say 'about so,' it must be ex-actly so. This wonderful gift served him as a soldier, for there, mirrored in his brain, lay before him, in the minutest detail, his work and the means by which his work was to be done."

Grant also gathered input from as many sources as he could before making important decisions. He read captured Confederate newspapers avidly, often discovering therein important information about Confederate movements. It was a Confederate newspaper account, for example, that tipped Grant to the fact that Sherman was about to be counterattacked as he closed the ring around Atlanta. Confederate president Jefferson Davis had been quoted as predicting that Sherman would be driven back from Atlanta "as Napoleon retreated from Moscow." "He neglected to say who would furnish the snow for this Moscow retreat," snorted Grant.

Sympathetic local people, who were usually, but not exclusively, black, often brought him timely and important news, as Paducah demonstrated.

A further, underrated but important, element in planning is quiet time. Grant's distaste for showy reviews and bombastic speeches served him well because he could use the time such excesses consumed in deciding how best to employ his troops. He would often spend hours in his tent, sitting at a camp desk, smoking a cigar, a candle illuminating a map, examining his options. Porter describes Grant on campaign, sitting outside his tent, smoking a cigar and staring off into space, looking for all the world like the most bored man in camp. Porter and the rest of the staff, of course, knew better. Grant was thinking.

## A Dynamic Process

Grant also never lost sight of the fact that the plan was meant to serve *him;* he did not live to serve *it.* The enemy plans as well, and he reacts to your plans. The unplanned and the unexpected, therefore, must be factored in. George McClellan did not do this well. Egotistically committed to his plan for the Peninsula Campaign, he stubbornly insisted on carrying it out even after Confederate forces unexpectedly abandoned their advanced positions in northern Virginia and pulled back nearly thirty miles closer to Richmond. That made the Peninsula plan, which was dependent on keeping Confederate forces out of the vicinity of Richmond for as long as possible, far less likely to succeed.

An even greater planning disaster was Major General Ambrose E. Burnside's Battle of Fredericksburg. Although today his name is a by-word for ineptitude, it is often forgotten just how close Burnside came to actually succeeding at Fredericksburg. After taking over from the fired McClellan on November 7, 1862, Burnside examined his predecessor's plans and found them unsatisfactory. He formulated a new plan and submitted it to President Lincoln for approval. The chief executive thought it would work but emphasized the need for speed. The approval process, however, had already consumed a full week.

The new commander's idea was to slip away from, rather than move toward, Robert E. Lee's Army of Northern Virginia. Burnside's immediate objective would be the strategic town of Fredericksburg, which dominated the crossings of the Rappahannock River between Richmond and Washington, D.C. If Burnside could seize the town before Lee's troops arrived, he could put the Army of the Potomac between Lee and his own capital. The Confederate commander would thus be forced to either surrender Richmond or fight in open country against odds that heavily favored the Federals.

It was a good plan, and, in spite of the week's delay, Burnside managed to slip away from Lee and beat him to the shores of the Rappahannock. There was just one problem: There were no bridges to cross the river when he got there. True, the stream was low enough that the troops could have forded it. But the Rappahannock was (and is) prone to flash flooding, and a sudden rise in the river would risk trapping the army on the south bank with no way to get back. The pontoon bridges that Burnside had been promised by the War Department were nowhere to be found. For days, the Federal army sat on its haunches, watching helplessly as thousands of Confederate troops poured into the town on the other side of the river, fortifying it against assault.

A change of plan was clearly called for, but none was forthcoming. This paralysis, concluded Bruce Catton in *Never Call Retreat,* brought into glaring relief Burnside's single greatest defect as a soldier: his inability to improvise. "He had to follow the original plan, even though the delay had ruined it," Catton wrote. "What followed was not so much a battle as a military tragedy."

Indeed, Fredericksburg proved that there was courage aplenty in the ranks of the Federal army, as they hurled themselves again and again against clearly impregnable Confederate defenses located behind a stone wall at the base of a hill called Marye's Heights. Still, there was opportunity to be seized if only Burnside could have grasped it. A division led by George G. Meade, the future victor of Gettysburg, made an unexpected breakthrough on the Confederate right, a success that—had it been immediately reinforced—might have allowed Union troops to pour through and attack the infamous stone wall from the rear. But Burnside's obstinate decision to stick with his plan (and to place his headquarters out of sight of the battlefield) filtered down to his commanders. Meade was not reinforced and had to fall back.

Grant's plans, by contrast, admitted of flexibility and change. What did not change was his vision: defeat of the enemy army and destruction of its ability to wage war.

"When [Grant] begins a campaign, he fixes in his mind what is his true objective point, and abandons all minor ones," Sherman recalled. "If his plan works wrong, he is never disconcerted, but promptly devises a new one, and is sure he will win in the end."

## *Planning in Action: The Vicksburg Campaign*

Rear Admiral David Dixon Porter, the son of a War of 1812 naval hero, was dining aboard a riverboat at Cairo, Illinois, in early December 1862 when a surprise guest interrupted the festivities. To the elegantly attired army and navy officers gathered around the table, the unimpressive-looking man dressed in rumpled civilian clothes did not seem important at first glance. "Admiral Porter, meet General Grant," said an army officer who was present.

The two men exchanged pleasantries and then moved off to a table by themselves. The prewar army and navy had occupied utterly separate worlds that rarely crossed paths. That would have to change. The great rivers that reached down into the heart of the Confederacy—the Tennessee, the Cumberland, and especially the mighty Mississippi—held the potential to serve either as barriers to Grant's plans or as highways. With Porter's help, they could be the latter; without it, they would be the former.

But Grant rarely went into a high-stakes game without having a good idea of the likely outcome. Porter was a fighter, like Grant himself. In the earliest days of the war, he jumped the chain of command and went straight to Lincoln with a plan for relieving Fort Pickens in Pensacola harbor. Impressed with a display of initiative that the president was to find all too rare in the war, Lincoln sent the brazen officer on his way, and Fort Pickens was duly saved. In short, if anyone in the navy was inclined to work closely with the army, it would be Porter.

Furthermore, Grant knew that Porter and Sherman had been exchanging letters for more than a month before the meeting and that Porter was favorably disposed toward helping the army move against the Confederate bastion at Vicksburg, Mississippi. The ground thus prepared, the two men talked for only about twenty minutes. Porter recalled detecting no hint of the sense of superiority or attitude of disdain that army officers were supposed to harbor toward their brothers in the naval service. When the two men rose, Porter was convinced that if anything was going to happen to win the war, Grant was the man who would make it happen. The plan to take Vicksburg began taking shape in that stateroom.

As previously noted, Grant was the first important commander in the Civil War to recognize the potential for army-navy cooperation. It was yet another example of Grant's thinking outside the box of rules, regulations, and organization charts. Simply because someone doesn't report to you in the chain of command doesn't mean you can't do business together for mutual benefit.

And the Union war effort would need every ounce of cooperation it could get. The Mississippi River was the single most important economic feature of the North American continent at the time of the Civil War. It was no exaggeration to call it the very lifeblood of America. Upon the secession of the Southern states, the river was closed to unfettered navigation, a situation that threatened to strangle the commerce on which the states of Illinois, Iowa, Ohio, and Minnesota depended. President Abraham Lincoln told his civil and military leaders, "See what a lot of land these fellows hold, of which Vicksburg is the key. The war can never be brought to a close until that key is in our pocket. . . . We can take all the northern ports of the Confederacy, and they can defy us from Vicksburg." Lincoln, who once patented a device to assist Mississippi riverboats over shoals, assured his listeners that "I am acquainted with that region and know what I am talking about, and as valuable as New Orleans will be to us, Vicksburg will be more so."

The capture of the bastion that Confederate president Jefferson Davis dubbed "the Gibraltar of the West" has justly been called Grant's greatest campaign. At a cost of fewer than 10,000 casualties (those who apply to Grant the tag "butcher of his own men" always overlook Vicksburg), he accomplished all of President Lincoln's ambitious goals. Rarely in the history of warfare has a target of such inestimable value been purchased at so meager a price.

Grant began formulating his move against Vicksburg in the fall of 1862 after a complex series of maneuvers in the north-central part of Mississippi had largely secured the area for the Union. As Grant pondered his options, he could safely draw but one conclusion: There was no doubt that the river city about 200 miles below Memphis and an equal number of miles above New Orleans would be a tough nut to crack.

Situated on the eastern bank of the Mississippi atop a series of commanding bluffs overlooking a hairpin turn in the river, Vicksburg was an almost perfect natural fortress. Any force landing from the river would confront those steep cliffs, which would be formidable to climb even if they were not bristling with Confederate artillery and sharpshooters. The overland approach from the north appeared superficially appealing, but a series of swamps and bayous curved like body armor around Vicksburg's northern reaches, making approach by a modern army dragging wagons and artillery impractical. An attack from the east offered firmer ground, but using it would mean that Union supply lines would snake tenuously back to Memphis over hundreds of miles of hostile country patrolled by Confederates. In addition, a series of steep gullies and ravines east of the town made for ideal defensive positions.

An approach from the south also offered dry ground, but how would Grant get his army there? Vicksburg itself lay between the southern approach and his army's base in Tennessee. And if he should somehow get the army there, how could it be supplied with the tons of ammunition and food it required every day? Confederates still held Port Hudson, Louisiana, another river fortress farther south, cutting off Grant's army from the Union forces occupying Baton Rouge and New Orleans. Graybacks sortieing from Port Hudson could also threaten his army's rear.

Just before Christmas 1862, Grant launched his first attempt, the one he had discussed with Porter. Settling on a two-pronged approach, Grant would march overland through Mississippi to distract Confederate general John C. Pemberton, who was in command at Vicksburg, while Sherman—who, since Shiloh, had been fast establishing himself as Grant's favorite lieutenant—would float the main assault force down the river route.

The result was a fiasco.

On December 20, Confederate cavalry commander Earl Van Dorn led a force galloping into the Mississippi town of Holly Springs, which Grant had selected as his advance supply base. The 1,500-strong Union garrison surrendered with indecent haste, and the Confederates burned what they could not carry off. Meanwhile, Confederate brigadier general Nathan Bedford Forrest was also active in Grant's rear, cutting telegraph and railroad lines snaking back to Grant's base at Columbus, Kentucky.

Cut off without supplies deep in enemy territory, Grant had little choice but to call off his end of the operation. Unfortunately, the break in communications meant there was no way of informing Sherman and Porter. They went ahead, with the result that Sherman was bloodily repulsed at Chickasaw Bayou, north of Vicksburg, just before New Year's. He lost 1,700 men and accomplished nothing whatever.

Or perhaps not. For Grant, the operation proved a vital learning experience. Faced with having to get his army home without the supplies that were lost at Holly Springs, he decided to repeat something he had seen in the Mexican War and ordered his men to live off the land. The results surprised even the commanding general:

> I was amazed at the quantity of supplies the country afforded. It showed that we could have subsisted off the country for two months instead of two weeks. . . . This taught me a lesson which was taken advantage of later in the campaign when our army lived twenty days with the issue of only five days' rations by the commissary. Our loss of supplies was great at Holly Springs, but it was more than compensated for by those taken from the country and by the lesson taught.

For now, however, Grant was faced with an unappetizing series of choices for getting at Vicksburg. The geographical barriers around the town dictated that the logical course for Grant was to pull the army all the way back to Memphis, reorganize, and essentially repeat the maneuver that had just failed. Indeed, Sherman favored this course. Grant would have none of it. Not only was he temperamentally averse to retracing his steps, but he also surely understood that, with the odor of Shiloh still clinging to him, any army that plodded into Memphis with its tail between its legs would sally forth again only under a commander other than Ulysses S. Grant. Retreat would mean personal oblivion.

But it would be a mistake to think that Grant was thinking only of himself. A patriot first and foremost, he was thinking of his country as well. Fredericksburg had happened only a few weeks earlier. A return to Memphis would be a further body blow to Northern morale. The country was heartily tired of defeats and retreats. Grant would stay where he was. Besides, staying where he was meant the initiative did not pass into Confederate hands.

The campaign would have to be based on the river, then. Van Dorn and Forrest couldn't cut that. But a riverine campaign posed its own set of problems.

Winter in central Mississippi is not particularly cold, but it is wet, and the winter of 1862–63 was the wettest in memory. The Mississippi and its tributaries rose and rose, causing much of the low-lying land nearby to disappear beneath the water. Soldiers had a hard time finding ground dry enough to pitch their tents. Disease ran rampant through the ranks.

Another general would have called a halt to all activity until spring. Not Grant. Idleness was something close to a mortal sin in his book. Talking with his headquarters staff, Grant concluded that there were four main possibilities before him. He decided to try them all.

Directly across from Vicksburg, on the Louisiana side of the river, a peninsula about four miles long and a mile wide aimed itself at the city like a dagger. The idea of digging a canal across the width of its base—thereby bypassing Vicksburg and its fearsome cannon altogether—had occurred to Union officers during the first abortive effort to take the city in the summer of 1862. Grant revived the idea. After receiving an engineering report that the idea just might work, Grant floated some dredging equipment and a bargeload of picks and shovels down from Memphis and got Sherman's men busy making the dirt fly.

At the same time, he wondered if he might not be able to use the rising waters to his advantage. On the Louisiana side of the river lies a bayou with the deceptively placid name of Lake Providence. Through a spaghetti-snarl of streams, swamps, and fallen trees, it flows eventually into the Red River, from which it would be possible to reach the Mississippi below Vicksburg. Grant dispatched engineers and work details to start digging and clearing trees. Meanwhile, on the other side of the Mississippi, a not dissimilar project began through the swamps known as Yazoo Pass. Here, Grant thought it might be possible to move troops through the marshes almost to the gates of Vicksburg.

Grant claimed in his memoirs that he had little faith in any of these plans, that he only really believed in the one that ultimately worked. But they served a purpose, nevertheless. They kept Grant's men active and physically fit throughout the winter months. Thus, by the time April rolled around and things were ready to get underway in earnest, those of Grant's men who survived the illness and privations of the winter were lean, mean, and ready to campaign.

More important, Grant's competition was utterly bamboozled by the beehive of activity. "Enemy is constantly in motion in all directions," lamented Pemberton in an April dispatch to Richmond.

All the while, Grant was formulating and refining his actual plan, the one that he thought would result in the fall of Vicksburg:

> I had had in contemplation the whole winter the movement by land to a point below Vicksburg from which to operate, subject only to the possible but not expected success of some one of the expedients resorted to for the purpose of giving us a different base. This could not be undertaken until the waters receded. I did not therefore communicate this plan, even to an officer of my staff, until it was necessary to make preparations for the start.

The necessity for secrecy caused Grant no end of grief:

> Because I would not divulge my ultimate plans to visitors, they pronounced me idle, incompetent and unfit to command men in an emergency, and clamored for my removal.

Having a president who knew something about the Mississippi was, at best, a mixed blessing. Lincoln was intensely interested in Grant's designs, especially the canal-digging project, and sent his man on the spot a series of "helpful" telegrams and requests for reports. The CEO, in other words, was peering over Grant's shoulder intently.

"Audacity" is not a word generally associated with Grant, but there is simply no other way to describe what he now proposed.

First, since there were no Federal shipping assets of any substantial nature below Vicksburg, he would have to get Porter's gunboats and transports past the town's deadly batteries so that they could ferry Grant's troops from the west (Louisiana) bank of the river to the east (Mississippi) bank. The admiral was keen but cautioned Grant: Once the ships were past Vicksburg—if they got past Vicksburg—there was no going back. The ships' engines simply weren't powerful enough to fight the current in any upstream attempt to run past Vicksburg. If the fleet were sunk or heavily damaged on the first pass, of course, the issue of a second run past the batteries would be academic.

Simultaneously with the navy's move, Grant would march his troops—divided into three corps under John A. McClernand, James B. McPherson, and the redoubtable Sherman—south down the Louisiana side of the river to a point several miles south of Vicksburg on the opposite bank. Porter's fleet, after running the gauntlet of Vicksburg's batteries (which it did, successfully, on the night of April 16), would then ferry the troops to the dry ground on the eastern bank. But before striking at Vicksburg, Grant planned to turn south and unite with Major General Nathaniel P. Banks to pinch off Port Hudson, Louisiana, a Confederate-held mini-Vicksburg further down the river. That would open the Mississippi to Union shipping from New Orleans and secure Grant's rear. Thus reinforced, Grant and Banks would combine, turn north, and overwhelm Vicksburg.

"His campaign plan was so flexible that it amounted to little more than a determination to move fast, deceive the enemy and take advantage of every opening," wrote Bruce Catton of the Vicksburg plan. And that flexibility was what saved it when the enemy, as well as Grant's fellow Union generals and Mother Nature, all did the unexpected.

To take the last first, the abnormally high waters of the Mississippi began dropping dramatically in late April, just as the campaign was getting underway. Grant had planned to rely on a makeshift canal parallel to the artificial road over which his troops would march down the Louisiana side of the river in order to haul supplies south past Vicksburg's still-dangerous guns. The falling water put paid to that idea as the boats became stuck in the tangles. Grant simply decided he would have to do with fewer supplies than he anticipated at the beginning. Besides, once he and Banks had taken Port Hudson, Grant could draw supplies up the river from New Orleans.

Shortly after the campaign began, however, N. P. Banks, whose first two initials were said to stand for "Nothing Positive," decided to live up to his nickname. He notified Grant in early May that he could not possibly make it to Port Hudson before May 10 because he was, incredibly, headed in the opposite direction. Grant was unhappy, but simply changed his plan:

> The news from Banks forced upon me a different plan of campaign from the one intended. To wait for his co-operation would have detained me at least a month. The reinforcements would not have reached ten thousand men after deducting casualties and necessary river guards at all high points close to the river for over three hundred miles. The enemy would have strengthened his position and been reinforced by more men than Banks could have brought. I therefore determined to move independently of Banks, cut loose from my base, destroy the rebel force in rear of Vicksburg and invest or capture the city.

Finally, there was the enemy to contend with. Grant had planned to land his troops on the Mississippi side at a spot called Grand Gulf, where the high ground south of Vicksburg meets the river. But the Confederates had arrived there first and strongly fortified the place. Porter's gunboats went at Grand Gulf on April 29 but suffered battle damage and casualties in exchange for nothing. A new landing spot had to be found. As at Paducah, Grant chose to take notice of someone most others would have ignored: a local black man. "[On] the evening of the 29th," Grant later wrote:

> It was expected that we would have to go to Rodney, about nine miles below [Grand Gulf] to find a landing; but that night a colored man came in who informed me that a good landing would be found at Bruinsburg, a few miles above Rodney, from which point there was a good road leading to Port Gibson some twelve miles in the interior. The information was found correct, and our landing was effected without opposition.

Grant built such flexibility and back-up plans into the orders he issued to his own subordinates. Consider this one he sent for the river crossing itself (still planned for Grand Gulf at the time the order was sent) to Major General John McClernand, commanding the XIII Corps, which was the lead element in Grant's army:

Perkins' Plantation, La.,
April 27, 1863

MAJOR-GENERAL J. A. McCLERNAND,
Commanding 13th A. C.

Commence immediately the embarkation of your corps, or so much of it as there is transportation for. Have put aboard the artillery and every article authorized in orders limiting baggage, except the men, and hold them in readiness, with their places assigned, to be moved at a moment's warning. . . .

Admiral Porter has proposed to place his boats in the position indicated to you a few days ago, and to bring over with them such troops as may be below the city. . . . It may be that the enemy will occupy positions back from the city, out of range of the gunboats, so as to make it desirable to run past Grand Gulf and land at Rodney. In case this should prove the plan, a signal will be arranged and you duly informed, when the transports are to start with this view. Or, it may be expedient for the boats to run past but not the men. In this case, then, the transports would have to be brought back to where the men could land and move by forced marches to below Grand Gulf, re-embark rapidly and proceed to the latter place. There will be required, then, three signals; one, to indicate that the transports can run down and debark the troops at Grand Gulf; one, that the transports can run by without the troops; and the last, that the transports can run by with the troops on board.

Should the men have to march, all baggage and artillery will be left to run the blockade. If not already directed, require your men to keep three days' rations in their haversacks, not to be touched until a movement commences.

U. S. GRANT,
Major-General

While all this was going on, Grant did not neglect the need to keep Pemberton's attention directed away from what was happening to his south. To that end, he dispatched Sherman on a feint back in the direction of his defeat the previous December at Chickasaw Bayou. But what Grant was really counting on had gotten underway up in La Grange, Tennessee, on April 17.

On that date, Colonel Benjamin Grierson, a onetime music teacher who carried a Jew's harp in his knapsack and bore scars from a horse that had kicked him in his youth—leaving him ever after fearful of the animals—led 1,700 Illinois and Iowa cavalrymen south straight through the heart of Mississippi. Their destination: Baton Rouge, Louisiana, 600 miles distant. This daring ride (which inspired John Ford's epic film *The Horse Soldiers*) cost Grierson just twenty-four men killed, wounded, and captured. A Confederate newspaper later informed Grant that the raid had achieved precisely the effect he desired: Pemberton had dispatched troops to pursue Grierson and his men, but they accomplished little beyond eating the raiders' dust.

Thus, Grant kept the initiative. These diversions were what allowed him to get away with the changes in his plans. Partly as a consequence, his troops came ashore at Bruinsburg without opposition.

Grant believed the worst was over. ("I was on dry ground and on the same side of the river with the enemy," he wrote.) But the true drama of the Vicksburg campaign now began. Moving light (Grant's personal baggage consisted of a toothbrush), the bluecoats charged, not due north at Vicksburg—that was what Pemberton was expecting—but north and east toward the Mississippi state capital at Jackson.

By threatening both cities, Grant would force the Confederates to divide their forces in order to cover both. Furthermore, the only rail line that could carry reinforcements to Pemberton ran through Jackson.

Over the eighteen days following the April 30 landing at Bruinsburg, Grant and his men undertook the first modern blitzkrieg, or "lightning war." In that time, Grant's men covered an incredible 200 miles, fought and won five battles, and drove the Confederates into the city's defenses. On May 1, Confederate forces at Port Gibson were defeated; on May 12, the same thing happened at Raymond. Two days after that, it was the turn of the state capital of Jackson.

Grant had not originally intended to take Jackson but changed his mind when he figured that capturing and burning the city was the safest way to keep it neutralized and discourage Confederate general Joseph E. Johnston from attempting to come to Pemberton's aid. In the event, this is exactly what happened. "Once more, Grant shifted in response to events," wrote Brooks D. Simpson in *Ulysses S. Grant: Triumph over Adversity*. "Once more, it would pay off."

Scarcely had the Stars and Stripes been hoisted above the statehouse, however, than a courier dressed in Confederate gray—who was actually a Union spy—handed Grant a dispatch that Johnston had intended should reach Pemberton. Johnston was regrouping after evacuating Jackson and looking for a way to join forces with the Vicksburg commander. "Time is all-important," Johnston urged. Grant was in absolute agreement. He immediately began writing dispatches:

> I ordered McPherson to move promptly in the morning back to Bolton, the nearest point where Johnston could reach the road. Bolton is about twenty miles west of Jackson. I also informed McClernand of the capture of Jackson and sent him the following order: "It is evidently the design of the enemy to get north of us and cross the Big Black, and beat us into Vicksburg. We must not allow them to do this. Turn all your forces toward Bolton station, and make all dispatch in getting there. Move troops by the most direct road from wherever they may be on the receipt of this order."

The contrast with McClellan on the Peninsula could not have been greater. Presented with potentially devastating news, Grant saw opportunity where others would likely have seen danger and immediately moved to take every advantage. After Grant issued his orders, Pemberton was soundly thrashed at Champion's Hill on May 16 and began falling back on Vicksburg (suffering a further ignominious defeat at Big Black River on May 17 to boot). And Joe Johnston? He was out of the game altogether by now, though he would continue to give Grant sleepless nights until Vicksburg surrendered on July 4.

## DECISION MAKING: WHEN IT'S YOUR CALL

PLANNING HELPS YOU narrow your options; it can be a group effort. Decision making is when you settle on what to do. There is no way to make this a group effort. The manager on the spot makes the call. Vicksburg shows Grant as a decision maker par excellence.

Grant's decisions at several points in the campaign could have brought his career to a shuddering end. Porter's fleet was irreplaceable. If Vicksburg's guns had smashed it to matchwood, Grant would have been heading back to his father's Galena leather goods store. His later decision not to wait for Banks and to leave Port Hudson in enemy hands to his rear could have been devastating had Confederates attacked him from there.

No one knew the risks Grant was running better than his friend Sherman, who, as previously noted, wanted to return to Memphis. When he discovered Grant's plan, he was most upset. As Grant described the scene in his memoirs:

When General Sherman first learned of the move I proposed to make, he called to see me about it. I . . . was seated on the piazza engaged in conversation with my staff when Sherman came up. After a few moments' conversation he said that he would like to see me alone. We passed into the house together and shut the door after us. Sherman then expressed his alarm at the move I had ordered, saying that I was putting myself in a position voluntarily which an enemy would be glad to maneuver a year—or a long time—to get me in. I was going into the enemy's country, with a large river behind me and the enemy holding points strongly fortified above and below. He said that it was an axiom in war that when any great body of troops moved against an enemy they should do so from a base of supplies, which they would guard as they would the apple of the eye, etc.

He pointed out all the difficulties that might be encountered in the campaign proposed.

Grant heard Sherman out but decided to go ahead anyway. He had considered all of Sherman's arguments and was aware of the risks he was running. The prize, however, was worth all the risks. It was Grant's decision, and once he made up his mind, he acted without hesitation. "He was perfectly sure of himself," said M. Harrison Strong, a member of Grant's staff.

That didn't mean he was sure that every decision was the right one. Far from it. When a staff officer asked him if he was certain of a decision he had just made, Grant's reply was disarmingly honest: "No, I am not, but . . . anything is better than indecision. We must decide. If I am wrong we shall soon find it out and we can do the other thing. But not to decide wastes both time and money and may ruin everything."

Decision making, therefore, is a planning tool. Only by trying, and perhaps failing, can managers see if their plans are adequate or need to be revised.

This kind of management, however, requires vast reserves of character. J. F. C. Fuller, the British military historian who did much early in the twentieth century to restore Grant's military reputation, discussed the role of this quality, which he called moral courage, in Grant's conduct of the Vicksburg campaign:

In the Vicksburg campaign, Grant's moral courage has seldom been equaled. His plan met with no support and Sherman strenuously objected to it. Grant, having thought it out, knew that it was good plan and refused to change it. Here his courage drew its strength from a firm knowledge of the situation. Courage is closely connected with self-discipline, for this teaches a man to rely upon himself. Grant unfailingly did so. Once he had made up his mind, he shouldered the full respon-

sibility for his actions. Yet he never adhered to a plan obsti-
nately. This we clearly see at Chattanooga, and in the Wilderness and Petersburg campaigns; but nothing would induce him
to give up the idea behind the plan.

Grant's willingness to listen to others—another leadership
trait—is revealed by his not holding Sherman's outburst
against him: "I did not regard either the conversation between
us . . . as protests, but simply friendly advice which the relations between us fully justified."

Sherman returned the favor when Governor Richard Yates
of Illinois and a retinue of worthies presented themselves
along the siege lines at Vicksburg. When someone suggested
that perhaps Grant did not deserve credit for the so-far-
successful campaign, Sherman reacted with heat.

"Grant is entitled to every bit of the credit for the campaign," the red-haired general declared. "I opposed it."

Thus was Grant's planning and decision-making process—
and the character that was the foundation of his leadership—
vindicated. "But for this speech," Grant wrote in his memoirs,
"it is not likely that Sherman's opposition would have ever
been heard of. His untiring energy and great efficiency during
the campaign entitle him to a full share of all the credit due for
its success. He could not have done more if the plan had been
his own."

## GRANT'S LESSONS

- The range of human activity is unlimited. Planning is designed to
narrow the options to what is achievable, given the constraints of
time and available resources.

- Planning is a dynamic process. Unforeseen events must be accounted for, as must the competition's plans. Allow yourself to become wedded to a sinking plan, and you will sink with it.

- Planning in a large organization is not for individuals. Bring your staff into the process in order to assess options and encourage a free flow of ideas.

- Decision making is the manager's alone. Once you settle on a plan, pursue your objective relentlessly.

CHAPTER 4

# PERSISTENCE AND DETERMINATION

## *"If It Takes All Summer"*

---

*What is the lesson of Grant's life? Foremost of all is the lesson of*
*tenacity, of stubborn fixity of purpose. In the Union armies there were*
*generals as brilliant as Grant, but none with his iron determination. . . .*
*Grant's supreme virtue as a soldier was his doggedness, the quality*
*which found expression in his famous phrases of "unconditional*
*surrender," and "fighting it out on this line if it takes all summer."*
—THEODORE ROOSEVELT

*It is the dogged pertinacity of Grant that wins.*
—ABRAHAM LINCOLN

THE TAKING OF Paducah and Smithland, Kentucky, by
Grant's forces in September 1861 was a critical step toward
winning Union control of the Tennessee and Cumberland
Rivers, both of which ran deep into the heart of Confederate
territory. But it was only a step. The Confederates had built
strongpoints on these rivers, notably Forts Henry and Donelson, to prevent approach by any Union force. Grant was eager
to move on them, but he ran up against the relentless lethargy
that seemed to infect the higher levels of the Union command.

In November 1861, Major General Henry Halleck, whose army nickname of "Old Brains" was not entirely complimentary, had replaced the hapless Fremont at St. Louis in command over Grant. In January 1862, Grant requested an interview with Halleck in St. Louis to explain his plan for moving against Forts Henry and Donelson. Halleck refused and urged Grant to get on with making a feint against Confederate positions in western Kentucky.

Grant loyally followed orders and, upon returning to Cairo, Illinois, once again asked to see Halleck about the forts. This time Old Brains assented. The meeting was a disaster. Grant scarcely knew Halleck before the war and was unprepared for the steely-eyed, imperious figure who now confronted him. Grant lost his usual composure and stumbled through his presentation. Halleck soon cut him off and sent the brigadier away, "as if my plan was preposterous."

Such a rebuff would have been enough to prevent most subordinates from ever mentioning the matter again. But Grant wasn't so easily discouraged. Realizing that his presentation was faulty but not his plan, Grant chose to make it in writing. Upon returning to Cairo, he sent Halleck a telegram and followed it up with a letter, explaining the plan in more detail. He also enlisted the support of a naval officer, Flag Officer Andrew Foote, who commanded the gunboats on the Ohio River that would be needed for the operation.

That did the trick. Halleck signed off on Grant's plan, in part because President Lincoln was impatiently demanding action of some sort somewhere. Until the moment the expedition cast off on February 3, 1862, however, Grant lived in dread that a last-minute telegram would arrive from Halleck either canceling the movement altogether or putting another officer in charge.

Very few Civil War battles took place in the winter for the simple reason that, in the days before paved roads and accurate weather forecasting, troops and their supporting horses and wagons could easily become mired in mud and snow. So Grant was taking a chance when he moved against the forts in February. And, indeed, Mother Nature was not to smile on this expedition. Grant's plan for a synchronized attack on Fort Henry on the Tennessee dissolved in a sea of rain, mud, and raging rivers. Fortunately for Grant, the rising waters had flooded the fort, making it indefensible. The Confederates fought only a delaying action after Foote's gunboats arrived and opened fire, the bulk of the garrison marching the twelve miles to Fort Donelson on the Cumberland.

Grant's troops were on their heels. A bit of unseasonably sunny, warm weather, however, caused many of the bluecoats to discard their heavy blankets and overcoats along the route. Those articles of clothing and equipment would be sorely missed in coming days, as rain, snow, and freezing weather quickly returned. Many troops were also afflicted with what army wits dubbed "the Tennessee two-step": chronic diarrhea.

Donelson was also a tougher target than Henry, situated as it was on a high bluff and mounting twelve large cannon. Grant decided to allow Flag Officer Foote to see if he could bombard Fort Donelson into submission in the same manner as at Fort Henry. The results were not nearly so positive: Foote couldn't elevate his guns high enough to do serious damage to the fort, and his ships were exposed to plunging fire from the Confederate positions. He pulled back, with many of his ships badly damaged.

The Confederate elation at driving back the gunboats was tempered by the sight of Grant's infantry investing the fort. The commander of the Union ground forces was far from ready to give up. The ranking Confederate officers convened a council of war—the result of which vindicated Grant's belief in the uselessness of such gatherings. Generals John Floyd, Gideon Pillow, and Simon Bolivar Buckner made a decision to "cut out" of the fort. They failed to make proper preparations, however, and when the attack was made on the morning of February 15, 1862, the graybacks were unprepared when the blue line showed signs of giving way.

Grant had been visiting Flag Officer Foote at the time of the Rebel attack. Galloping to the scene, he quickly restored order and morale by pointing out that the Confederates must be in worse shape than the Union troops if they were trying to run away. Grant's steady nerves and determination were tonic to the demoralized Union troops. "This worked like a charm," noted a member of Grant's staff. "The men only wanted someone to give them a command."

Panicked when Union troops suddenly counterattacked, the Confederate commanders hastily ordered their men back to their original positions. Now they were trapped again. A second council of war was held within the fort, and Floyd and Pillow both decided to escape, leaving poor Buckner to dicker with Grant over terms of surrender. The two ranking generals then ignominiously fled. When Buckner—who had known Grant before the war and had lent the Union commander money when he was in dire straits—asked for surrender terms, Grant sent back one of the most famous replies in military history. "No terms except unconditional and immediate surrender can be accepted," he wrote. With little choice, Buckner agreed. "Unconditional Surrender" Grant thus acquired a nickname.

Grant's was the first major Union victory of the war and one of the most significant. The loss of the two forts opened the Tennessee and Cumberland Rivers to Federal navigation and forced the Confederacy to evacuate western Tennessee and Nashville. It would never recover these areas. From that point on, Grant would only move forward. It was in his nature.

## GRANT'S DETERMINATION

FROM AN EARLY AGE, Grant developed an aversion—indeed, a positive superstition—against retracing his steps. "He often put himself to the greatest personal inconvenience to avoid it," wrote Horace Porter of his chief's peculiar predilection. "When he found he was not traveling in the direction he intended to take, he would try all sorts of crosscuts, ford streams, and jump any number of fences to reach another road rather than go back and take a fresh start. . . . The enemy who encountered him never failed to feel the effect of this inborn prejudice against turning back."

The origin of this unusual habit is obscure, but it is a constant in Grant's life from an early age. It is one of the things that helped keep him going when things became very difficult indeed and might have caused another man with a different constitution to give up altogether.

Grant was born in a two-room house in Point Pleasant, Clermont County, Ohio, about twenty-seven miles upriver from Cincinnati, on April 27, 1822. He was the first-born child of Hannah Simpson Grant, a devout Methodist, and Jesse Root Grant, a leather tanner who would later become quite successful. His given first name was Hiram, suggested by Hannah's father, but it was never used. Instead, the family favored his middle name, Ulysses, after the Greek hero.

The leather trade brought the Grants prosperity, but no amount of money could make Ulysses love the process of stripping animals of their hides. The stench of the tannery turned the young man's stomach, and the sight of blood, human or animal, would become a lifelong aversion.

The young man preferred the company of live animals, particularly horses. At age two he had his first pony ride, when a circus came to town, and it was love at first sight. As he matured, the young Ulysses would often take long, unsupervised rides around the neighborhood, sometimes not returning for days.

His love of horses also spawned one of the most embarrassing of Grant's childhood experiences. At about age eight, he spotted a colt owned by a farmer named Ralston and was determined to own him. Jesse, however, thought Ralston's asking price of twenty-five dollars too steep and told his son to offer the farmer twenty dollars up front and go to twenty-five only if Ralston would not take less. When the young man confronted the farmer, however, he blurted out his top price. "It would not require a Connecticut man to guess the price finally agreed upon," Grant mordantly recalled later in his memoirs.

This story has often been repeated by biographers looking for early evidence of Grant's lack of business acumen. But as biographer Brooks D. Simpson has pointed out, another lesson can be drawn from it: Grant *came* for the colt, and he was not going to allow his father's tightfistedness to force him to leave without it. (Also rarely mentioned, Simpson says, is the fact that Grant sold the horse several years later—when it was nearly blind—for twenty dollars.)

Grant's tenacity thus displayed itself at an early age. It would reappear at West Point. The academy's obsession with military minutiae and the omnipresent marching band (Grant was tone deaf and music annoyed him) caused him initially to detest the school. His spirits rose early on in his tenure when Congress debated abolishing the military academy. That would have given Grant an honorable excuse to return home. But Congress chose not to act, and so Grant stayed. He struggled, but he refused to be beaten. He also came to respect the product West Point turned out, later calling the academy "the best school in the world" because of the way it built character. Though Grant managed during the war to work well with some "volunteer" officers who were not professional soldiers—notably John A. Logan and Frank P. Blair, Jr.—he displayed a marked preference for West Point–trained officers. Having run the gauntlet himself, he held in high regard anyone else who survived the experience.


## GRANT'S "WILDERNESS YEARS"

GREAT LEADERS OFTEN have in common a time spent in "the wilderness"—that is, a period when they meet with frequent failure and frustration or are out of favor following a period of triumph. Winston Churchill, Charles de Gaulle, and Richard Nixon are among those who have experienced this kind of isolation prior to achieving great success.

So did Ulysses S. Grant. His "wilderness" years came between his resignation from the army in 1854 and his return to active service eight years later. During this period, Grant was a fish out of water. A man of motion who craved action and adventure, he sought to make a living in the most rooted and unexciting of all occupations: farming. He compounded this poor career choice by seeking to supplement his income by working in other occupations equally unsuited to his nature.

To be sure, anything following the Mexican War would have seemed an anticlimax. The war had been a grand, romantic adventure for Grant in the Kipling tradition. It's not hard to see why. By any standard, the young lieutenant had had a "good war." In spite of several close calls, he came home physically unscathed. It is interesting to note that, in spite of his later doubts about the war's wisdom and morality, the man who was so reluctant in later life to discuss his Civil War experiences was rarely so reticent when the subject was Mexico. The war gave him a larder of stories and observations he would draw on for the remainder of his life.

The peacetime army, in contrast, held few charms. Its primary mission in the immediate wake of the war was garrisoning the Western territories newly won from Mexico. After a spell of duty in Detroit and upstate New York, Grant was assigned to Fort Vancouver at the mouth of the Columbia River in the Pacific Northwest. The journey to the West Coast was no simple matter in those days, and Grant and the 4th Infantry made the trip over the Isthmus of Panama, with many lives lost along the way. Grant was relieved he had left his pregnant wife and young son Fred behind, bitter though he was to be without their company.

The two years Grant spent on the West Coast make for depressing reading. It was one long emotional tailspin. Loyal to the institution that had educated him, Grant had every intention of remaining a career army officer, and he hoped that the separation from Julia and his two sons (one of whom he had never seen) would be brief. There was no question of their joining him. The journey was too hazardous. Besides, his army pay barely covered his own modest expenses in Gold Rush California, let alone the cost of a wife and two children.

Re-posted to isolated Fort Humboldt 250 miles north of San Francisco, the newly promoted Captain Grant missed his wife and family almost beyond description. His army duties were light and usually occupied only a few hours daily. For a family man with an active mind, the boredom of Fort Humboldt must have been close to unbearable. Making it worse was the presence of the irascible post commander, Lieutenant Colonel Robert C. Buchanan. "Old Buck" seemed to have little use for anyone below his rank—and he seems to have taken an exceptional dislike to Grant.

This period in his life appears to be have been the only one in which it can be said with a fair degree of certainty that Grant experienced a period of heavy drinking. Depression and isolation seem to have been the main reasons. Part of his difficulty also seems to have been that he didn't "hold" his liquor well. Two or three drinks, which might have scarcely affected many of his hard-drinking army comrades, slurred Grant's speech and made him appear utterly inebriated.

The exact circumstances under which Grant left the army remain murky. What is certain is that on April 11, 1854, Grant sent two letters to the War Department in Washington, D.C. One indicated that he had received and accepted his promotion to captain in the regular army, and the other resigned that commission. Grant was going home to his family in St. Louis.

Things did not start off auspiciously. On the way back, Grant tried collecting some debts he was owed, without notable success. (It was at this time, in New York, that Simon Bolivar Buckner lent him some money.) His father, Jesse Root Grant, was so displeased with his son's decision that he unsuccessfully implored Secretary of War Jefferson Davis to reconsider accepting the resignation. Intent on becoming a "well-off Missouri farmer," Grant soon began working a sixty-acre tract that Julia's father had given the couple as a wedding present.

Although his first year's crops were good, prices were down, and Grant soon found himself in debt. This was the time when he began selling firewood in St. Louis in an effort to supplement his income. At the same time, the government was periodically dunning him for the thousand dollars that had disappeared from Army quartermaster funds under Grant's jurisdiction in Mexico. (This obligation, which was imposed in spite of a finding that Grant had not been negligent, was not relieved until Congress passed a special bill during the Civil War.)

Meanwhile, two more children came along, a daughter and a son. Jesse Root Grant said he was willing to help his oldest son. But he would not do so as long as Ulysses insisted on making his home among "that tribe of slaveholders," the Dents. For his part, Frederick Dent, Grant's father-in-law, was always close at hand to remind his daughter that going north to accept Jesse's offers of assistance would mean doing without her slaves. (On the whole, however, Grant's relationship with Dent seems to have been good, though complicated. For more on Grant and slavery, see chapter 12).

The Grant family's situation went from difficult to serious in 1857, when the economy experienced one of its periodic "panics," or what would today be called a deep recession. Now everyone was finding it hard to make a living. Grant fell so far behind in his debts that he pawned a gold watch that Christmas for twenty-two dollars. On top of it all came bouts with sickness, including malaria. Finally, almost in desperation, he turned to the real estate business, though a man less suited to the task of collecting rents and debts would be hard to imagine.

Yet, amid all this darkness, Grant refused to give up. Another man similarly situated might have crawled into a liquor bottle, abandoned his family, and drifted off somewhere to die in obscurity. Not U. S. Grant. He is often described in this period as a "failure," but that is too harsh. He was more devoted than ever to Julia and the children and wanted desperately to provide for them. The trouble was he couldn't bear to be parted from them. That factor limited his occupational choices to those for which he was unsuited. Still, Grant showed flashes of his true calling. In conversations with neighbors and friends, he perked up noticeably when the subject was foreign or military affairs. He would animatedly discuss the Italian wars of unification then ongoing and even trace out on newspaper maps his own impressions of the likely course of the campaigns.

Grant was also laboring under another disadvantage in divided St. Louis as regional tensions reached the boiling point. Because he was a Northerner by birth, Southerners in St. Louis did not wholly trust him, while his marriage into the slaveholding Dent clan meant Northerners also were wary of his loyalties. In August 1859, these crosscurrents swept away Grant's last remaining hope for a steady, paying job in St. Louis as county engineer. At a time when just a handful of Americans had enjoyed a college education, Grant had not only attended college but also studied engineering. He was thus eminently qualified for the post. But the five-member county board was controlled three to two by Republicans, and Grant lost out. According to Simpson, one of the Republican members was a friend of Grant's but later told him that he could not vote for Colonel Dent's son-in-law.

As the new decade dawned, Grant had to face facts. St. Louis simply had not worked out for him, and he badly needed a fresh start. One does not need to be Sigmund Freud to guess the emotional pain Grant was experiencing—caught between his feuding parents and in-laws, while dependent on them both. No doubt swallowing hard, he decided to accept his father's (conditional) offer of employment in the family leather business. The condition was that Grant and his family move north—*sans* slaves—and that Grant work as an employee until he learned enough about the business to be made a partner. With little choice, Grant packed up his family and headed north for Galena, Illinois, in March 1860.

The nearly thirty-eight-year-old West Point graduate and war hero now began learning the trade of a clerk, a job he performed adequately, but certainly with little enthusiasm. He was under the supervision of his younger brothers Simpson and Orvil. Still, Grant sought to be as optimistic as possible and even expressed enthusiasm at the prospect of becoming a partner.

All the while, the nation's political temperature was rising steadily. Grant sought to stay above the fray. "I don't know anything of party politics, and I don't want to," he insisted to any that inquired. Grant was sympathetic to the presidential candidacy of Illinois senator Stephen A. Douglas but could not vote for him because Grant had not lived in Galena long enough to satisfy the residency requirement. Still, Grant's status as a West Point graduate and former army officer was well known enough that the local Douglas Club invited him to help drill their marchers, an offer Grant declined. But when a group of Republican marchers, who called themselves the "Wide Awakes," seemed to have difficulty getting their act together, Grant stepped in and offered some unsolicited advice.

Unlike many of his fellow Northerners, Grant was under no illusions that a good swift kick would be all that was required to bring the new Confederacy crashing down once states began leaving the Union following the election of Illinois Republican Abraham Lincoln that November. "The South will fight" was his grim prediction.

But so would Grant. After attending a tumultuous meeting in the Galena courthouse after Fort Sumter was fired upon (the featured speaker was a local lawyer named John Rawlins, who would serve later in the war as Grant's chief of staff), the old soldier made up his mind. "I think I should go into the service," he said to his brother Orvil as they walked home. Orvil didn't discourage him, and Ulysses S. Grant never walked back into the leather store again.

Getting back into the army, however, proved far more difficult than leaving it, despite the fact that President Lincoln's call for 75,000 volunteers and the resignation from the service of so many talented Southern-born officers meant experienced military men were at a premium. The local Galena volunteer company offered to elect him their captain, but Grant refused. Captain, after all, was the rank Grant had held those eight long years earlier in California. Besides, in addition to his military education, there was his combat experience in Mexico. If he consented to serve as a volunteer captain, it almost certainly would mean that this man who had already proved himself under fire would end up serving under volun-

teer officers who had little or no military background. Grant
had enough confidence in himself and his abilities—not to
mention pride—to realize his talents could be put to better
use. A colonelcy, he decided, was his proper place.

Though Grant later claimed that he had never sought a
position but waited to be sought out, his quest for those
colonel's eagles was a notable exception that consumed three
nerve-wracking months. Elihu B. Washburne, a Republican
who represented Galena in Congress, got him in front of Illinois governor Richard Yates, and Yates thought Grant could
help drilling and mustering in new regiments. But when the
legislature passed a bill appointing drill officers, Grant's name
was not on the list.

Preparing to go home to Galena in discouragement, Grant
had a chance meeting with the governor. Calling Grant "Captain," Yates asked if Grant would delay his departure and
come to the governor's office the next day. There, Yates offered him a position in the adjutant-general's office. No commission went with the job, but for the moment, it would do.

Paper shuffling was not Grant's forte, but he performed
competently enough. Still, after a few weeks of it, he once
again considered returning home. Yates asked if instead he
would travel around the state and help with drilling newly
mustered regiments. Grant agreed, though once again, no
commission was forthcoming. "I find all those places are
wanted by politicians who are up to logrolling," a frustrated
Grant wrote his father.

On May 23, 1861, Grant left Springfield to look into the
possibilities in his native state of Ohio. At the same time, he
sent a letter to the War Department in Washington, D.C., directly requesting command of a regiment. The letter was
never answered. (After the war, it was discovered in a War Department file folder, where it had apparently been placed and
forgotten.)

Ohio's volunteer troops had been placed under the command of George McClellan, who had left the army several years before the war for a career as a railroad executive. McClellan, too, had been a captain when he resigned from the army, and he was now wearing major general's stars. Grant hoped McClellan would remember him from the army and perhaps Little Mac did—though not in a way that was flattering to Grant. After cooling his heels in McClellan's outer office for two full days, Grant took the hint and left. He had no better luck in Indiana.

It began to look as though the war, which everyone expected to be short, might pass Grant by. Then the help he needed came, not from some powerful, well-connected politician, but from a most unexpected quarter.

The 21st Illinois was one of the regiments that Grant had helped muster in. Command, however, had gone to one Simon Goode. He was one of those comic-opera figures from the early days of the war who spouted endlessly about Napoleonic theory while chaos reigned around him. Locals quickly dubbed the 21st "Governor Yates' Hellions" as they smashed up Springfield saloons and raised hell generally. Even so, they managed to hoodwink the great McClellan, who rode by on an inspection tour on June 15, 1861, and pronounced himself well satisfied.

The regiment's junior officers, however, weren't fooled. Going into combat under Colonel Goode would mean an unappetizing choice between death and dishonor. This they told Governor Yates, who no doubt worried about being blamed for the antics of the 21st Illinois. The regiment desperately needed a new colonel. What about that fellow who had mustered them in? He seemed to know what he was about. What was his name? Grant?

On the same day as McClellan's visit, Yates made out Ulysses S. Grant's commission as a colonel of volunteers and gave him command of the 21st Illinois. Persistence had paid off.

# THE LESSONS OF GRANT'S TENACITY

"I PURPOSE TO FIGHT it out on this line if it takes all summer" has become one of Grant's most famous quotations. (A newspaper correspondent thought the word "propose" fit better than Grant's "purpose," and so it has come down to us.) Of course, in the immediate context in which it was made—the murderous Battle of Spotsylvania—it was inaccurate. Grant did not fight on that same line all summer. By June, he was far to the south, around Petersburg. But he was still fighting. That was the key. "If we were under any other general except Grant I should expect a retreat, but Grant is not that kind of soldier, and we feel that we can trust him," wrote Elisha Hunt Rhodes, an officer in the 2nd Rhode Island at around this time. Lincoln said something similar to one of his intimates. Cartoonists of the period often depicted Grant as a bulldog.

Persistence and tenacity are underrated leadership tools. Even the best ideas—indeed, *especially* the best ideas—are going to encounter resistance and opposition. Failures and rebuffs are inevitable. A true leader, however, keeps the goal in mind and keeps on plugging. Grant allowed neither the high waters around Vicksburg nor Robert E. Lee's brilliant defensive tactics in the late spring of 1864 to deter him.

At the same time, care must be taken to see that persistence doesn't tip over into fanaticism. The difference is that persistence involves keeping the goal in mind while being flexible about the means of achieving it, whereas fanaticism involves continuously repeating the same failed method over and over with ever increasing zeal. Grant was not a fanatic. Unlike Japanese commanders in the South Pacific in World War II, who hurled wave upon wave of suicidal banzai charges at American positions, Grant in 1864–65 constantly sought to sidle around Lee's right flank. The habitual slowness of the Army of the Potomac's officer corps in executing orders, however, meant that

Lee always managed to get his troops into position just in time to meet Grant's assaults.

Tenacity of the kind Grant displayed during his career is clearly, to some extent, innate. But he was not a superman and, on at least one occasion, became sufficiently discouraged that only the intervention of the man who would become his most trusted lieutenant prevented Grant from walking away into obscurity.

The period immediately following the Battle of Shiloh on April 6–7, 1862, was one of the darkest in Grant's military career. Although he had salvaged the situation after being surprised, the 13,000-plus casualties suffered by the Union army profoundly shocked public opinion in the North. Soldiers wrote home with grisly tales of the carnage. In a little less than two months' time, the hero of Fort Donelson had seen himself transformed in the public mind into a blundering incompetent. Rumors of Grant's being drunk at the battle were rife, though unsupported. Nevertheless, he proved an easy figure on which to focus blame. The lieutenant governor of Ohio attacked Grant viciously. A grim Major General Henry Halleck arrived to assume command in person. Although Abraham Lincoln famously refused to fire Grant on the grounds that "he fights," he did nothing to prevent Halleck from shunting Grant into the supernumerary role of second in command.

Grant didn't want to be an embarrassment to anyone. He asked for thirty days' leave to go visit his family. The "leave" request, however, didn't fool William T. Sherman when he heard about it. He knew that if Grant actually left, he would be leaving the army for good.

Sherman rode over to Grant's headquarters tent and there found trunks and boxes being packed for Grant's planned departure the next day. Sherman entered the tent and found Grant tidying up his correspondence.

We have only Sherman's word, in his memoirs, for what happened next; Grant doesn't even mention the incident in his own memoirs. Was it true, the flame-haired general asked, that Grant was leaving?

"Sherman, you know that I am in the way here," a weary Grant replied. "I have stood it as long as I can and can endure it no longer."

Grant couldn't leave, Sherman thundered. Events would go along, and he would be left out. Put up with Halleck for the time being; endure the barbs from empty-headed politicians and the press. A man of Grant's abilities could not be kept down for long. Some "happy accident" was bound to occur that would give him another chance. After all, hadn't Sherman himself been labeled insane by the press not long before?

Sherman left Grant's tent uncertain of his friend's decision. Grant had said he would think it over. A short time later, while in the field, Sherman received a short note from Grant announcing his decision to stay. "You could not be quiet at home for a week while armies were moving," Sherman replied.

## GRANT'S LESSONS

- "If at first you don't succeed, try, try again" may be a cliché, but like most clichés, it contains more than a grain of truth. Don't be easily discouraged if your plans or proposals meet initial resistance.

- Don't accept an inferior position simply because it is the first one offered. If you don't place a high value on yourself and your abilities, no one else is likely to do so.

- Always keep your ultimate goal in mind while remaining flexible about how you will achieve it.

- All the determination in the world, however, won't help if you have fundamentally miscast yourself in an occupation for which you are not suited. "*I* would have failed too selling firewood, farming, clerking in a store and bill collecting," said General H. Norman Schwarzkopf of Grant's wilderness period.

CHAPTER 5

# MISTAKES

*Everyone Makes Them;
Not Everyone
Learns from Them*

———

*Cold Harbor, is, I think, the only battle I ever fought that
I would not fight again under the circumstances. . . . [It
belongs] to the category of mistakes which men necessarily
see to have been mistakes after the event is over.*
—ULYSSES S. GRANT

W ILLIAM  TECUMSEH  SHERMAN  once told a friend
what he thought was the secret of Grant's leadership: "Wilson, I am a damn sight smarter than Grant. I know a great
deal more about war, military history, strategy, and grand tactics than he does; I know more about organization, supply
and administration, and about everything else than he does.

"But I tell you where he beats me and beats the world,"
Uncle Billy concluded this uncharacteristically introspective
statement. "He don't care a damn for what the enemy does
out of his sight, but it scares me like hell. . . . I am more nervous than he is. I am more likely to change my orders, or to
countermarch my command than he is. He uses such informa-

tion as he has according to his best judgment. He issues his orders and does his level best to carry them out without much reference to what is going on about him."

This quotation is often used to show Grant at his best; and, indeed, it is generally more positive to be concerned with what you are going to do to the competition than worry about what he is going to do to you. The failure to do this, Grant firmly believed, is what crippled the leadership of the Army of the Potomac.

But our worst qualities are often mirror images of our best qualities. The flip side of Grant's determination to keep the initiative, the tenacity with which he made war, and his determination to ignore the enemy "out of his sight" also led him into one of the costliest mistakes of his leadership—a mistake that very nearly ended his reborn military career just as it was beginning.

## SURPRISED AT SHILOH

ON THE AFTERNOON of April 4, 1862, Colonel Everett Peabody reviewed his brigade of the 6th Division of Grant's Army of the Tennessee. A sudden downpour cancelled the scheduled drill, but a squadron of Confederate cavalry was seen riding in a leisurely manner through the woods to the south. The Union soldiers who beheld this curious sight thought it odd that the enemy should be allowed to move unmolested so close to their encampment. But then, most of the troops were green and, for all they knew, such things were normal.

The next day, however, the scene was repeated, this time as the division commander, Brigadier General Benjamin Prentiss, was reviewing his entire command. Prentiss immediately ordered a reconnaissance party into the woods. After marching about a mile and a half, the bluecoats encountered some local blacks, who told them they had seen hundreds of Rebels nearby.

Dark was falling, however, with visibility becoming difficult. Colonel David Moore, the party's commander, elected to turn back and reported to Prentiss that he had seen nothing.

But his soldiers had *heard* something. "We could hear the enemy moving in every direction," one of them recalled later. Captain Gilbert D. Johnson of the 12th Michigan heard the distinct sound of movement in the woods to his front and passed the report on to his colonel, who passed it to Prentiss. Don't be alarmed, the general said.

But Johnson was not convinced. He took his story to Colonel Peabody. A thirty-one-year-old Harvard graduate, Peabody had already been captured and exchanged once in the war, after the Battle of Lexington, Missouri, seven months earlier. He had no taste for repeating the experience. Unable to sleep and acting without orders, he dispatched several companies into the dark woods around midnight, determined to discover what was making the racket.

The Union men groped their way forward in the inky blackness of the Tennessee woods. Near dawn, they stumbled on a Confederate skirmish line that they mistook for a much smaller force and attacked with gusto. The Confederates fired back, forcing the Union troops to turn on their heels. Prentiss, who at that moment was upbraiding Peabody for bringing on a fight without orders, realized something more than an isolated skirmish was occurring and gave orders to begin turning out his division for action.

Indeed, an entire 40,000-strong Confederate army, under the command of Albert Sidney Johnston, Jefferson Davis's favorite general, was advancing on the camp of the 40,000 unsuspecting Union troops. The bluecoats were awaiting 30,000 reinforcements under Major General Don Carlos Buell for a move south against the rail center of Corinth, Mississippi, where Grant expected to meet Johnston's by-then-outnumbered force and destroy it.

But thoughts of Corinth were a long way away as a bright sun rose over the Tennessee countryside that Sunday, April 6. "Get in line! The Rebels are coming," shouted a wounded Ohio soldier as he stumbled back into camp to warn his comrades. A captain who went into the woods to investigate came running back shouting, "The Rebs are out there thicker than fleas on a dog's back!" The colonel in command dispatched an urgent message to division commander Brigadier General William T. Sherman, who had admonished the same colonel a few days earlier for crying wolf. "You must be badly scared over there," was Sherman's dismissive reply.

Riding forward to investigate, however, Sherman arrived just in time to see a large Rebel force advancing across a field in his front. "My God, we are attacked!" he exclaimed, just as the first Confederate shots cut down the aide who was riding next to him.

Sherman's surprise was understandable, for he had been pooh-poohing reports of Rebels in the woods around the Federal lines for some time. "Take your damned regiment back to Ohio," he had snarled at the jumpy Ohio colonel the day before the battle. "There is no enemy nearer than Corinth."

It was a sentiment shared by his chief, Major General Ulysses S. Grant. "There will be no fight at Pittsburg Landing," he told another officer the day before the battle. "We will have to go to Corinth, where the Rebels are fortified."

Unfortunately for Grant and his army, the enemy was unwilling to wait for him to attack them.

In retrospect, the potential for Union disaster seems obvious. The Union troops had been camped at Pittsburg Landing, a day's march from Corinth, for two weeks, plenty of time for hostile locals and Confederate scouts to learn of their position. Since the Tennessee River wound its way down to the Confederate concentration at Corinth, it would not take much to guess at the bluecoats' likely target. The Confederates under Johnston, not unnaturally, decided to strike first.

Even as he scrawled his memoirs while lying on his deathbed, Shiloh remained Ulysses S. Grant's worst embarrassment. While Grant and Sherman were accurate in their claims afterward that their men were not caught in their beds—most of the Union troops had at least a few minutes' warning to get into line—it was not accurate to claim that they had not been surprised. Grant deserves credit for restoring the situation (see chapter 1). He kept his head when many other commanders would have lost theirs and given in to panic. He organized the arrival of Buell's forces that night and attacked the next morning without hesitation when the Confederates were still off balance.

The Confederates retreated to Corinth. Grant and Buell chose not to pursue.

Grant's success on the second day went largely unnoticed, however. The staggering casualty list (over 13,000 Federals) stunned Washington, which demanded a scalp. Grant came near to filling that role but instead found himself shunted into the meaningless role of serving as Major General Henry Halleck's second-in-command. The hero of Fort Donelson found himself a national goat in less than two months' time. But Grant learned from Shiloh. Never again would he be surprised on a battlefield. Never again would an enemy be permitted to skulk away, but instead would be pursued with a vengeance. Grant had made a mistake on the first day, but he was determined not to let it happen again.

## GENERAL ORDERS NO. 11: THE "JEW ORDER"

ULYSSES S. GRANT was a man out of his time when it came to race and religious relations. In mid-nineteenth-century America, attitudes that would today be considered patronizing at best and racist at worst were common elements of the American lexicon. Grant, however, did not share in them.

His Southern neighbors in St. Louis thought he treated his black slaves and employees too kindly. As president, he vigorously enforced the Reconstruction laws designed to ensure equal political and civil rights for the ex-slaves and their white Republican allies in the postbellum South. Upon Grant's death, Frederick Douglass, the greatest African American leader of his day, paid tribute to the late general and president as a friend of Negroes. At Appomattox, the surrender terms were written out by one of Grant's closest aides, Colonel Ely S. Parker, a Seneca chief.

In light of this record, then, Grant's issuance of General Orders No. 11, his infamous order expelling all Jews from his military department in December 1862, is difficult to understand:

> The Jews, as a class violating every regulation of trade established by the Treasury Department and also department orders, are hereby expelled from the department within twenty-four hours from the receipt of this order.
>
> Post commanders will see that all of this class of people be furnished passes and required to leave, and any one returning after such notification will be arrested and held in confinement until an opportunity occurs of sending them out as prisoners, unless furnished with permit from headquarters.
>
> No passes will be given these people to visit headquarters for the purpose of making personal application for trade permits.
>
> By order of Maj. Gen. U. S. Grant:
> JNO. A. RAWLINS,
> Assistant Adjutant-General

Because the order was actually signed by Grant's chief of staff, John Rawlins, many of Grant's defenders have sought to put the responsibility for it on the aide's shoulders. It is hard to believe, however, that a martinet-like lawyer such as Rawlins would have issued such an obviously inflammatory order in Grant's name without his knowledge. So what would have provoked Grant to issue it?

Part of the reason can certainly be found in Grant's enforced inactivity for months following Shiloh. Although he got his command back when Halleck was called east, things were far from good. Grant spent much of his time fruitlessly chasing Confederate cavalry raiders around west Tennessee. Meanwhile, a desperate President Lincoln had agreed to allow John A. McClernand, a well-connected Illinois politician with dreams of martial glory that he hoped would carry him to the White House, to form an army-within-an-army in Grant's department that clearly threatened Grant's own position in command. And in the midst of all this came the general's father, Jesse Root Grant.

The elder Grant was completely unlike his general son. Where the son was gentle and did little to attract attention to himself, the father was a born huckster and salesman. When it became clear that this would be no "ninety-day war," many businessmen saw that there was money to be made in the carnage and were quick to take advantage. Jesse was no exception.

What drew Jesse Grant's attention was cotton. When the war began, the Southern states deliberately withheld their cotton crop from world markets, hoping the resulting economic pressure would bring the states of Europe into the war on the side of the South. Prices soared. At ten cents a pound in December 1860, the "white gold" of the South was selling for sixty-eight cents a pound two years later. Smuggling became so rampant that the government in Washington felt compelled to at least partially legalize the trade, allowing local army commanders to issue trading permits to favored merchants. It was Ulysses S. Grant's misfortune to be in command of an area that not only was ideal for growing cotton—western Tennessee, northern Mississippi, and eastern Arkansas—but also happened to border on the North. If Jesse Grant concluded he had been handed the key to the kingdom, it would have been hard to blame him.

If so, however, Jesse Grant had badly misread his son. Cotton smugglers and speculators had been, after Confederate raiders such as Nathan Bedford Forrest, the bane of Grant's existence for months. The patriotism of such men, he fumed in a letter to Julia, "is measured in dollars and cents. Country has no meaning to them."

Memphis, Tennessee, had a small but well-established and influential Jewish community that had been active in river trading before the war. Thus, it was inevitable that many of the men with whom Grant was frustrated would be Jewish. Even before General Orders 11, Grant had occasionally expressed anti-Semitic sentiments in his correspondence. In November, he had written to General Hurlbut in Jackson, "The Israelites especially should be kept out." The next day he wrote General Webster a dispatch that stated, "Give orders to all the conductors on the road that no Jews are to be permitted to travel on the railroad south from any point . . . they are such an intolerable nuisance that the department must be purged of them."

When Jesse Grant arrived at his son's headquarters, he brought along with him the Macks, three Jewish brothers from Cincinnati who were in business together. Unbeknownst to the general, who treated his father and guests warmly, the four had an arrangement: The three business partners would pay all of Jesse's expenses on the trip in return for Jesse's persuading his son to issue them a cotton trading permit.

It wasn't long before the details of the shady scheme came out. Ulysses S. Grant was enraged. He instantly ordered the three Mack brothers placed under guard and escorted to the first northbound train. Jesse was allowed to hang around camp for a few more weeks, perhaps hoping that he could somehow persuade his general son to change his mind. General Orders 11 was issued almost as soon as the Mack brothers' train pulled out of the station.

The consequences were immediate and ugly. Jewish traders who were legally selling goods to the Union army found themselves hustled out of army camps at bayonet point. At Paducah, Kentucky, thirty Jewish families were rounded up and deported. More than 1,000 Memphis Jews were forcibly removed after having their personal possessions confiscated. Jewish soldiers in the army were taunted and threatened. At least one Jewish Union army officer resigned his commission in protest.

In Washington, the Lincoln administration was still reeling from the fallout of the Battle of Fredericksburg on December 13 (the same day Jesse Grant and company hit camp in Mississippi). This was a distraction that it most certainly did not need. After meeting in the White House with Cesar Kaskel, a prominent Jew who had been designated a spokesman for his people, Lincoln commanded the order be revoked, and Grant did so.

Six years later, the Jew Order came back to haunt Grant's first presidential campaign. Historian Stephen D. Lutz recounts that Democrats were exploiting the issue in an effort to swing Jews away from their traditionally Republican allegiance. Grant's spokesmen did everything they could to divert blame from the candidate. Grant, however, would have none of it. In a letter to his old friend Isaac Morris, the future president stepped up to his responsibility.

> I do not pretend to sustain the order. At the time of its publication I was incensed by a reprimand received from Washington for permitting acts which Jews within my lines were engaged in. There were many other persons within my lines equally bad with the worst of them, but the difference was that the Jews could

pass with impunity from one army to the other, and gold in violation of order, was being smuggled through the lines. . . . The order was issued and sent without any reflection and without thinking of the Jews as a sect or race to themselves, but simply as persons who had successfully . . . violated an order, which greatly inured to the help of the rebels. . . . I have no prejudice against sect or race, but want each individual to be judged by his own merit. General Orders, No. 11 does not sustain that statement, I admit, but then I do not sustain that order. It never would have been issued if it had not been telegraphed the moment it was penned and without reflection.

Grant had indeed acted hastily and without thinking. So upset was he at his father's crude attempt to use him and his position for personal profit that he chose to lash out at the nearest and most obvious available target, his father's Jewish business partners and all like them. It was a mistake and Grant owned up to it. Later, as president, Grant put force behind his words and appointed several Jews to important posts in his administration.


## COLD HARBOR

COLD HARBOR IS about three miles north of the Chickahominy River and eleven miles north and east of Richmond. Grant considered it an important point as several roads converged there, offering facilities for the movement of troops in almost any direction.

No one knows exactly how Cold Harbor got its name, for there was nothing cold about it in early June 1864, and there was no harbor anywhere nearby. Regardless, the name acquired a chilling significance among Union soldiers who survived it. After the war, Union veterans visited the old battlefields—

Gettysburg, Chancellorsville, Vicksburg. But, it was said, no one wanted to go back to Cold Harbor.

The assault there, made at dawn on June 3, 1864, was the biggest mistake Grant admitted to making in the course of the Civil War. (He also regretted the second assault at Vicksburg on May 22, 1863, although he noted that it was McClernand who had requested it.)

Tempers were growing short around Grant's headquarters in the days prior to the assault. For nearly a month, the Army of the Potomac had battered its way south across the Virginia countryside, seeking to trap and destroy Robert E. Lee's Army of Northern Virginia. The two forces had butted heads at the Wilderness, Spotsylvania, and now this desolate crossroads called Cold Harbor.

Lee's army resolutely refused to come out and fight in the open, where Grant's superiority in numbers and artillery would tell. Instead, it preferred to crouch behind prepared fieldworks and blast away at the attacking Federals. The cost to both sides had been fearful, but especially to the bluecoats: By the beginning of June, nearly 50,000 men out of the 118,000 that had begun the campaign had been killed, wounded, or captured. Worse, the bulk of those lost were among the best, bravest, and most experienced men Grant possessed. Replacements had largely made good the losses on paper, but they consisted substantially of inexperienced garrison troops, unwilling draftees, bounty jumpers, bewildered immigrants fresh off the boat, and "galvanized Yankees"—that is, former Confederates who had changed sides and whose ultimate allegiance was dubious.

Grant probably was also finding the Army of the Potomac more difficult to handle than he had anticipated. Technically, Grant did not command the army; Major General George G. Meade did. To save time, however, Grant often issued orders directly to the army's corps commanders, bypassing Meade's headquarters and making the army commander feel superfluous.

One reason Grant felt he had to give personal direction was the fact that those corps commanders were of wildly uneven quality. The best by far was Winfield Scott Hancock, commanding the II Corps. Gouverneur K. Warren, commanding the V Corps, was not incompetent but was of too cautious and careful a nature for Grant's taste. John Sedgwick, commanding the VI Corps, had been killed at Spotsylvania in early May. His successor, Horatio Wright, was still feeling his way but showing no signs of brilliance. As for Ambrose Burnside, the IX Corps commander, the less said the better. William F. "Baldy" Smith, commanding the XVIII Corps, had been a Grant favorite since his brilliant performance as an engineer in helping break the siege of Chattanooga the previous November. As a corps commander, however, he was out of his depth. Grant's grand strategy appeared open to question. Lee's army was battered, but far from beaten. Sherman was making progress in Georgia, but it was slow. Meanwhile, in the election campaign underway in the North, "Peace Democrat" charges that the war was pointless seemed to ring with increased validity by the day.

Even Grant's up-to-now-rock-steady nerves were showing signs of fraying. On June 1, as the two armies were racing for possession of Cold Harbor, Grant came upon a teamster who was beating a horse. In Horace Porter's long book, *Campaigning with Grant,* this is the only time he reports witnessing the general publicly lose his temper—Grant ordered the teamster tied to a tree for six hours. Porter reports that the incident upset Grant for the rest of the day.

The stage was thus grimly set for the worst day of Grant's generalship. A series of frustrating mistakes and wrong turns had essentially wasted June 2, the day for which the attack on Lee's rapidly fortifying positions at Cold Harbor had been planned. Grant, concerned about Meade's prickly pride, had stepped back and let the army commander handle the actual preparations for the assault. This was a mistake. Meade issued no overall attack plan and made no coordinated reconnaissance of the ground. As Brooks Simpson reports, he didn't seem to realize or care that Lee's army would be incomparably better entrenched following the twenty-four-hour delay. The men weren't fooled, however. Horace Porter reported seeing them carefully writing their names and hometowns on slips of paper that they then pinned to the backs of their uniforms.

The attack went ahead at 4:30 A.M. on June 3 and achieved some initial success. But it was short-lived. Reports filtering back to Meade were not encouraging. The latter, instead of stepping up to his responsibility and suspending the attack, sent Grant a message in the rear asking what he should do. Grant sent back a matter-of-fact reply that if the attack had failed, it should be suspended, but that if it had succeeded it should be pressed. Meade then passed the buck to the corps commanders, letting each of them decide whether or not to press the offensive.

This confused state of affairs persisted until late morning, when Grant visited the front. What he saw convinced him to order Meade to suspend the attack. "I remember meeting the General as he returned from Cold Harbor and he was much depressed," recalled Grant's cousin, W. W. Smith, in later years. "He dismounted and took a seat on the stone. 'What is the situation,' I asked? 'Bad—very bad,' he replied."

That was putting it mildly. A head-spinning 7,000 Union soldiers lay dead and wounded on the field, most of them cut down in the early minutes of the dawn assault. The homemade dog tags Porter saw the soldiers pinning to their uniforms turned out to be a wise precaution.

Those who have called Grant a "butcher of his own men" have traditionally pointed to Cold Harbor. But what then to say of Pickett's Charge? Or of Lee's assault on Malvern Hill during the Peninsula Campaign? Confederate general John

Bell Hood's ordering of a suicidal charge at Franklin, Tennessee, in November 1864 was undertaken with far less justification than Grant's at Cold Harbor. The attack at Cold Harbor was indeed a terrible mistake, but it was far from unique in the war and not at all typical of Grant's style of leadership.

For his part, Grant stepped up to his responsibility for the attack, admitting that it was mistaken not because it had been undertaken at all, but because "no advantage whatever" was gained to compensate for the losses incurred.

Grant learned important lessons from Cold Harbor. There would be no more frontal assaults against entrenched positions. Instead, he would move to cut Lee's supply lines by crossing south of the James River and capturing the crucial railway junction at Petersburg.

The crossing of the James is an achievement that gets remarkably little attention in Civil War histories. After Grant's men evacuated their positions in front of Cold Harbor on the night of June 12, 1864, the supposedly omniscient Robert E. Lee was dumbfounded. Where was Grant going?

Deep inside enemy territory, the Union general's engineers had built a 700-yard-long pontoon bridge, more than twice as long as any previously built. Achingly vulnerable to Confederate naval bombardment or attack by Lee (if the Confederate had any inkling of what was happening), this slender ribbon of wood and rope was the highway over which Grant proposed to move more than 100,000 men, with all their artillery, horses, wagons, and equipment.

For two days and one night, with Grant calmly smoking a cigar as he surveyed the scene from atop a nearby knoll for much of the time, the bluecoats trudged across the makeshift span. The entire host made the crossing while losing not so much as a musket ball to enemy action.

If Grant got south of the river, Robert E. Lee had commented earlier, "it will become a siege, and then it will be a mere question of time." Grant had taken his biggest gamble of the war—and made a prophet of his opponent.

---

## GRANT'S LESSONS

- Everyone makes mistakes. The critical factor is how you react to them.

- Don't let mistakes get you down. Sulking isn't going to solve anything.

- If your mistake has injured someone, do your best to own up to it and try to make it up to him or her.

- Make the best of a bad situation. If mistakes ruin your initial plans, look for a way to redeem the situation.

# PART II

# MANAGING PEOPLE

# CHAPTER 6

# GETTING ALONG WITH SUPERIORS

## *Remember Who's Boss*

———————

*Grant is the first general I have had. You know how it's been with all*
*the rest. As soon as I put a man in command of the army, they all*
*wanted me to be the general. Now it isn't so with Grant. He hasn't*
*told me what his plans are. I don't know and I don't want to know. I*
*am glad to find a man who can go ahead without me. He doesn't ask*
*impossibilities of me, and he's the first general I've had that didn't.*
—ABRAHAM LINCOLN

SUBORDINATION WAS A very crucial attribute in the
estimation of Ulysses S. Grant. The word pops up again and
again in the pages of his memoirs, which are littered with
tales of generals scheming against their superiors or sulking if
they did not get their way. Grant made it plain that he disap-
proved of all such conduct. The same orderly worldview that
rejected the idea of a state seceding from the Union was re-
pelled by the thought of any individual seeking to undermine
or defy legitimately constituted authority.

The mid–nineteenth century was a romantic period much
obsessed with matters of personal honor and standing. Prior

to the war, duels were one of the major causes of mortality among army and navy officers. During the Civil War, at least one Northern general and several Confederates fell, not in battle, but in what were termed "personal encounters." Most of the time, things did not degenerate that far. But in the pre-war army, promotion was based strictly on seniority, and any deviation from it was severely frowned upon by those passed over and could even be interpreted as a personal affront. This stratification caused endless problems during the war on both sides, with various generals refusing to serve under one or another because of disputes over who was senior.

Such nonsense held few charms for Grant, to whom the cause was everything. He had no time for officers who placed personal ambition or prerogative ahead of that cause. Don Carlos Buell was an example. Grant owed Buell a great deal; it was thanks to Buell's timely arrival at Shiloh, after all, that Grant was able to stave off total disaster. A talented but rigid officer, Buell fell into disfavor following the bloody and indecisive Battle of Perryville in October 1862 and was removed from command. Upon becoming general in chief in 1864, Grant recalled in his memoirs, he sought to have Buell restored to a command. But Buell preferred to nurse his wounded pride rather than fight:

> I . . . recommended to the [War] Secretary the assignment of General Buell to duty. I received the assurance that duty would be offered to him; and afterwards the Secretary told me that he had offered Buell an assignment and that the latter had declined it, saying that it would be degradation to accept the assignment offered. I understood afterwards that he refused to serve under either Sherman or [E. R. S.] Canby because he had ranked them both. Both graduated before him and ranked him in the old army. Sherman ranked him as a brigadier-general. All of them ranked me in the old army, and Sherman and Buell did as brigadiers. The worst excuse a soldier can make for declining service is that he once ranked the commander he is ordered to report to.

Loyalty is a two-way street, though. Grant gave it as well as expected it, even when doing so made things more difficult than they needed to be. For example, Grant could not have been more pleased by the accommodating attitude of Major General George G. Meade when Grant made his first visit to the Army of the Potomac in March 1864 as general in chief:

> Meade evidently thought I might want to make still one more change not yet ordered. He said to me that I might want an officer who had served with me in the West, mentioning Sherman specially, to take his place. If so, he begged me not to hesitate about making the change. He urged that the work before us was of such vast importance to the whole nation that the feelings or wishes of no one person should stand in the way of selecting the right men for all positions. For himself, he would serve to the best of his ability wherever placed. I assured him that I had no thought of substituting anyone for him. As for Sherman, he could not be spared from the West.
>
> The incident gave me even a more favorable opinion of Meade than his famous victory at Gettysburg the July before. It is men who wait to be selected, and not those who seek, from whom we may always expect the most efficient service.

Meade stayed in command of the Army of the Potomac right to Appomattox. The arrangement was awkward and frequently created unnecessary delay and confusion in the transmission of orders, but Grant knew it was important that the officers and men of the Army of the Potomac understand that Grant had confidence in them and would not willy-nilly replace them with his own loyalists.

Grant's admiration for his superior in the Mexican War, the plainly dressed, straightforward General Zachary Taylor, who stood in such contrast to the elaborately uniformed General Winfield Scott, has already been described. Grant's relationships—one good and the other terrible—with his two most important superiors, Presidents Abraham Lincoln and

Andrew Johnson, also reveal much about Grant's character and leadership abilities.

## GRANT AND LINCOLN

GRANT WAS CERTAINLY the top commander with whom Lincoln had the most harmonious relationship, as the quotation at the beginning of this chapter illustrates. But it was not fated to be so and could well have gone badly.

Grant and Lincoln had never met prior to the tumultuous White House reception on the evening of March 8, 1864, at which the general was very nearly trampled to death by the excited crowd. (Indeed, it was only Grant's second visit to the nation's capital in his life, and the first in twelve years.) On the surface, the two men couldn't have been more dissimilar. Lincoln was tall and given to making points by telling stories that were often taller. He was one of the greatest—probably *the* greatest—speechmaker in American history. Grant was well under six feet and reserved, with a horror of public speaking. But the chief executive and the new general in chief were alike in many subtler ways. Each had an active, probing mind that critics often missed. Both men were also adept at hiding their intentions from the gaze of those with no need to know.

The partnership that would win the Civil War began on a wary note. Some have found it odd that eight months were permitted to elapse between Grant's great victory at Vicksburg and his being called east to take full command of the Union's armies in the field. But as John Y. Simon has pointed out in his essay "Grant, Lincoln and Unconditional Surrender," it doesn't seem unusual when the totality of the circumstances are taken into consideration.

Grant had voted for Democratic presidential candidates before the war and said he would have supported Stephen A.

Douglas for president in 1860, rather than Lincoln, had he met the residency requirement for voting in Galena, Illinois. Grant had tolerated slavery under his own roof. After Grant's victories at Vicksburg and then Chattanooga, the northern Democrats made no secret of courting the new hero. Discontented Republicans, too, were looking for someone who would help them unseat Lincoln.

The president, facing a difficult reelection in 1864—the third year of civil war, with the end nowhere in sight—thus had good reason to be wary of the rising young general in the West. He had already had experience with one general, George B. McClellan, who was clearly preparing to make a run for the White House. As Simon points out, not until J. Russell Jones, a friend of both men from Galena, Illinois, assured Lincoln that Grant had no presidential ambitions did the president's fears ease.

At the same time, Grant could not have felt entirely at ease with Lincoln from afar. After all, even though Lincoln might or might not have said, "I cannot spare this man, he fights," in response to calls for Grant's scalp after Shiloh, it is a fact that Lincoln did nothing to prevent Grant's being temporarily sidelined when Major General Henry Halleck arrived to take command in the West after that near debacle. Upon accepting promotion to lieutenant general, however, Grant did not make McClellan's mistake of forgetting who was in charge. From the start, he knew that his job was to carry out the administration's policy, not make it himself, a distinction that McClellan, for all his brilliance, never seemed able to grasp. Also, despite Lincoln's claim that he "did not want to know" Grant's plans, it is evident that the general took the president wholly into his confidence and described his overall plan for a simultaneous movement against Confederate forces all across the board. Lincoln was content to leave the details to Grant.

Those who believe "face time" with the boss is the secret of success ignore the example of Grant and Lincoln. Not only had the two men never met prior to March 1864, but they actually spent relatively little time together during that visit as well, and much of what time there was occurred in the presence of the cabinet. Grant let his actions speak for themselves, and there was little need—even if Grant had felt the inclination—to butter up the boss.

Nevertheless, there was friction between the two men. It is possible that Grant might have interpreted his mandate more broadly than Lincoln intended. Grant seems to have been under the impression that Lincoln had given him a free hand in the field. While Lincoln certainly gave Grant more slack than any other general, there definitely was a leash. This Grant discovered after Confederate general Jubal Early came perilously close to leading a Confederate raid into the heart of Washington, D.C., in July 1864. Lincoln met with Grant alone at Fortress Monroe on the Chesapeake and—while there are only some sketchy surviving notes of the meeting in the president's hand—it is clear that Lincoln was tough with Grant. That the general omitted the encounter from his memoirs—his usual method of dealing with unpleasant memories—shows how difficult an experience it had been.

Grant sent a steady stream of reports back to the War Department on his progress, though he was careful never to tax his superior's time with unnecessary communications or demand things he knew it was not within the president's power to grant. Lincoln appreciated this regard for his time immensely. The level of confidence that he had in his new general is evidenced by the fact that, as casualties mounted in the Army of the Potomac during the summer of 1864, Lincoln allowed Grant to strip the Washington fortifications of their garrison troops to reinforce the front line. McClellan could only have dreamed of such consideration.

Still, Lincoln refused to stop looking over Grant's shoulder. When Grant appointed Major General Philip H. Sheridan to drive Early from the Shenandoah Valley, Lincoln cautioned Grant that decisive results were unlikely unless Grant himself "watched it every hour of every day and forced it." In early March 1865, Confederate lieutenant general James Longstreet, who was Julia Grant's cousin, proposed a meeting between Grant and Lee to discuss peace possibilities. Grant's enquiry to Washington brought back a sharp reply signed by Stanton (but composed by Lincoln) reminding Grant to stay out of political controversies and "press to the utmost your military advantages."

Grant performed two of his greatest services for his commander in chief outside of the strictly military arena, however.

The first was Grant's ill-concealed effort at helping Lincoln win reelection in 1864, both by facilitating soldier voting in the field as well as by a series of carefully worded letters to political friends (which Grant fully expected would be circulated publicly), making it clear that the administration's return to office was essential to secure a just and lasting peace.

The second was related to the first. Grant was not completely free to select his own subordinates. Early in the war, Lincoln had appointed a number of "political" generals with little or no professional military training to high posts. John McClernand, who gave Grant grief in the Vicksburg campaign, was one of these. Another was Ben Butler.

A highly successful Massachusetts Democratic politician before the war, Butler was one of the first to offer his services to the nation after Fort Sumter, and Lincoln appointed him a major general, eager as the president was to showcase "loyal" Democrats who backed the war effort. Unfortunately, this made the military amateur Butler one of the most senior officers in the Union army.

Eager for martial glory that he hoped would lead to the White House, Butler took the opportunity to carve out for himself a military record remarkable for its ineptitude even in a war where command incompetence was commonplace. He lost what is widely regarded as the war's first large skirmish, at Big Bethel, Virginia, in June 1861. He failed to take Petersburg in June 1864, when the city lay all but defenseless before him, a failure that necessitated Grant's undertaking a nine-month siege operation.

Grant would have loved to fire Butler, but the reasons that Lincoln had for appointing him in the first place still applied: Butler was politically influential, and the president needed his support in the fall campaign. Grant thus tolerated Butler's ongoing blunders until November 1864, when he was sent home to "await orders." Butler insisted on leading one last disaster in early 1865, when he failed to take Fort Fisher, North Carolina. After that, he was out of uniform for good. The lesson of Grant, Lincoln, and Butler is, Sometimes you have to do what you have to do.

## GRANT AND ANDREW JOHNSON

GRANT HEARD ABOUT President Lincoln's assassination while traveling with his wife from Washington to New Jersey. The Grants had declined the president's invitation to attend Ford's Theater on the fateful night so the Grants could go to New Jersey to see their children. Now Grant had a new commander in chief, President Andrew Johnson.

"I dread the change," Grant told Julia of the prospect of working for Johnson. It isn't hard to see why. None of us likes to lose a boss with whom we have established not merely a strong working relationship, but a close personal bond as well. Grant hardly knew Johnson, and what little he knew he didn't much like.

A Democrat and the only Southern senator who had refused to secede with his state, the Tennessean vice president
was born poor and rarely let anyone forget it. He detested the
slaveholding bourbon aristocracy that had fathered the Confederacy and was known as a man in favor of treating the defeated South much more harshly than Lincoln had planned.
He had been placed on the ticket as a gesture toward national
unity rather than with any view toward the type of president
he would make. His naturally dyspeptic disposition could not
have been helped by his tenure as military governor of Tennessee during the war, a position in which his very life was under constant threat.

It wasn't long before the two men clashed. Johnson
wanted to try all the major Confederate leaders for treason—
including Robert E. Lee—and have them hanged. Grant objected strenuously. The terms at Appomattox exempted from
punishment all former Confederate officers who swore an
oath of allegiance and promised to obey the laws.

This was not the answer Johnson wanted. "When can
these men be tried?" he demanded of Grant.

"Never," Grant replied, "so long as they do not violate
their paroles."

It was downhill from there. The Johnson administration
was almost certainly the most difficult period of Grant's public career. As a military officer, he sought to stay out of
politics, but Johnson—and, to a lesser extent, the Radical
Republicans—kept dragging him in. Grant soon came to detest his chief.

Johnson made several efforts to secure Grant's goodwill,
consulting him frequently and inviting him to sit in on cabinet
meetings. He arranged for Grant's son Fred to attend West
Point and he supported legislation creating the rank of full general, adding a fourth star to Grant's shoulders. But whatever

goodwill he might have secured through these efforts was lost by the crass ways Johnson sought to use the war's greatest hero to prop up his faltering administration.

Senator Carl Schurz, a former Union army general, toured the defeated Confederacy in the months after the war and brought home grim tidings. Despite being defeated, he found the whites increasingly sullen and resentful toward the idea of black political equality and the newly freed slaves increasingly fearful of violence. Johnson, who might have hated the Confederacy but who hated the idea of black political equality even more, was anxious to squelch Schurz's report. He asked Grant to undertake a whirlwind, two-week visit to Virginia, the Carolinas, and Georgia to take his own soundings.

Reluctantly, Grant agreed. Perhaps still a bit besotted with "the spirit of Appomattox," Grant reported back that things were not as bleak as Schurz made them out to be. Johnson seized upon Grant's survey to justify ignoring and disparaging Schurz's reportage. The Radical Republicans were outraged.

Grant now began walking a career tightrope between loyalty to his constitutionally designated commander in chief and the swelling ranks of Johnson's critics in Congress. The president continued to impose on Grant's sense of duty, even dragging him along on a whistle-stop political tour of the Midwest in 1866, using Grant as a prop to imply his support of Johnson's lenient Reconstruction policies. Though Grant sought to maintain his dignity in public, he privately wrote Julia that he found Johnson's speeches against black political equality "a national disgrace."

Grant's personal popularity remained unsullied through all this political maneuvering, though his opposition to Johnson was becoming increasingly obvious. The president decided to solve the problem by getting Grant out of the country—specifically, by sending him on a diplomatic mission to Mexico. Johnson planned to fire Secretary of War Edwin M. Stanton—

his leading critic in the cabinet—while Grant was away and re-place him with Grant's lieutenant, William T. Sherman.

The political explosion this plan would have ignited can be imagined. Regardless, it never happened because Grant simply refused to go. "No power on Earth can compel me to do it," he boldly declared to Johnson's face at a cabinet meeting. In essence, he was daring the president to fire him. Johnson wasn't ready to do that and backed down, but the relations between the two men deteriorated further.

All the while, with Johnson refusing to enforce the Civil Rights and Reconstruction Acts that Congress had passed over his veto, the burden of enforcing Reconstruction and black equality fell to Grant and the military. The shrinking Union army, however, was hard-pressed to maintain order as Southern resistance increasingly took the form of terrorism and brutality. All this combined to push Grant into the camp of the Radical Republicans and toward a political future for himself—a future he once swore to avoid.

The nadir of the Johnson/Grant relationship came when the president finally "suspended" Stanton in August 1867, while Congress was out of session. (The Tenure of Office Act, passed to protect Stanton from Johnson, required the Senate's approval to remove him from office.) The president then thrust the position of acting secretary on Grant, who took it simply because he was fearful that Johnson would give it to someone worse if he refused.

Grant labored in this highly uncomfortable position for five months, until the Senate voted to confirm Stanton in of-fice. Grant returned the keys to his former superior, an act that enraged Johnson.

In response to Johnson's ongoing efforts to remove Stan-ton, the House of Representatives moved to impeach the pres-ident in May 1868. But, by a single vote, the Senate failed to convict him. Grant was greatly disappointed.

## GRANT'S LESSONS

- Remember who's in charge. If you forget who's boss, your superior might remind you by firing you.

- Never consider a job beneath your competence or dignity.

- If you find yourself stuck with a selfish or inconsiderate superior, serve him to the best of your ability until either you or he moves on.

CHAPTER 7

# BUILDING A WINNING TEAM

*Finding Your Sherman*

━━━━◆━━━━

*While I have been eminently successful in this war, in at least gaining*
*the confidence of the public, no one feels more than I how much of*
*this success is due to the energy, skill, and the harmonious putting*
*forth of that energy and skill, of those whom it has been my good*
*fortune to have occupying subordinate positions under me.*
—ULYSSES S. GRANT TO WILLIAM T. SHERMAN,
MARCH 4, 1864

GRANT'S SARCOPHAGUS in New York City is sur-
rounded by the busts of five of his most prominent subordinates:
William T. Sherman, Philip H. Sheridan, James B. McPherson,
George H. Thomas, and E. O. C. Ord. They are the army officers who rose to prominence in the Civil War and came to be
known (not always kindly) as "Grant's men." They were the
team that he painstakingly assembled to help him win the war.

The old saw that "if you want a job done, do it yourself"
has a deceptive ring of truth to it. But if what you are setting
out to accomplish is anything much more complicated than
building a model airplane kit, you probably can't manage it

on your own. Even a boxer, alone in the ring, has a team of managers and trainers who helped get him there. You, too, need to build a team.

What did Grant look for in building his winning team? Men like himself, generally. This is a great deal more difficult than it appears. Many managers tend to hire "yes-men" who will do as they are told and employ no imagination. Grant looked for people who were eager to take the fight to the enemy rather than make excuses for not moving. He was fighting a war, and he wanted fighters. He set high goals and made it clear he expected his people to attain them.

Let's take a closer look at some of "Grant's men."

## WILLIAM TECUMSEH SHERMAN

ON THE SURFACE, Grant and William Tecumseh Sherman could not have been more dissimilar. Where Grant was quiet to the point of imperturbability and could sometimes sit for hours without saying a word, Sherman was tightly wound and explosively volatile; he tended to say whatever came into his head. Both smoked cigars, but whereas Grant smoked them slowly and down to a nub, Sherman smoked his furiously and frequently discarded them after only a few vigorous puffs, lighting a fresh one almost immediately. Whatever their differences on a personal level, however, both men overcame them to meld into the most lethal combination in American military history.

Sherman and Grant first met at West Point, when Sherman was a first classman about to graduate and Grant a seventeen-year-old plebe. Separated in age and responsibility, they were not particular friends at the academy. Nor did they know each other in Mexico, for Sherman was one of the few young regular army officers who saw no action there.

The most striking similarity between the two men, however, was their pre–Civil War experience of grim times. Like Grant, Sherman grew frustrated with garrison life in the peacetime army and resigned, unsuccessfully seeking to make a career as a banker and as a lawyer. Frustrated in his efforts to rejoin the army, he accepted the presidency of the new Louisiana Military Seminary (now Louisiana State University), a position he resigned when Louisiana left the Union in January 1861.

Unlike almost everyone else in the war's early days, Sherman foresaw a long struggle, one that would require the services of hundreds of thousands of troops to achieve victory. When he put these views to Secretary of War Simon Cameron, the secretary branded them as "crazy," a characterization that found its way into the newspapers and lost Sherman his command of the Department of the Cumberland. (Thus was born Sherman's lifelong hatred of newspaper reporters, though he was such good copy that it was impossible to keep them away entirely.)

That might well have been the end for Sherman. Thanks to his influential father-in-law (who was also, interestingly, his foster father) and his brother John, both of whom were or had been U.S. senators, Sherman won a second chance. He was placed in command of the troops at Paducah, Kentucky, which Grant had captured in 1861. Sherman was ordered to support and supply Grant's move against Forts Henry and Donelson.

His efficiency and timeliness in performing this important task won Grant's attention:

> At the time he was my senior in rank, and there was no authority of law to assign a junior to command a senior of the same grade; but every boat that came up with supplies or reinforcements brought a note of encouragement from Sherman, asking me to call upon him for any assistance he could render, and saying that

if he could be of any service at the front I might send for him
and he would waive rank.

You could never go wrong with Grant if you offered to put
your personal prerogatives aside for the sake of the cause.

Their partnership would be forged in steel on the field at
Shiloh several months later, where Sherman commanded one
of Grant's divisions. Together they went through the confused
and confusing campaign against Iuka and Corinth in northern Mississippi, where Sherman claimed to have dissuaded
Grant from resignation. As a team, they shared the glory of
Vicksburg, where Sherman opposed Grant's bold plan and
later admitted he was wrong and Grant was right.

Sherman was extremely self-aware. Like a great football
running back, Sherman knew he worked best with a strong
"quarterback" calling the plays. With Grant as that quarterback, Sherman blossomed. "When you have completed your
best preparations you go into battle without hesitation . . . no
doubts, no reserve; and I tell you it was this that made me act
with confidence," he wrote Grant in a revealing letter. "I
knew that wherever I was you thought of me, and that if I got
in a tight place you would come—if alive."

Grant's regard for Sherman sometimes escalated to absurd
levels, and Grant's determination to protect his protégé's back
sometimes did injustice to others. At Chattanooga in November 1864, Sherman's command performed indifferently while
Major General Joseph Hooker's was instrumental in winning
the battle. Yet, in his final report, Grant praised Sherman
highly while downplaying Hooker's role.

When Grant went east after being named general in chief
in 1864, he named Sherman as his successor in the West.
While still a subordinate, Sherman would be largely on his
own. Did the man the papers once called "insane" have the
mettle to stand the test?

Fortunately for the Union cause, he did. "Uncle Billy" proved the most formidable campaigner of the war, moving his "bummers" from Tennessee through the heart of Georgia to the Atlantic coast and then up into North Carolina by war's end. An indifferent tactician, he was nevertheless a brilliant strategist, engineer, and logistician. He had an almost mystical view of the importance of the Mississippi River, viewing its capture as the signing of the Confederacy's death warrant. His decision to ignore Confederate general John Bell Hood's Army of Tennessee after the fall of Atlanta and march to the sea is his most controversial decision and one that made Grant and the rest of the Union high command shudder with apprehension. But Sherman insisted that the psychological blow that would be delivered to Confederate morale by the sight of a Yankee army marching unmolested through the heart of the South would be incalculable. Given the way the name "Sherman" sticks in the throats of Southerners to this day, he was certainly right.

Sherman was that kind of soldier, a political philosopher almost as much as a military man. "I attach more importance to these deep incisions into the enemy's country, because this war differs from European wars in this particular," he wrote in a letter. "We are fighting not only armies but a hostile people, and must make old and young, rich and poor, feel the hard hand of war, as well as their organized armies." Grant, though he did not put it quite so colorfully, was in complete agreement.

Sherman repaid Grant's loyalty with loyalty. After the success of the March to the Sea, a bill was introduced in Congress to create a second lieutenant-generalcy and raise Sherman to a rank equivalent to that of Grant. Most other men would have seen this as an unparalleled career opportunity. Not Sherman. He used all his considerable influence in Washington to squelch the bill. "I would rather have you in command that anyone else," he wrote Grant, "for you are fair, honest and have at heart the same purpose that should animate us all. I should emphatically decline any commission calculated to bring us into rivalry."

When Sherman made a mistake, Grant came to his rescue. At the end of the war, Sherman offered Confederate general Joseph E. Johnston exceedingly generous terms of surrender that encompassed political as well as military issues. When the terms became known in Washington, they ignited a political firestorm. Secretary of War Edwin Stanton published them in the newspapers as though he were unmasking a traitor. He ordered Grant to North Carolina to take command and finish off Johnston as he had Lee.

Grant was not about to humiliate his old friend in that way. Instead, he slipped quietly into Sherman's headquarters and told him to offer Johnston the same terms Lee had accepted at Appomattox or face extermination. Grant then took his leave, declining Sherman's offer to be present at the interview with Johnston. Johnston accepted Sherman's offer, and the war effectively ended.

The two men remained close after the war, with Grant promoting Sherman to his place as full general upon Grant's assumption of the presidency. There were some rough spots, such as in 1875 when early reviews of Sherman's memoirs indicated he had slighted Grant. This proved not to be so, and relations between them were restored. A decade later, when Grant lay on his deathbed, Sherman was a frequent visitor. Grant said that his talks with Sherman about old times were worth more than all the physicians and medications in the world.

When Stonewall Jackson was accidentally shot in the left arm by his own troops, Robert E. Lee lamented, "He has lost his left arm, but I have lost my right!" The Army of Northern Virginia was to feel Jackson's loss keenly, for it never again won a major victory after his death. Sherman was Grant's right arm, the subordinate on whom Grant could rely without close supervision. Fortunately for him and the Union cause, Sherman lived throughout the war.

## PHILIP H. SHERIDAN

EARLY ON THE MORNING of October 19, 1864, Major General Philip Henry Sheridan was breakfasting with a Pennsylvania cavalry regiment while returning from a conference in Washington to rejoin his troops, who were camped about twelve miles distant near Cedar Creek, in the Shenandoah Valley of Virginia. Scattered firing from the direction of the camp began increasing in tempo and volume, however, and Sheridan became concerned. Mounting his big jet-black charger Rienzi, Sheridan galloped off to the sound of the guns.

As he approached the site of his army's bivouac, Sheridan was chagrined at the sight of blue-coated soldiers streaming toward him along the road, telling of a major Confederate attack that had overrun their camp. Chagrin turned to anger as Sheridan put the spurs to Rienzi, calling out to the fugitives, "Turn back! Turn back! Sheridan's here!"

The demoralized soldiers now began responding to their commander, chanting his name over and over. "Don't cheer me! Fight, damn you! Fight!" he shouted.

And fight they did, re-forming their lines and counterattacking the Confederates, who had been unable to resist the temptation to stop and loot the abandoned Yankee camp. Surprised, the graybacks were rocked back on their heels and found themselves now fleeing the field they had captured only a few hours before. Cavalry led by the Boy General, George Armstrong Custer, smashed a hole in the Confederate center and completed the victory.

Grant was elated when he heard the news of Sheridan's victory, firing a one-hundred-gun salute into Robert E. Lee's defenses at Petersburg in celebration. He called Sheridan's rallying of his men the greatest single feat of personal battlefield leadership in the entire war. Sheridan thus more than justified the confidence Grant had shown in entrusting such responsibility to a man who was only thirty-three years old.

Philip Henry Sheridan didn't impress many people upon first meeting. There is dispute about his exact height, but it was probably in the neighborhood of five feet five inches, and he weighed barely over a hundred pounds. His features were almost Asian in appearance, leading many to believe that something strange had happened back there in his parents' native Ireland. "The officer you brought on from the West is rather a little fellow to handle your cavalry," someone in the War Department told Grant after Sheridan reported for duty in the Eastern theater in April 1864.

"You will find him big enough for the purpose when we get through with him," Grant replied coolly.

It is a tribute to Grant that he was able to see Sheridan's merits, for Grant himself had a poor first impression of the fiery young officer. They first met in the railroad station at Corinth, Mississippi, in September 1862, as the newly promoted Colonel Sheridan was entraining his regiment, the 2nd Michigan Cavalry, for Kentucky. Grant had intended for the 2nd Michigan to stay with his army and sought to persuade Sheridan to let another regiment take the assignment. Sheridan, who sensed action in the Bluegrass State, was having none of it. His refusal was "brusque and rough," leaving Grant both hurt and annoyed. "I don't think Sheridan could have made a worse impression on me," he said years later.

Sheridan found what he was looking for in Kentucky, commanding a division at the Battle of Perryville on October 8, 1862. Nearly three months later, in the fierce fight at Stone's River, Tennessee, Sheridan showed himself "a perfect tornado in battle." At Chickamauga in September 1863, Sheridan joined George Thomas in refusing to be swept from the field by the Confederate onslaught and joined "the Rock of Chickamauga" on Snodgrass Hill.

Clearly, the bantam Irishman was the kind of fighter Grant was looking for, and he wasted no time overlooking the unpleasantness of their first meeting to bring Sheridan forward. Although Sheridan was an infantryman by training, Grant thought him just the man to put some iron into the Army of the Potomac's dispirited cavalry corps, which had spent most of the war up to that time eating the dust of J. E. B. Stuart, Robert E. Lee's legendary cavalry commander.

He didn't disappoint. Sheridan conceived a plan to lure the great Stuart into a head-on battle. Trotting south slowly and deliberately, virtually daring Stuart to attack him, Sheridan finally confronted his adversary on May 11, 1864, at Yellow Tavern, a crossroads just outside Richmond. There, the Union troopers achieved victory, along with the grim satisfaction of the death of Stuart.

When Confederate general Jubal A. Early was dispatched by Robert E. Lee to make a diversionary raid on Washington, D.C., in July and August 1864, spooking President Lincoln and his administration badly in the midst of an election campaign, Sheridan was the man to whom Grant turned. Not only was Early to be defeated and driven back, Grant told his subordinate, but the entire Shenandoah Valley was also to be burned and leveled, so that it could never again be used to supply Lee and his army.

Sheridan was a bit too slow in starting for Grant's taste, and the general in chief visited Sheridan at his headquarters with a plan of his own in hand. But Grant asked to see Sheridan's plan first and, finding it satisfactory, quickly left Sheridan's headquarters, allowing his subordinate to go ahead. Grant didn't want anyone to give him the credit for Sheridan's achievement.

The successful 1864 Valley campaign created one of the great "what ifs" of the Civil War, one that didn't escape Ulysses S. Grant. Suppose the great Thomas J. "Stonewall" Jackson had found himself confronted with Sheridan instead of the second-raters he in fact faced during Jackson's great Valley Campaign of 1862?

> I shall always be sorry that Stonewall Jackson never fought Sheridan. The result of that battle would have given him the place in history which he dies without attaining.

Little Phil, as he came to be known, ran a close second only to Sherman in Grant's affections. When Sherman was promoted to full general in March 1869 to succeed Grant, the latter promoted Sheridan to succeed Sherman as lieutenant general, a move that did not sit well with George H. Thomas and George G. Meade, both of whom felt slighted. Grant, however, had no doubt he had made the right decision. As Grant later told Otto von Bismarck,

> As a soldier, as a commander of troops, as a man who is capable of doing all that is possible with any number of men, there is no man living greater than Sheridan. He belongs in the first rank of soldiers, not only of our country but of the world. I rank Sheridan with Napoleon and Frederick and the great commanders of history.

Hyperbole, perhaps, but Sheridan fully reciprocated the feeling:

> He guided every subordinate with a fund of common sense and superiority of intellect, which left an impression so distinct as to exhibit his great personality. When his military history is analyzed after the lapse of years, it will show, even more clearly than now, he was the steadfast center about and on which everything else turned.

# JAMES B. MCPHERSON

THE OHIO CONNECTION with Grant is strong, though there is no evidence that it was anything other than coincidence. Still, it is interesting to note that, in addition to Grant himself, Sherman and Sheridan either were born in the state or grew up there. Add to those illustrious names another not as well known, but one that Grant held in equally high esteem: James Birdseye McPherson.

First in his West Point class of 1853, McPherson holds the distinction of having been described by Grant as "my best friend." Unlike with Sherman and Sheridan, who won great victories, it is hard to point to one single achievement by McPherson that caused him to rise so high in his chief's estimation (though Grant was highly impressed with McPherson's skill as an engineer). But he was present with Grant from the capture of Fort Donelson in February 1862 until Grant went east, and then he served with Sherman until being ambushed and killed on a road outside of Atlanta in July 1864 before he could achieve distinction in independent command.

Nevertheless, all accounts agree that McPherson knew his trade as an engineer officer. In the campaigns around Iuka and Corinth, he kept the army moving and the supplies coming. In the Vicksburg campaign, when only thirty-four years old, he was a major general leading the XVII Corps of Grant's army, winning the Battle of Raymond, near the Mississippi state capital of Jackson. He also played a large part in moving Grant's army around the bogs and bayous in that part of Mississippi and Louisiana.

So high was McPherson's standing in the army at the time of Vicksburg that a whispering campaign began soon after the great victory that the daring plan must have been McPherson's idea. He never claimed authorship, however, and never encouraged anyone to give him credit for Grant's victory.

In the campaigns around Atlanta, Sherman used McPherson's corps effectively as his "whiplash" to outflank and push back the Confederate army led by Joseph E. Johnston. Sherman came to regard him so highly that he believed McPherson would have risen to eclipse both Sherman and Grant by the end of the war.

That seems a bit of a stretch. Given that he never exercised independent command, the best that can be said about McPherson was that he was an exceptionally able corps commander. Still, the "might-have-beens" have always surrounded his reputation. Tall in stature, with a handsome face and powerful Christian faith, McPherson came close to being the beau ideal of a Civil War soldier. The metaphor of a medieval knight recurs again and again in descriptions of McPherson. Sherman was stunned by his death; Grant wept.

## GEORGE H. THOMAS

FEW RELATIONSHIPS have puzzled those who study the career of Ulysses S. Grant as much as that with George H. Thomas. Certainly Grant could not quarrel with Thomas's commitment to the Union cause, for few had made so great a sacrifice to serve it. A native Virginian, Thomas had, unlike Robert E. Lee, chosen to remain loyal to his flag and his oath at the expense of his family and Southern friends. Like Grant, Thomas counted William T. Sherman among his closest friends and comrades-in-arms. No one could gainsay the willingness and ability of "the Rock of Chickamauga" to fight.

Yet there was tension between Grant and Thomas, a tension whose source has been a topic of speculation for nearly one hundred and fifty years. Thomas is reliably on record as disparaging Grant on a number of occasions. For his part, Grant showed himself to poor advantage when, in a remarkable fit of impatience, he came within an ace of relieving Thomas of command in Tennessee in 1864. The two men had known one another at West Point (Thomas was three years ahead of Grant) and also in the Mexican War, though their first Civil War contact came after the Battle of Shiloh, where Thomas and his men arrived too late to take part in the battle. As we have seen, Grant was willing to overlook poor first impressions. Still, what happened next might have cut more deeply. When Grant was scapegoated following Shiloh and given the empty honor of being Henry W. Halleck's second-in-command, most of his troops were given to Thomas. Though the latter had no control over this, some of Grant's friends traced the beginning of their feud to this moment.

Others say it came later, specifically, the night Grant arrived at Thomas's headquarters in the besieged town of Chattanooga in 1863. Sopping wet, ravenously hungry, and in considerable pain after suffering a fall from his horse, Grant was offered little more than a seat in front of a fire by Thomas. When prompted, Thomas finally offered Grant a change of clothes and a hot meal, both of which Grant icily declined.

Holding a grudge was unlike Grant. Still, he might well have been surprised at such treatment by Thomas, who, after all, owed his appointment at Chattanooga to Grant. For his part, Thomas may have resented the fact that Grant saw it necessary to come to Chattanooga in person and apparently did not trust Thomas to get the job done himself. Later, during the Battle of Missionary Ridge, Thomas gave the impression of seeming to ignore an order from Grant in Grant's own presence. Of course, Thomas might well have been merely engaging in his predilection for slow, deliberate movement. Grant, however, might have interpreted it as insubordination, which, as we have seen, was a cardinal sin in Grant's book.

Thomas's great moment came at Nashville in December 1864. Sherman, as we have seen, elected to strike out from

Atlanta to the sea rather than find and destroy Confederate general John Bell Hood's Army of Tennessee. Hood didn't simply disappear; instead, he headed back into his army's namesake state for a move northward. Sherman—anticipating such a maneuver—had left Thomas behind to garrison Nashville against just such a movement by Hood.

Thomas was unhappy with the assignment but did his part with his customary thoroughness. On November 30, 1864, an advance guard of Thomas's army shredded much of Hood's at the furious Battle of Franklin. Two weeks later, the ragged remnants of Hood's army were gathered before Nashville. This situation caused Grant no end of anxiety. Daily, then almost hourly, he bombarded Thomas with telegrams demanding that he attack Hood immediately. Thomas, ever patient, replied that he would not strike until he was ready and the weather was favorable. Enraged, Grant toyed with the idea of removing Thomas from command but hesitated to so ignominiously end the career of the hero of Chickamauga.

Finally, on December 15, 1864, the ice storm that had hampered Thomas's operations broke, and he attacked. Hood's army crumbled like a wet Saltine, and Thomas won one of the most complete victories of the war. Afterward, Grant recommended Thomas's promotion to major general in the regular army—a little tardily, Thomas thought.

Whatever their differences during the war and after it— Thomas was affronted when President Grant appointed Sheridan over his head to be full general—the fact is that the two men managed to work together well for the larger cause. Thomas was slow and deliberate, a fact that Grant couldn't understand. Yet it was part of Thomas's makeup.

"If he (Thomas) had the quality of inertia, he possessed momentum as well," said Adam Badeau, Grant's military secretary and historian of his campaigns. "He was like an elephant crossing a bridge and feeling his way with ponderous feet before every step. But woe to the enemy he met on the opposite side."

## GRANT'S STAFF

GRANT'S SENIOR LIEUTENANTS could be described, in a business sense, as his division heads. But Grant also had what might be called "line managers": his military staff.

In the days before the command and leadership of armies was truly professionalized, commanders tended to gather around themselves a military "family." Often, these were actual family members, with generals naming their own sons or other relatives as aides. Personal friends and acquaintances, often with little or no military experience, were also commonplace in the role.

At the war's beginning, Grant's staff was little different. His early choices included William S. Hillyer, a St. Louis attorney who had helped Grant during his trying days as a bill collector and was one of the witnesses at Grant's manumission of the slave William Jones; Clark B. Lagow, a volunteer officer with the 21st Illinois, Grant's first command; and John A. Rawlins, a Galena, Illinois, attorney who represented the Grant leather business and had inspired the future general with a fiery pro-Union speech after Fort Sumter was attacked. None was a professional military man. Only Rawlins would still be with Grant by war's end.

Rawlins is worth a closer look, given that his precise relationship with Grant remains a matter of stormy controversy even today. Just thirty years old when the war broke out, Rawlins was the polar opposite of the quiet, undemonstrative Grant. A bundle of nerves and energy, he was fascinated by the Mexican War and wasted no time beating a path to Jesse

Grant's leather store when he heard that a real live veteran of the conflict was employed there.

Grant, shy around strangers, did not at first take to this excitable young man who asked so many questions. But he eventually accepted Rawlins's sincerity and admitted to being impressed with the lawyer's powerful sense of patriotism. When Grant became a brigadier general in August 1861, he turned to Rawlins to help organize his staff. So devoted was Rawlins to his chief that he accepted the offer just days after burying his wife, who had died of tuberculosis, and left behind his three young children.

Rawlins is best known for his intense, bordering on fanatical, detestation of alcohol. His father had been an alcoholic, and Rawlins had pledged himself to a life of total abstinence. This aspect of Rawlins's makeup has led many to believe that his primary, or even only, job was to keep Grant away from the bottle.

This is ridiculous. There are certainly several overwrought letters from Rawlins to the general on the subject. But Rawlins seems to have been man who could get excited if someone asked him to pass the salt at the mess table. Given the vehemence of his opinions of the subject, the merest rumor that Grant had taken even a sip of alcohol would be enough to send Rawlins into an epistolary rage. Endeavoring to keep an alcoholic away from the bottle against his will is a hopeless task. Grant clearly possessed the self-control to keep himself sober.

What, then, was Rawlins's role? Many wondered at the time. Because Grant was so quiet and Rawlins so animated, many assumed that the chief of staff was the real "brains" of the army. Untrue. Rawlins was the classic "desk jockey," spending his days on the drudgery of administrative detail involved in running an army headquarters that freed Grant to think about strategy. Also, as a familiar face from back home,

Rawlins seems to have fulfilled Grant's need for stimulating company in the absence of his family.

"Rawlins," said another member of the staff, "could argue, could expostulate, could condemn, could even upbraid without interrupting for an hour the fraternal confidence and goodwill of Grant." Indeed, Rawlins often didn't hesitate to talk back to Grant and even use blue language to underline his points. Witnesses wondered how he managed to get away with this behavior. It seems likely he earned these privileges with his almost puppy-like devotion back in Galena, before Grant was anybody.

Unfortunately, this special position probably fed Rawlins's sense of his own indispensability and he became intensely jealous of anyone else becoming close to his chief. In the war's last months and the years of peace that followed, the presence of Mrs. Grant and the children meant Grant no longer needed Rawlins's companionship as much as before. This might have been the source of the distancing in their relationship that many noticed.

Some of Grant's friends later thought the general had sold Rawlins short, slighting him with only two brief mentions in his memoirs. But Rawlins was a major general by war's end and was, briefly, secretary of war in Grant's cabinet before dying of the same disease that had killed his wife in 1861. Grant could be forgiven for thinking he had done quite a lot for Rawlins. The general was under no obligation to provide him with emotional succor as well.

As the war went on, the amateurs were gradually weeded out and Grant developed, by fits and starts, the makings of a modern staff system. Young, West Point–trained professionals began appearing, such as Cyrus B. Comstock, class of 1855, an engineer who had caught Grant's eye during the Vicksburg campaign. Another was Orville E. Babcock, a Vermonter in the class of 1861 who had served with Comstock on the engineering staff of the Army of the Potomac. There was also Horace Porter, class of 1860 and an engineer as well. His classic memoir, *Campaigning with Grant,* is an invaluable source for the workings of Grant's staff.

Frederick T. Dent, Grant's brother-in-law, also found a place on the staff. But any whiff of nepotism surrounding the appointment was dissipated by the fact that Dent had been at West Point with the general and was a major in the Regular Army when Grant tapped him for his staff. Grant was adamant that new staffers be well qualified for their posts, even turning down an application from a Captain Kinney that was endorsed by Lincoln himself, on the grounds that Grant did not know Kinney and so could not vouch for his competence.

Grant did not overlook talented non–West Pointers. Most notable among these was Ely S. Parker, a Seneca chief and trained engineer whom Grant had known in Galena. Because Indians were not American citizens in 1861, Parker had a hard time getting into the army. Grant eventually endorsed his application for a commission, however, and Parker joined Grant's staff. This is an excellent example of Grant overcoming the prejudices of his time. Parker would eventually achieve general's rank and serve as the stenographer at Appomattox.

The staff would be more than mere clerks, however. Grant intended to use these men as his eyes and ears on the battlefield. In effect, they were to be his ambassadors to some of his more problematic field commanders, impressing Grant's vision of the campaign on the likes of Ambrose P. Burnside with the full force of Grant's authority. The night before the Overland Campaign was to begin in May 1864, Grant assembled his staff and outlined their duties:

> I want you to discuss with me freely from time to time the details of the orders given for the conduct of a battle and learn my

views as fully as possible as to what course should be pursued in all the contingencies which may arise. I expect to send you to the critical points of the lines to keep me promptly advised of what is taking place, and in cases of great emergency, when new dispositions have to be made on the instant, or it becomes suddenly necessary to reinforce one command by sending to its aid troops from another, and there is not time to communicate with headquarters, I want you to explain my views to commanders, and urge immediate action, looking to cooperation, without waiting for specific orders from me.

"Grant had moved into the realm of modern staff usage," writes R. Steven Jones, author of *The Right Hand of Command: Use and Disuse of Personal Staffs in the Civil War,* of this development. "[The staff] did not just facilitate communications between headquarters and field commands; they carried with them full authority to act in Grant's stead, to make critical spot decisions and issue orders in his absence. . . . They embodied all of the general's plans, ideas and hopes for this campaign. They were to be, in effect, Grant himself."

The system worked well, but not well enough to overcome the Army of the Potomac's seemingly inbuilt caution and lack of command surefootedness. Visits from staff officers seemingly could do nothing to help improve the performance of military incompetents such as Burnside, Franz Sigel, and Ben Butler. Nevertheless, Grant was the only top commander on either side in the Civil War to even approach the potential inherent in his staff. "Only Grant improved his personal staff, changing it from a group of amateur volunteers to trained professionals with expanded duties," states Jones. "[He] prov[ed] himself as much an innovator within his headquarters as he was on the battlefield."

## GRANT'S LESSONS

- Delegation of responsibility is unavoidable in all but the smallest of organizations. Team building is essential.

- Don't fall into the trap of seeking "yes-men" and subordinates with no opinions of their own. Find people who share your goals and want actively to achieve them.

- First impressions are often most lasting, but don't let them govern you. Look beneath the surface.

- Personal connections should not be the sole criterion for hiring someone. Make sure he or she possesses the qualifications needed to perform well.

- Don't let personality clashes blind you to the value a person brings to the organization. Put your feelings aside if the person is otherwise serving your organization's objectives.

CHAPTER 8

# DEALING WITH DIFFICULT PEOPLE AND AWKWARD SITUATIONS

*They're Both Unavoidable*

———————

*[Halleck] is a man of gigantic intellect and well-studied*
*in the profession of arms. He and I have had several little spats*
*but I like and respect him nevertheless.*
—ULYSSES S. GRANT ON HENRY W. HALLECK,
ONE OF THE MOST DIFFICULT INDIVIDUALS
WITH WHOM GRANT EVER HAD TO DEAL

ON THE LATE AFTERNOON of May 21, 1864, during the Overland Campaign through Virginia, Grant and his staff reached a small crossroads called Guinea Station. As was his wont when on campaign, Grant took a seat in a chair on the front porch of a house owned by a Mr. Chandler. Before long, the lady of the house came out and discovered her uninvited guest was the Federal general in chief.

"This house has witnessed some sad scenes," she declared, according to Horace Porter of Grant's staff. "One of our greatest generals died here just a year ago—General Jackson— Stonewall Jackson of blessed memory." Clearly trying to get

Grant's goat, the Virginia lady went on about what a "great and good man" was the late Jackson.

It was potentially an awkward situation. Grant, however, immediately defused it. "Indeed," he replied. "He and I were at West Point together for a year and we served in the same army in Mexico. . . . He was a sterling, manly cadet, and enjoyed the respect of everyone who knew him. . . . He was a gallant soldier and a Christian gentleman, and I can understand fully the admiration your people have for him."

"After taking a polite leave of his hostess," Porter then recounted, Grant gave orders that a guard was to be posted at the woman's house to see that no harm came to her or her property.

The encounter was vintage Grant. He rarely raised his voice or was impolite to anyone he encountered, even if he was treated with less than full respect. It's a quality few of us are born with, but one all would be advised to cultivate. People tend to remember perceived slights and insults far longer than compliments.

## THE BOSS FROM HELL: HENRY W. HALLECK

Few people claimed to actually like Henry Wager Halleck. (Curiously, the irascible William T. Sherman was one of the few.) A fountainhead of knowledge about all military subjects (but without a day's combat experience to back it up), Halleck was known throughout the army as "Old Brains." If Grant was a man who craved action and movement, Halleck was comfortable pushing paper and intriguing with politicians. In other words, he was the type who tends to get promoted. And until Grant himself became general in chief in the last year of the war, he was Grant's boss.

Halleck scarcely knew Grant when the war started, but the pre–Civil War army was a small place and Halleck had heard the rumors about Grant's supposed weakness for drink. He made little secret of his distaste for Grant. As we have seen previously, Halleck gave short shrift to Grant's first, halting proposal to attack the Confederate Forts Henry and Donelson in Tennessee. After that unsuccessful meeting, Halleck began intriguing with General in Chief George B. McClellan to replace the young, vigorous Grant with Ethan Allen Hitchcock, an old army warhorse of unproven ability who was reluctant to replace Grant.

Ironically, it was McClellan who unintentionally came to Grant's rescue, passing on to Halleck an (erroneous) report that major Confederate reinforcements were headed for Tennessee. With no time to waste, Halleck allowed Grant's attack plan to go forward, fully expecting to hear news of a disaster.

When the forts surrendered to Grant, however, Halleck, who had never left his headquarters desk in St. Louis, wasted no time claiming credit for the spectacular victory and seeking to capitalize on it. "Make [Don Carlos] Buell, Grant and [John] Pope major generals of volunteers and give me command in the west," he wired the War Department. "This I ask for Forts Henry and Donelson."

Grant was indeed made a major general, but Halleck's grand designs did not include him. Instead of realizing that having a subordinate like Grant would make Halleck look good, Old Brains continued scheming to have Grant shelved, even as Grant champed at the bit to pursue the beaten and retreating Confederate armies in Tennessee. Grant even hijacked a division that Buell had sent him for the capture of Fort Donelson (it had arrived too late for that) to grab the Tennessee capital of Nashville.

Was Halleck pleased? Far from it. He soon began complaining that he hadn't heard from Grant in some time and that—incredibly—the victor of Fort Donelson was content to rest on his laurels! That Halleck had heard nothing from

Grant after the fall of Fort Donelson was palpable rubbish. The files of Halleck's headquarters show at least a dozen letters and telegrams from Grant to his chief during this time. Some of Grant's communications did indeed go astray, but because a telegraph officer turned out to be a Rebel turncoat. Primed with this supposed "evidence" of Grant's unfitness for command, combined with rumors that Grant had "resumed his bad habits" (in other words, was drunk), Halleck asked McClellan for Grant's removal.

Now, any right-thinking commanding general would have reacted to such a request with horror and certainly would have raised questions regarding the mental stability of the man who made it. Grant was a national hero. His capture of Forts Henry and Donelson was the first important Union victory of the war. Firing him—and on the flimsiest of pretexts at that—would, at a minimum, invite a close examination of the circumstances. But, as we have seen, McClellan had a tin ear for politics and blithely granted Halleck permission to remove Grant.

The telegram ordering Grant to turn his troops over to another general was the first inkling Grant had that anything was amiss between him and Halleck, whom he thought he had served faithfully and to the best of his ability. A witness said tears welled in Grant's eyes as he read it. But Grant calmly complied with the order, protesting his innocence in an even-tempered tone to Halleck and asking to be relieved of all duty if his performance was not satisfactory. Later, Grant renewed his request to be relieved but, ominously for Halleck, demanded a court of inquiry.

While all this was going on, however, McClellan was suddenly relieved of *his* position as general in chief by a frustrated Lincoln. Halleck had been counting on McClellan's support in any showdown over Grant's future. Overnight, Halleck's ace in the hole had turned into a joker. Pressed by

Lincoln—who had heard from Grant's friend Congressman Washburne—to substantiate his charges against Grant, Halleck let the matter drop and restored Grant's command.

Grant was too relieved to look into the intricacies of what had actually happened, and he appears not to have suspected Halleck as the author of his troubles.

A few months later came Shiloh; and in its aftermath, Grant was shunted into a meaningless post as Halleck's second-in-command. Perhaps Halleck had learned a lesson: If he couldn't actually fire Grant, he could make his life so miserable that he would feel obliged to quit. A dissembler of the first order, Halleck all the while kept reassuring Grant that he, Halleck, was his protector and friend and that it was unnamed "others" who were seeking his removal and disgrace. The ploy very nearly worked, as we have seen. Only the faithful Sherman dissuaded Grant from resigning.

Failing upward yet again, Halleck was soon appointed to succeed McClellan as general in chief, and Grant was back in command in Mississippi. Halleck went to Washington and, for the moment, was out of Grant's hair.

It wasn't until after the war that Grant became aware of how truly two-faced had been his treatment at Halleck's hands during this period. Still, Grant knew enough that when he was appointed lieutenant general on March 9, 1864, there would have been little stopping him from merely accepting Old Brains's proffered resignation as general in chief and putting him out to pasture. Instead, Grant recognized Halleck's bureaucratic talents and appointed him the first army chief of staff, responsible for supplying and administering the armies in the field that Grant commanded. It was a position in which Halleck excelled.

A troublesome boss can be a nightmare, but so can a troublesome subordinate who has ideas very different from yours and who sees you as an obstacle to his plans.

## THE SUBORDINATE WITH HIS OWN
## AGENDA: JOHN A. MCCLERNAND

John Alexander McClernand has been called
many things: vain, ambitious, insubordinate, and incompetent. All more or less true, though he was perhaps more competent than is generally recognized. He may not have been a
professional soldier, but he was eager to fight.

Grant wanted fighters, and his willingness to promote
competent "political" officers such as John A. Logan and
Francis P. Blair shows he was not averse to recognizing
non–West Point talent. Why, then, did Grant and McClernand
clash like fire and water? Probably because Grant wanted to
win the war, while McClernand wanted *credit* for winning the
war.

That McClernand was ambitious few could doubt. A Democrat in Congress before the war, he represented Lincoln's
home district in Illinois and was on good terms with the new
president, in spite of their differing party affiliation. A "War
Democrat," McClernand early on grandly resigned from
Congress to enter the army as a brigadier general. Like many
another politician of the time, he no doubt thought a strong
war record would be his ticket to bigger things.

Perhaps the first bit of bad blood came on the very day of
the commission. There were four Illinoisans on the brigadier
general's list in August 1861. McClernand's name was on it,
to be sure, but so was Grant's—in first position. That meant
this erstwhile captain who was rumored to have drunk his
way out of the army seven years earlier actually ranked Mc-
Clernand. We can only speculate on how well this sat with a
man who came within an ace of being elected Speaker of the
House.

Speaking. That was something else McClernand loved to
do. The first time he and Grant probably encountered each

other was when then-representative McClernand came to inspect the 21st Illinois under Colonel Grant's command. As was the style of the time, McClernand gave a long stemwinder about duty, honor, and patriotism. After McClernand had finally finished, he turned to Grant, expecting the newly minted colonel to make a similar flowery address. Grant, who detested public speaking and hardly ever addressed his men, simply dismissed his troops to their quarters.

McClernand failed to take the hint that soldiers (or any other subordinates, for that matter) want to get the job done, with as little muss and fuss as possible. For Grant, victory would be its own inspiration. McClernand, however, went right on speechifying. Accounts of his generalship are littered with tales of McClernand making speeches at the most inopportune moments: in the midst of the Battle of Belmont, for example, when his troops should have been pursuing the fleeing Confederates. During the Vicksburg campaign, he jumped up on a stump and gave his troops a political harangue while bullets were flying.

McClernand seems to have sensed that he would never win personal glory while Grant was around. In early 1862, he may have intrigued with a Captain William J. Kountz, a pedantic nag whom Grant finally had placed under arrest and who was now retaliating by seeking Grant's court-martial for drunkenness and incompetence. It never went anywhere, but it provided a dark hint of how far McClernand might be willing to go to see Grant out of his way.

If he couldn't have Grant fired, then McClernand would simply bypass him by persuading the president to allow him, McClernand, an independent command on the Mississippi aimed at taking the river fortress of Vicksburg. The Illinois Democrat promised his friend in the White House that legions of loyal Democrats would flock to the colors if McClernand were in command. Lincoln, ever eager to showcase

Northern Democratic support for the war effort and fed up
with McClellan's excuses for inaction, agreed and told Mc-
Clernand to go ahead.

Ironically, it was Halleck who now came to Grant's rescue.
Old Brains didn't much like Grant, as we have seen, but at
least Grant was a West Pointer and a professional soldier. Mc-
Clernand was neither, and Halleck wasn't about to entrust
tens of thousands of soldiers to the care of a militarily inexperienced and politically ambitious general. The details are
murky, but Halleck (with help from Admiral David Dixon
Porter) seems to have impressed his views upon Lincoln, who
no longer backed the idea of an independent command for
McClernand quite so enthusiastically. It was under these circumstances that Grant and Sherman "hijacked" McClernand's army of Democrats in Memphis to attack Vicksburg
(unsuccessfully) in December 1862 after McClernand had unwisely gone home to Illinois to wed his late wife's sister.

Halleck had authorized Grant to fire McClernand if the
good of the army required it. But Grant, still under the cloud
of Shiloh, wasn't about to move against the powerful McClernand without real cause. He decided to bide his time and wait.
McClernand, given his past record, would provide justification
enough eventually. Still, Grant was taking a chance. McClernand had direct access to Lincoln and wasn't shy about using
it. When Grant decided, in January 1863, to exercise personal
command of the next campaign against Vicksburg—using the
seniority that the list of brigadier generals had given him sixteen months earlier—McClernand was outraged.

It's hard not to sympathize with McClernand to a limited
extent here. Lincoln had (most unwisely) promised him an independent command if McClernand would raise an army,
and McClernand had kept his part of the bargain. Now, it appeared, he had been euchred out of his command by a cabal
of West Pointers. Grant, Sherman, and Halleck were right on

the merits: McClernand was not equipped by knowledge or temperament to lead a mighty army against so critical a point as Vicksburg. But McClernand's participation in the coming campaign in a subordinate position under Grant would undoubtedly mean trouble.

The Vicksburg campaign was marked by many bitter exchanges between Grant and McClernand, though it seems clear that Grant was doing his level best to make use of McClernand as a corps commander. Early in the campaign, McClernand's XIII Corps led the way for Grant's army, while the favored Sherman was generally left behind to deal with the pots and pans. Still, Grant's orders to the politician-general were lengthy and highly detailed, while those to Sherman and McPherson, his other two corps commanders, were much shorter and more general.

Nonetheless, it couldn't have been far from Grant's mind that if anything should happen to him, McClernand would take command by virtue of seniority. Given McClernand's poor relations with Sherman and McPherson, as well as Admiral Porter, this would have been an intolerable situation for the army before Vicksburg.

Grant's opportunity to rid himself of the politician-general came shortly after the failed initial assault on the defenses of Vicksburg on May 22, 1863. Repeatedly, McClernand dispatched notes to Grant urging him to renew the assault, stating that McClernand's troops had captured Confederate fortifications and would win through if only Sherman's and McPherson's corps would support him. Grant told Sherman he didn't believe a word of it, but McClernand's notes had the aroma of a man building a record. Grant put aside his misgivings and ordered the assault renewed, with nothing more to show for it than several thousand more dead and wounded Union soldiers.

McClernand followed up this failure by issuing to his troops a typically bombastic proclamation hailing their efforts

and, by implication, criticizing Sherman's and McPherson's
corps for not attacking more vigorously. The text found its
way to a newspaper, which published it in full. Grant obtained
a copy and demanded to know if it was genuine. McClernand
answered that it was, and Grant had him relieved on the tech-
nical point that statements by a subordinate had to be cleared
by the commanding general before being made public.

McClernand pulled strings galore in an effort to get his
job back and see Grant cashiered. Such efforts were pointless
once Grant took Vicksburg on July 4, 1863, and became the
toast of the nation. McClernand's ultimate failing was the
cardinal sin in Grant's eyes: insubordination. McClernand's
sense of his own importance precluded the taking of orders
from anyone he thought his social inferior.

## THE SPY AT HEADQUARTERS:
## CHARLES A. DANA

"MR. DANA WAS with the General [Grant] from the time
we left Memphis in 1863," wrote General James H. Wilson to
Adam Badeau, Grant's military secretary, after the war:

> We all regarded him as a confidential agent of the War Depart-
> ment. His duties, it was always understood, were to keep the
> Secretary of War and the Government informed of everything
> important transpiring in the army.
>
> As you know, my first impression in regard to this matter
> was unfavorable to Dana. I rather looked upon him as an in-
> former upon the General's actions, and this idea was shared by
> others, but at that time, his relations with the General were of
> the most cordial and friendly character. He was treated with
> great friendliness by the General, and recognized as holding re-
> lations of confidence with the Secretary of War. It was no un-

common thing for the General to ask him to telegraph to the Secretary for instructions and to give information. I know what they conferred together freely during this entire campaign in regard to men and things.

Dana during the entire campaign was with us, and his relations if anything continued to grow more intimate and confidential with Grant, and from my own mind all doubt of his position and his relations with the War Department was removed as I became well acquainted with him.

From the first moment Lincoln became aware of this general named Grant, he had gotten mixed reports about him. Some said he was a drunkard and an incompetent who ought to be relieved immediately. Others swore to the general's sobriety and reliability under pressure. Lincoln, from more than a thousand miles away in Washington, didn't know whom to believe. There was only one way to find out: dispatch a reliable individual to Grant's headquarters on some pretext and endeavor to learn the truth.

That individual was Charles A. Dana, a former editor of Horace Greeley's *New York Tribune,* who had won national notice for his fire-breathing "on to Richmond" editorials. Greeley, however, blew hot and cold on the war, and Dana eventually found himself looking for work. Edwin M. Stanton, the new secretary of war, appreciated Dana's editorial support and offered him appointment as assistant secretary of war. After some initial assignments in the West, Dana was on his way to Grant's headquarters at Milliken's Bend, Louisiana; officially, he was to look into reported irregularities in the army pay service.

No one on Grant's staff bought that cover story for even one moment. Dana was a spy, and many of the members of Grant's military "family" favored freezing him out and giving Dana as little information as possible.

Grant, encouraged by Chief of Staff Rawlins, realized that any such move would be a mistake. Instead, Grant immediately invited Dana to dine at his own table and placed at his disposal a horse and the service of an orderly.

Grant even took the unusual step of bringing the man from Washington into his confidence about plans for taking Vicksburg. Impressed, Dana began filing glowing reports about the general. Within a matter of weeks, Dana had forgotten all about the conditions of the army pay service as well as his true mission of spying on Grant to become, in effect, a member of Grant's staff. He also, not incidentally, sent back poor reviews for the generalship of John A. McClernand, preparing the ground for the latter's dismissal. Winning Dana over was definitely the right approach for Grant.

The wrong approach was illustrated a few months later when Dana arrived at the headquarters of Major General William S. Rosecrans on a mission similar to that with Grant. "Old Rosey," as he was universally known, was a long-winded blowhard who enjoyed keeping members of his staff awake until all hours discussing fine theological points. His combat record was mixed, and his chief attribute seems to have been a belief in the limitless appetite of Secretary Stanton and President Lincoln for long, highly detailed telegrams of complaint from Rosecrans.

Old Rosey took an instant dislike to Dana and made no effort to hide it, berating Dana at their first meeting with a speech about meddling bureaucrats. Unsurprisingly, Dana began filing a series of damaging reports about Rosecrans's competence, even to the point of questioning the general's sanity. "The practical incapacity in the general commanding is astonishing," Dana wrote in one of his reports. "It often seems difficult to believe him of sound mind. . . . His imbecility appears to be contagious." Dana was present when Rosecrans's army was all but swept from the field by the Confederate Army of

Tennessee at the Battle of Chickamauga, and he lost no time telegraphing Washington about the disaster. "Chickamauga is as fatal a name in our history as Bull Run," he said.

Rosecrans's career was finished. Grant (who disliked Rosecrans's insubordinate attitude in any case) replaced him with George H. Thomas.

---

## GRANT'S LESSONS

- Anyone who aspires to a leadership position is going to meet unpleasant people both above and below. Read the situation carefully and react rationally, not emotionally.

- If given a subordinate you don't want, try your best to work with that person and get the best you can out of him or her for the greater good of the organization. If that proves impossible, let the subordinate go when shortcomings prove manifest.

- Don't engage in mindless hostility toward someone who can do you harm.

Part III

# MANAGEMENT:
# WORDS INTO DEEDS

# CHAPTER 9

# COMMUNICATIONS
## *Clear and Distinct*

———◆———

*Grant never mumbled, he spoke distinctly and he never lolled around*
*to attract any attention. I never heard him raise his voice and he was*
*always alert and the reputation he has of having a "lazy brain" is as*
*far from the truth as you can get.*
—M. HARRISON STRONG, ONE OF GRANT'S AIDES

THE FIRST DAY of the Battle of Gettysburg had gone
splendidly for Robert E. Lee's Army of Northern Virginia.
The Union Army of the Potomac's I and XI Corps had been
pushed back from their positions north of the town of Gettysburg, ceding it and its neighboring seminary to the graybacks while retreating to defensive positions on the ridges and
hills south of the town. Lee recognized the danger of leaving
the bluecoats in possession of the commanding heights. Late
in the day, he issued an order to General Richard Ewell, commander of one of Lee's infantry corps, to "secure possession
of the heights . . . *if practicable*" [emphasis added].

Lee probably didn't think twice when issuing this order.
Ewell had previously served directly under Lieutenant General Thomas J. "Stonewall" Jackson (who had died at

Chancellorsville nearly two months earlier), and Lee had frequently issued such discretionary orders to Jackson, secure in
the knowledge that he would interpret them aggressively. But
this was Ewell's first battle serving directly under Lee, and
Ewell's corps had taken heavy casualties earlier in the day.
General A. P. Hill's corps had also been roughly handled, and
Ewell could not count on its support. Further complicating
the issue was Lee's qualification, "if practicable." Ewell hesitated. After waiting for more than an hour for the attack to
begin, Lee rode toward Ewell's headquarters to inquire into
the reason for the delay. By the time Lee arrived, the Union III
and XII Corps had come up, and the opportunity for a quick,
relatively easy Rebel success had gone aglimmering.

This was probably the most famous example of miscom-
munication in the entire Civil War, and one that Ewell was to
spend the rest of his life endeavoring to live down. Assigning
blame to Ewell, however, was completely unfair, because he
was merely interpreting the order he had received in light of
the battlefield situation as he saw it. If Lee had wanted the hill
taken at all hazards, he should have said so. But the postwar
Southern effort to canonize Lee as a military saint meant he
could not be blamed for the ultimate failure at Gettysburg.
Scapegoats had to be found. Ewell was one.

## GRANT'S INTELLECTUAL DEVELOPMENT

GRANT'S CRITICS HAVE saddled him with a reputation
for being a dullard and a slow thinker. "The type was pre-
intellectual, archaic, and would have seemed so even to the cave-
dwellers" was the famously sneering assessment of Grant by the
self-consciously intellectual Henry Adams. That reputation is
hard to square with the record, however. Jesse Grant always
claimed his son was a studious youth who enjoyed school, and
young Grant himself expressed a desire to attend college, an

odd ambition for someone who was supposedly a poor student. Of course, he ultimately produced a memoir that many consider the greatest ever written by an American.

Despite his modest class rank at West Point (itself misleading, as we have seen), in disciplines such as mathematics, engineering, and horsemanship, Grant stood quite high among his classmates. Interestingly, Grant also did well in drawing—then an important subject at the Point—and his sketches and landscapes are very well rendered.

Grant was not a grind at the military academy. Since so much of the curriculum revolved around mathematics, which came easily to him, he spent much time reading, especially the fiction of James Fenimore Cooper and Sir Walter Scott. The cadet literary society elected him its president in his senior year.

Sherman thought Grant knew too little about the theory of warfare and its history. Actually, Grant seems to have understood both well enough. During the boring garrison duty in California following the Mexican War, other officers were surprised at Grant's precise dissections of the war's campaigns, as if he had "the whole thing in his head." When he returned east to take command of all the Union armies, he told aide Horace Porter that he had followed the fighting in Virginia in great detail. And during his post-presidential trip around the world in 1877, as historian John Keegan recounts, he entertained reporter John Russell Young with commentary on many of Napoleon's campaigns. Clearly, Grant got plenty of reading done when no one was looking.

Unlike many of his contemporaries, however, Grant understood that book learning had to be tempered by real-world experience, a lesson neither Halleck nor McClellan ever learned. As Grant also told Young,

> Some of our generals failed because they worked out everything by rule. They knew what Frederick did at one place and Napoleon

at another. They were always thinking about what Napoleon would do. Unfortunately for their plans, the Rebels would be thinking about something else. I don't underrate the value of military knowledge, but if men make war in slavish obedience of rules, they will fail.

There is considerable evidence for Grant's intellectual growth—for example, his vision of the war as an ideological battle between two peoples, one or the other of whom "had to yield principles they held dearer than life itself" before it could come to an end. Nothing at West Point would have prepared him for this leap of understanding, one he shared with Sherman and Lincoln. Later, as president, he envisioned a constitutional order where everyone's rights—regardless of the color of their skin—would be equally protected. Quite a leap for a man who once had slaves in his own household.

## GRANT AS COMMUNICATOR

GRANT POSSESSED tremendous powers of concentration and intellectual stamina—attested to again and again by those who worked closely with him during the war. According to M. Harrison Strong,

> The first days I would hand him dispatches and he would answer them rapidly, without being annoyed by outside conversation. He was never in a hurry. Let me give an example: Grant had a black body servant named Bill at this time and he annoyed me a good deal. He slipped in one day and stole my feather duster and ran away into the General's tent. I almost ran over General Grant in trying to get Bill. I said, "If you take that again, I will break your neck!" Grant was alone in his tent and never once looked up and never noticed us. He was above anything small and was wholly wrapped up in thought.

At night the General wouldn't sleep much. I would bring in dispatches and find him lying in bed, smoking. I know he was awake many times, waiting for a dispatch that he had to answer and he always did his duty.

Horace Porter tells a similar tale:

Nothing that went on around him, upon the field or in his quarters, could distract his attention or interrupt him. Sometimes, when his tent was filled with officers, talking and laughing at the top of their voices, he would turn to his table and write the most important communications. There would then be an immediate "Hush!" and abundant excuses offered by the company; but he always insisted upon the conversation going on, and after awhile his officers came to understand his wishes in this respect, to learn that noise was apparently a stimulus rather than a check to his flow of ideas, and to realize that nothing short of a general attack along the whole line could divert his thoughts from the subject upon which his mind was concentrated.

You probably won't be called upon to think and write in conditions as chaotic as Grant encountered in the midst of a war. The ability to concentrate and work under less than ideal conditions, however, is an important leadership tool.

Grant might well have possessed a photographic memory. Porter noticed that any map Grant examined "seemed to become photographed indelibly on his brain, and he could follow its features without referring to it again."

Porter also painted a memorable pen portrait of Grant's method of writing dispatches:

My attention was soon attracted by the manner in which he went to work at his correspondence. At this time, as throughout his later career, he wrote nearly all his documents with his own hand, and seldom dictated to anyone even the most unimportant dispatch. His work was performed swiftly and uninterruptedly, but without any marked display of nervous energy. His thoughts flowed as freely from his mind as his ink from his pen; he was never at a loss for an expression, and seldom interlined a word or made a material correction. He sat with his head bent low over the table, and when he had occasion to step to another . . . to get a paper he wanted, he would glide rapidly across the room without straightening himself, and return to his seat with his body still bent over at about the same angle at which he had been sitting when he left his chair.

As Grant finished each page, he would simply brush it off the desk and onto the floor. When he had finished writing, he would simply gather up all the pages and sort them out for copying and distribution. Porter was amazed at the high quality of the dispatches so written and found that they were "directions . . . for the taking of vigorous and comprehensive steps in every direction throughout the new and comprehensive command." That opinion was shared by Theodore Lyman, chief of staff to General George G. Meade, who noted, "there is one striking feature of Grant's orders; no matter how hurriedly he may write them on the field, no one ever had the slightest doubt as to their meaning, or even [had] to read them over a second time to understand them."

Military historian John Keegan gives four examples of dispatches written by Grant to his various subordinates on May 16, 1863, during the Vicksburg campaign.

To Francis P. Blair:

Move at early dawn toward Black River Bridge. I think you will encounter no enemy by the way. If you do, however, engage them at once, and you will be assisted by troops further advanced. . . . [Later] If you are already on the Bolton Road continue so, but if you still have the choice of roads take the one leading to Edward's Depot—Pass your troops to the front of your train, except a rear guard, and keep the ammunition wagons in front of all others.

## To John A. McClernand:

I have just obtained very probable information, that the entire force of the enemy has crossed the Big Black, and was at Edward's Depot at 7 o'clock last night. You will therefore disencumber yourself of your trains, select an eligible position, and feel the enemy. . . . [Later] From all information gathered from citizens and prisoners the mass of the enemy are south of Hovey's Division. McPherson is now up to Hovey and can support him at any point. Close up all your other forces as expeditiously as possible but cautiously. The enemy must not be allowed to get to our rear.

## To James B. McPherson:

The enemy has crossed Big Black with the entire Vicksburg force. He was at Edward's Depot last night and still advancing. You will therefore pass all trains and move forward to join McClernand with all possible dispatch. I have ordered your rear brigade to move at once and given such directions to other commanders as will secure a prompt concentration of our forces.

## To William T. Sherman:

Start one of your divisions on the road at once with its ammunition wagons—and direct it to move with all possible speed till it comes up with our rear beyond Bolton. It is important that great celerity should be shown in carrying out this movement, as I have evidence that the entire force of the enemy was at Edward's Depot at 7 o'clock yesterday evening and still advancing. The fight might be brought on at any moment—we should have every man on the field.

Note the definitiveness of Grant's orders: "start," "at once," "move forward," "engage them," and so forth. The words "if practicable," or any approximation of them, are nowhere to be seen. Grant clearly expects his subordinates to achieve the goals he has set for them.

And for a man who was supposedly lacking in gray matter, Grant coined or popularized many memorable phrases and statements: "I propose to fight it out on this line if it takes all summer," "unconditional surrender," "I will take no backward steps," "I propose to move immediately upon your works," "Let us have peace," and "Let no guilty man escape."

Reading these orders and statements, Grant's critics refused to believe that the taciturn, unimpressive-looking man they knew had written them. Rumors spread that chief of staff John Rawlins was the actual author of these dispatches. Rumor persists to this day that Mark Twain "really" wrote Grant's famous memoirs. There is no truth to any of these allegations. Grant had a substantial intellectual and literary gift, a novelist's ability to set a mood or paint a pen portrait that gets at the essence of an individual.

## GRANT AND NEW TECHNOLOGY

WHILE VIRTUALLY ALL Civil War generals on both sides made use of the telegraph, Keegan notes that few used it to such effect as Grant. An invention not even into its third decade when the war began, the telegraph enabled a general to conquer that unique feature of fighting in the North American heartland: space. Grant simply could not have been the general he was—controlling armies spread out over thousands of miles of territory—without the telegraph. It was a rare day in Virginia when Grant did not insist on reading Sherman's daily situation report, even though the dispatch had to travel a circuitous 1,500-mile route to reach him.

Everywhere he went, Grant gave high priority to the stringing of new telegraph wires, to ensure he stayed in touch with his commanders as well as with Washington. "Headquarters," he wrote in his memoirs, "were connected to all points of the command." Grant had a telegraph operator in his office and would spend considerable parts of the day sending telegrams to his various subordinates. Lee, by contrast, tended to rely more on couriers.

The lesson is clear: If new technology that enables better communication becomes available, use it. This is especially true in an age when communication technology is advancing by leaps and bounds. E-mail attachments, for example, have already made the fax machine—which seemed like revolutionary technology only fifteen years ago—virtually obsolete.

But Grant's example of concise, direct, and clear communications remains the most important example of all. Well-developed communications skills are indispensable to an executive. The best ideas and vision in the world are of no help if a leader can't get them across to the people who will be executing them.

## GRANT'S LESSONS

- Instructions to subordinates and reports to superiors should be as clear, direct, and concise as possible. Get the information across without taxing the reader's time.

- Where possible, spice up your communications with colorful and memorable words or phrases.

- Read widely and as much as possible. Develop good habits of concentration and memory.

- Be open to new technology and means of communication.

CHAPTER 10

# KNOW YOUR TRADE

### *"I Was No Clerk"*

——————

*The campaign of Vicksburg, in its conception and execution,*
*belonged exclusively to General Grant, not only in the great whole,*
*but in the thousands of its details. I still retain many of his letters*
*and notes, all in his own handwriting, prescribing the routes of*
*march for divisions and detachments, specifying even the amount*
*of food and tools to be carried along. . . . No commanding general*
*of an army ever gave more of his personal attention to details.*
—WILLIAM T. SHERMAN

*I would say: know your trade.*
—COLONEL DAVID HACKWORTH,
AMERICA'S MOST DECORATED LIVING SOLDIER,
ON WHAT MAKES FOR A SUCCESSFUL LEADER

W HEN GRANT ARRIVED in Cairo, Illinois, as a
newly minted brigadier general in August 1861, the scene that
confronted him was one of almost complete disorganization.
His superior, General John C. Fremont, was far away in St.
Louis and was suspected of tolerating corruption.

Grant's troops lacked modern arms and reliable transportation on the rivers, because steamboat captains were

charging top dollar for their services. Grant soon discovered that the quartermaster he had inherited was corrupt, agreeing to pay exorbitant amounts to contractors and steamboat captains who were in league with him. Grant replaced him without delay and refused payment to contractors whose charges, Grant believed, were far above market rates.

"My reply to them was that they had got their contract without my consent," he recalled of his meeting with the angry contractors. "I would not approve a voucher for them under that contract if they never got a cent. Hoped they would not. This forced them to sell . . . for what it was worth."

## GRANT AS LOGISTICIAN

GRANT KNEW WHEREOF he spoke. During the Mexican War, he had been appointed acting regimental quartermaster and commissary officer for the 4th Infantry. That meant he was responsible for outfitting and equipping the troops and seeing to it they had everything they needed to live and fight, including arms, ammunition, food, and blankets. Greatly preferring to be where the shooting was, young Lieutenant Grant hated the assignment. But he performed his job with his customary vigor, soon winning the (in his eyes) dubious honor of promotion from acting quartermaster to permanent quartermaster.

Although he held a staff position that theoretically kept him out of combat, Grant found that having food and provisions for the men meant he frequently had to lead "foraging" (i.e., stealing) expeditions into the countryside near where the army was based. This meant frequent clashes with Mexican forces or guerrillas. Though Lieutenant Grant was told to avoid such conflicts where possible, he seems to have taken the position that, while he would not go out of his way to harm civilians (he paid for goods as well), he would not brook resistance or interference either. He carried this philosophy into the Civil War, when he told Southern civilians who rejoiced at the destruction of his supply bases by Confederate raiders that they could not expect men with arms in their hands to go hungry in the midst of plenty.

Though he might have disliked being a quartermaster, Grant did the job well.

"He was always up with the regiment and his services as a quartermaster were splendidly done and he was even complimented from the War Department for his services," said J. D. Elderkin, drum major of the 4th Infantry. "He would have everything ready for the regiment each night; cattle to kill and wood for the campfires, for he was always prepared. When the regiment got there at night, they would have nothing to do but pitch their tents. He bought all his supplies from the Mexicans and paid for them too."

The experience, he admitted, came in handy later on:

> My old army experience I found to be of very great service. I was no clerk, nor had I any capacity to become one. . . . But I had been quartermaster, commissary and adjutant in the field. The army forms were familiar to me and I could direct how they should be made out.

Grant's experience of logistics also told him what an army in the field could do *without* as well as what it needed. His foraging expeditions in Mexico told him an army could rely on the local countryside for its food, a lesson that was reinforced after his supply base at Holly Springs was burned in December 1862. Therefore, his army did not require a huge train of food wagons encumbering its movements across the country. During the Vicksburg campaign, Grant gave orders that the army was to carry mostly ammunition in its supply train rather than food.

His time as a quartermaster wasn't entirely positive, however. On two occasions, funds entrusted to his care vanished. The first instance, involving three hundred dollars, the government was prepared to overlook. The second instance, however, was a matter of one thousand dollars, serious money in 1847. While a court of enquiry attached no blame to Grant for the money's disappearance, he was obligated to repay it. This debt would dog Grant until 1862, when a grateful Congress relieved the hero of Fort Donelson of the obligation.

One of Grant's iron rules, however, was that friends and family were to receive no special favors. While at Cairo, Grant received a visit from his tiresome father, Jesse, who wanted to sell leather goods to the army. Grant turned his father down flat: "It is necessary both to my efficiency for the public good and my reputation that I should keep clear of government contracts." This policy extended even to his errant brother-in-law John Dent, a Confederate sympathizer, who ended up in a Southern jail when he tried to take up residence in the South during the war. John didn't come home until the general exchange of prisoners after the war.

Grant's quartermaster's experience helped sharpen the eye for detail that Sherman noted. In this he was helped by an excellent memory. James Elderkin again:

> His memory was a marvelous instrument. There was no one else, I feel, that could tell as good a story as he could about Mexico or remember precisely each detail. He never exaggerated or changed stories, he told the facts of the battle or situation exactly as they occurred, without altering the outcome or spicing up the particulars. I could listen to him by the hour retelling events of which I had been a part.

Sometimes this tendency could be wearisome. Horace Porter relates that Grant would tell an anecdote about having conversed with a person "inside his tent," for example. Half an hour or so later, however, Grant would return as if on a matter of most urgent importance to correct himself. The meeting had occurred not inside the tent, he would say, but *outside* of it.

But to Grant, this *was* a matter of importance. "He hates only two kinds of people: liars and cowards," chief of staff Rawlins once remarked. And it was a point of pride for Grant that he numbered himself among neither group.


## GET ON YOUR HORSE
## AND SEE FOR YOURSELF

GRANT PUT HIS entire career on the block—not for the last time—on the night of April 16, 1863. The fleet that would transport his army across the mile-wide Mississippi south of Vicksburg had to first run the gauntlet of the fortress city's batteries. Not only were the ships irreplaceable, but, in addition, they could not be brought back north of Vicksburg if need be: Moving against the southward flow of the river's current, they would be sitting ducks for the city's guns. The ships *had* to get through if Grant's plan were to have any chance of success.

With furnaces banked for minimal smoke and movement onboard muffled, the seven ships rounded the bend just above Vicksburg. "Ten minutes later," writes Civil War historian Shelby Foote, "all hell broke loose."

Watching as if from a box in a darkened theater, Grant, along with his military and personal families, waited on the deck of a nearby steamer to watch the "show." The flash and roar of Vicksburg's mighty guns did little to inspire confidence that the fleet might get through. "Magnificent, but terrible," was Grant's later recollection of that night.

After ninety minutes of uproar, the river once again fell black and silent, telling those on deck nothing of the fleet's fate. Grant's legendary imperturbability now failed him. Calling for his horse, he mounted up and headed down the west bank of the river. "This was quite unlike the old Grant, who had never seemed in a hurry about anything at all," writes Foote. An officer on his staff who had never seen Grant ride at even a fast trot now watched in amazement as the general rode forward at a full gallop. Not until nearly midday the next day, when he arrived at New Carthage to find the fleet riding at anchor, battered but intact, did he relax.

Getting accurate information and getting it quickly was always one of the biggest difficulties in the Civil War, and Grant often decided to get it in person. His ride on the night of April 16–17 was more dramatic than many of his other personal inspections, but it was not unique. A natural horseman, the general liked nothing better than getting out of headquarters, mounting Cincinnati, his favorite horse, or Jeff Davis, a pony that had been captured on the Confederate president's Mississippi plantation, and going out to see for himself the conditions at the front.

The accounts of Grant at the front are numerous. We have already seen him in action at Shiloh, riding back and forth across the field all that terrible day. At Fort Donelson, he galloped for eight miles to turn back the Confederate attempt to break out of the trap in which Grant had snared them.

At Shiloh, Grant and two staff officers blundered within range of some Confederate riflemen, who immediately began taking potshots at the bluecoat party. Grant and his two aides turned and bolted as fast as their horses could carry them for, as Grant estimated later, one full minute. When they slowed down, they found that one aide's horse was mortally wounded, the other aide had his sword scabbard bent by a bullet, and

Grant had lost his hat. "All were thankful it was no worse," one of the aides recorded later.

Though Grant would have plenty of such close calls later in the war ("Ulyss don't scare worth a damn," commented a Wisconsin private watching Grant under fire during the Vicksburg campaign), he never went out of his way to put himself in personal danger. Though he would never admit it, Grant perhaps sensed his own indispensability and sought to avoid exposing himself if he could help it. The introduction of the long-range infantry rifle in the 1840s and 1850s meant that soldiers could shoot accurately over a longer range than in Napoleon's day. Officers were always a prime target, and generals in particular. Maybe more than mere modesty was involved in Grant's decision to eschew an elaborate uniform on the field of battle.

## GRANT'S LESSONS

- Approach unpleasant or undesired assignments as learning opportunities. The knowledge gained from the position can be employed later on.

- Try to know as many aspects of your profession as possible, not merely those that immediately concern you. That way, you will understand the problems others are having when you are working with them.

- Reports from the field, when given by reliable subordinates, often provide all that you need. But never underrate the importance of that personal visit or phone call. It not only can provide information, but also underlines to your subordinates the importance you attach to the task at hand.

CHAPTER 11

# INNOVATION
## *Try New Things Always*

———————

*We could not and ought not be rigidly bound by the rules laid down*
*under circumstances so different.*
—ULYSSES S. GRANT

*It is expected that all commanders will especially exert themselves . . .*
*not only in organizing colored regiments and rendering them efficient,*
*but also in removing prejudice against them.*
—ULYSSES S. GRANT

THE MEXICAN WAR was a triumph of American pluck
and gall over common sense. The U.S. Army was miniscule
and stayed that way, even after the addition of volunteers who
enlisted for the war. The Mexican army, whose officers to all
intents and purposes governed the country, was by no means
insubstantial. Further, it would be fighting on its home territory. In short, the Mexicans had every reason to be optimistic
about the outcome.

What they hadn't counted on was American daring. Using
their naval power, the Americans landed troops at points
along the Mexican coast where the Mexicans didn't think it
was possible to land troops, and they placed artillery in places
the Mexicans didn't think it possible to place artillery.

Such as in a church belfry.

Mexico City is built on an island, and the city can be approached only by a series of causeways. The Mexicans had barricaded these, preventing the Americans from advancing.

Young Grant noticed a church nearby with a tall belfry. It would be an excellent vantage point from which to examine the enemy position. Taking some men with him, Grant banged on the heavy church door and told the priest in halting Spanish that if he did not open the door, Grant's men would admit themselves. The priest complied, and Grant and his men ran up the stairs.

The steeple did indeed prove an excellent observation post, but Grant noticed that there just might be room for a mountain howitzer, which would bring the enemy position under direct fire. Dashing back down the stairs, Grant and his team went in search of such a weapon.

Finding the small but powerful gun, they quickly disassembled it and hand-carried it back to the church. Dragging the heavy parts up the rickety stairs, they reassembled the gun on the roof and opened fire on the startled Mexican defenders. The effect was immediate, demoralizing the Mexicans and allowing the Americans to make progress.

"This is mighty fine work, sir," said General William Worth, Grant's division commander. "Every shot tells. I'll find you another gun." Grant didn't bother telling the general that there was barely room in the belfry for the one gun, let alone another.

We all carry around a "box" in our heads, the way we look at the world and do things because that is the way we were taught. Rules are important and usually exist for a reason. But changing technology and circumstances can change rules too. Grant thought outside the box in Mexico and in so doing helped win a crucial battle. It was a habit he formed and developed throughout his career.

## GRANT VERSUS NAPOLEON

"His principal aversion was to Napoleon," wrote reporter John Russell Young, who traveled the world with Grant after the latter left the White House. "I endeavored once, without success, to persuade him to go to the Invalids and see the Emperor's tomb. We were at the very door of the church, but he continued his walk. It was an opinion based upon a study of the Emperor's character—the greatest man of modern times, but a monster!"

Grant's dislike of Napoleon was highly exceptional among mid-nineteenth-century soldiers, most of whom worshiped him as something akin to the god of war. French was the language of warfare as well as of love, with phrases such as *coup de main* and *hors de combat* being commonplace officer parlance. We have already seen (in chapter 2) the influence of Dennis Hart Mahan and his Napoleon Club on West Point cadets in the 1830s and 1840s. That Napoleon's career ended in defeat and exile seems to have garnered rather less attention than it probably merited.

Napoleon's signature was the grand, climactic battle, a clash that would shatter the enemy psychologically as much as militarily and make him sue for peace. (Austerlitz and Jena spring to mind.) In this sense, Robert E. Lee was the classic disciple of the great Corsican. In his correspondence with Confederate president Jefferson Davis, Lee repeatedly states his desire to destroy the Union army. Any number of Union generals, including the star of the Napoleon Club, George McClellan, also thought the war could be won in an afternoon.

Those who slavishly admired Napoleon and sought to imitate him, however, seemed to lose sight of an essential fact: Napoleon himself was no imitator, but an innovator. He thought outside the box. He pioneered the close-in use of artillery to blast holes in the lines of enemy infantry, through which his own infantry would pour. He was constantly surprising the enemy with unexpected maneuvers, such as his transportation of cannon over the St. Bernard Pass in winter, which was not unlike Grant's feat at Mexico City.

Grant may have despised Napoleon because of his bad character, but that didn't mean he ignored him as a military leader. John Russell Young, during his round-the-world trip with Grant, recalled Grant's admiration for Napoleon's willingness to break the rules.

"My impression is that his first success came because he made war in his own way, and not in imitation of others," he told Young. "War is progressive, because all the instruments and elements of war are progressive."

The most notable sign of progress in war since Napoleon's time was the introduction in 1855 of the Springfield rifled musket. The smoothbore muskets of Napoleon's day did not have an effective range beyond 200 yards or so. As Grant himself once said about these weapons in the hands of the Mexican army, a fellow could fire at you all day long without your even being aware of it.

The rifled musket changed all that, moving effective range out to between 500 and 600 yards. In the hands of a skilled soldier, it could be extended even farther. Thus, moving artillery up to the firing line, as Napoleon did, was no longer practical, since infantry could pick off the gunners at long range. It also made a victory on the scale of an Austerlitz highly unlikely. Even so seemingly complete a Confederate victory as Chancellorsville in 1863 occurred only because Union generalship failed. The army itself was quite intact and, indeed, Union soldiers wrote home after the battle telling their families that they thought they had won a victory.

Grant did not believe that individual battles, however seemingly decisive, would end the war. The American Civil

War was a contest of peoples, not merely of armies. The men in the ranks were not simply pieces on a chessboard, and their will was unlikely to be broken by setbacks. This gave Grant the long view and kept his eye on the ultimate objective: the defeat of Lee's army. For his part, the Napoleonic Lee had little to offer once his prospects for a war-winning battle vanished after Gettysburg.

There are many examples of how Grant "made war in his own way." The Vicksburg campaign, which we have already seen, was one. His pioneering use of economic warfare was another. Let's look at a few more:

## ENLISTING BLACK SOLDIERS

FROM THE BEGINNING of the war, both sides exploited black labor. The South did so, most obviously, via the institution of slavery. The North did so, less obviously, by using escaped slaves to dig fortifications and canals and perform general labor. Northern abolitionists wanted to employ blacks as fighting soldiers, an idea that President Lincoln tended to resist until after the Emancipation Proclamation. He had reason for caution. Though the prejudice against blacks was much less in the North than in the South, the belief in the idea of Negro inferiority to the white race was still strong. Few whites were willing to concede that blacks might be as capable of fighting for the Union (and, not incidentally, their own freedom) as whites.

Still, the idea of enlisting blacks as soldiers had several attractions. One was simple manpower. By 1863, the North had had to introduce conscription to fill the ranks of the Union army, a measure that was to prove so unpopular that the deadliest riot in American history exploded over the issue in New York City in July 1863.

But the second, and perhaps more important, reason was psychological. "The bare sight of 50,000 armed and drilled black soldiers upon the banks of the Mississippi would end the rebellion at once," Lincoln wrote to one skeptic. And now that slavery was to end, it would be critical that blacks know that they had fought for their own freedom. "There will be some black men who can remember that with silent tongue, and clenched teeth, and steady eye, and well-poised bayonet, they have helped mankind on to this great consummation," Lincoln said.

Grant was in agreement with Lincoln on this issue, which many found surprising given his prewar tolerance of slavery under his own roof. But Grant was without a prejudiced bone in his body. He was willing to believe that any man could make of himself what he would. When Adjutant General Lorenzo Thomas appeared in Grant's camps around Vicksburg in the spring of 1863 to look into organizing black regiments, Grant welcomed him and gave him the run of his camps to get white Union soldiers used to the idea.

Grant's open-mindedness was repaid on June 7, 1863, when some of the newly recruited black units drew first blood in a vicious little engagement near Milliken's Bend, Louisiana. After initially falling back, the black troops reorganized and counterattacked, spurred on by reports that blacks captured in the initial engagement had been murdered in cold blood by Confederate troops. Grant endorsed the report of the Union commander in the battle by noting that the blacks "had but little experience in the use of fire arms," but their conduct had been "most gallant and I doubt not but with good officers they would make good troops."

While not quite as dramatic as Lincoln had hoped for, the psychological effect of armed and drilled black troops was indeed a powerful one. Confederates found fighting blacks to be unnatural and quite unnerving, and atrocities against captured black soldiers (and their white officers) were not uncommon. It should be noted here that if the "chivalrous" Robert E. Lee had any objection to the mistreatment of captured black Union soldiers, it is unrecorded.

The endorsement of the most successful Union general of the war was crucial for the acceptance of black troops in the United States. (However, Grant could never get Sherman to come around to this point of view.) Eventually, more than 178,000 blacks enlisted in the service, serving in 449 engagements, 39 of them major. One-third of them died in service. At the end of the war, the total number of blacks enlisted in U.S. armies almost equaled the number of Confederate troops still present for duty.

## ACQUIRING SANTO DOMINGO

WHEN U. S. GRANT became president, one of the issues that engaged his interest most strongly, almost to the degree of passion, was acquiring the Caribbean nation of Santo Domingo as a U.S. possession.

There were strategic reasons for making the purchase. Now that the country stretched from sea to sea, the next most obvious region of concern for the United States would be the Caribbean basin. Grant had led an expedition across the Isthmus of Panama while still a young army lieutenant, and he had never forgotten the difficulties and deaths that took place along the journey. In his first message to Congress as president, Grant proposed the construction of a Panama canal and dispatched no less than seven survey parties to the area during his time in office.

Such a canal, if it were to become reality, would need protection, and Santo Domingo seemed to offer an ideal base at the Bay of Samaná. It helped that the country's government was so hopelessly corrupt that the majority of the island's inhabitants, who were a mixture of Indians, Hispanics, and escaped slaves from Haiti, would probably support annexation.

But Grant had another, more idealistic, reason for wanting Santo Domingo. One of the most critical problems he faced was the continuing second-class citizenship of black Americans. Slavery had been abolished, but blacks were still treated with disdain in the South and were not welcome in large numbers in the North.

Santo Domingo could help solve this difficult problem. The island was large enough to potentially carve out three or four states, each of which would elect two black senators and at least one black representative. Senators and representatives from the newly restored Southern states would thus be forced to reckon with black political power in Washington, even if they denied it at home. In addition, the existence of a black-dominated homeland would give former slaves in the Southern states a place to go if they continued to be maltreated at home. With this leverage, they would thus be in a better position to demand equal rights.

It was a perfect example of Grant thinking outside the box. Alas, it was much too far outside the box for the American political system in 1871. Even nonracist liberals such as Senator Charles Sumner refused to support the treaty of annexation that Grant had negotiated. Despite several efforts, Grant couldn't get the two-thirds vote he needed in the Senate, and the annexation of Santo Domingo failed.

## THE "MULE SHOE" AT SPOTSYLVANIA

THINKING OUTSIDE the box can be contagious—to your benefit. Grant was not only willing to ignore the rules himself but willing to encourage such behavior in others as well.

From the beginning of the war, a brilliant young (West Point class of 1861) officer named Emory Upton had wrestled with the problem presented to attacking infantry by the rifled musket. The accepted means of attack by Civil War soldiers had been to form up in two long lines, one behind the other, facing the enemy and then bang away at each other until one side or the other yielded.

To the modern mind, this seems like insanity, and that's how it struck Upton, too. Incredibly, he was almost the only person to consider doing something about it.

Upton's idea was to form his men into columns rather than lines, rushing the enemy's position edge-on rather than head-on and not stopping to fire. That way, the men would present a smaller target to enemy infantry and have a greater chance of piercing the enemy's fortifications and getting inside his works.

Today, this seems like basic common sense. At the time, it was revolutionary. To his credit, Grant agreed to let Upton try it with twelve picked regiments. The test came at the spot known as "the Mule Shoe" at Spotsylvania on May 10, 1864.

Upton's attack developed exactly as he had planned, with his men piercing the Confederate lines with relatively light losses. Unfortunately, they were too few for the task that now faced them. Their success was so quick and unexpected that Union reinforcements failed to move up to exploit the breakthrough, and the Confederates were able to seal the gap. Upton was forced to pull his men back.

Grant was impressed, however, and promoted Colonel Upton to brigadier general on the spot. Grant ordered that the attack be resumed the next day and this time with an entire corps rather than a mere brigade. After eighteen brutal hours of close-quarters combat, much of it in the driving rain, Union troops took the Mule Shoe, though at fearful cost. Unfortunately for Grant's men, Lee was able to plug the line farther back. Upton, however, went on to become one of the army's most brilliant and original thinkers.

———————

## GRANT'S LESSONS

• Don't do things simply because "that's the way we've always done it." Be open to new and better ways of getting the job done.

• Study the ways of successful people, but don't merely imitate them. Times and conditions change.

• Make certain your subordinates know you value original thinking and are not simply looking for automatons who will do what they are told.

PART IV

# PERSONAL LEADERSHIP: SETTING THE EXAMPLE

CHAPTER 12

# DO THE RIGHT THING

*Especially When It Hurts*

—————

*Grant has a great moral breadth and stability, a reliable honesty and
certainty of character which make him the superior of all such men as
Sherman, however brilliant.*
—JAMES HARRISON WILSON

ULYSSES S. GRANT did not want to be president. "I
am not a party politician and hope never to be one," he said
during the war. But as Grant knew better than most, men are
not masters of their own fate. Forces bigger than Grant's own
formidable will were conspiring to pull him into the political
arena after the war.

Aside from Grant's distaste for politics generally, there
was another strong reason for him to avoid the presidency:
money. Grant biographer Geoffrey Perret points out that his
salary as a full general was $21,000 per year. Along with in-
come from some other investments that he had, he cleared
about $25,000 per year. In the days before inflation and in-
come taxes, that was very good money indeed.

The president's salary in 1868 was $25,000 per year. With
the income from his investments, Grant would see his total

income rise slightly. But as president, he would be expected to entertain lavishly and often, a cost that would have to be covered largely out of his own pocket. Nor did presidents in those days receive pensions. At the end of four or eight years, he would be unemployed and mired in debt. The attractions of simply remaining in the peacetime army were powerful.

But Grant saw that larger issues were at stake. What had the war been for? The Union had been preserved, to be sure, but the attitude of Southern whites after three years of peace could at best be described as sourly reconciled. The idea of black political equality was still viewed as an outrage by many, perhaps most, Southern whites, and vigilante groups, notably the Ku Klux Klan, had been formed to violently resist it. Politically active blacks and their white Republican allies took their lives in their hands.

To Grant, this situation was intolerable. Civil rights for the freed slaves were among the fruits of victory for which the Union had expended so much blood and treasure. He couldn't simply walk away from that.

Weary of her husband's endless evasions on the subject, Julia finally confronted him one night in 1868. This is the account she gives in her memoirs:

"Ulys, do you want to be president?"

"No," he responded. "But I don't see that I have anything to say about it. The national convention is about to assemble and, from all I hear, will nominate me, and I suppose if I am nominated, will be elected."

Grant's presumption proved correct, though only just. Although nominated handily, he received barely 51 percent of the popular vote in the November 1868 election. With much of the South still not voting, it was hardly a ringing endorsement.

Sherman, Grant's friend and no fan of politics or politicians, was one of the few who refused to flatter him with congratulations on his nomination.

"I will not congratulate you because I believe you are sacrificing personal interests and comforts to give the Country a civil victory," he wrote Grant.

Indeed, that was exactly what Grant had done. Many thought he had made a mistake, but, given who he was, he could have done nothing else.

## FREEING A SLAVE

HOW GRANT CAME to own a slave remains murky. Perhaps he was a present from Julia's interfering, slaveholding father. In any case, Grant disliked slavery and, according to the testimony of one of the Dent family slaves, let it be known he wanted to see them all freed one day.

That was easier said than done, however. Julia saw nothing wrong with slavery and felt she could not do without her own slaves. Missouri laws also discouraged manumission, requiring that any slave freed by his owner and desiring to remain in the state had to post a bond to guarantee good behavior. Grant didn't have much money to spare in 1859, and the slaves certainly didn't.

Nevertheless, Grant decided to make his feelings known about the "peculiar institution" in the most unmistakable fashion. Biographer Brooks D. Simpson notes that on March 29, 1859, Grant filed papers in St. Louis for the manumission of one William Jones, a thirty-five-year-old mulatto slave. A healthy male of working age was quite valuable: Grant might have secured $1,000 or more for Jones on the auction block, and Grant needed money badly. But he did not do so, giving Jones his freedom instead. What became of Jones afterward is also unknown.

Grant had never claimed to be an abolitionist, though he later came to realize that slavery was the ultimate cause of the

Civil War and had to be ended if the war was to be ended. It was also questionable how much Julia's four slaves benefited him economically. (They were household servants, after all, not field hands, and they were four more mouths to feed.)

But Grant refused to be defensive about the subject. He had done his best to make his own personal protest known when it counted.


## ENDING PRISONER EXCHANGE

PRISONERS HAD BEEN informally exchanged between North and South from the earliest days of the conflict. With a much smaller manpower base to work from than the North, the South was eager to make the arrangement a formal one. This was a step that President Abraham Lincoln was loath to take, since it would involve a tacit recognition of the Confederacy. Still, political pressure in the North from the families of captured soldiers was great, and he agreed to the establishment of a formal system.

Concluded in July 1862, the so-called cartel provided for an elaborate system of exchange: A general could be traded for an enemy general of equivalent rank, a private for a private, and so on. Exchanges of different ranks were also possible: A general, for example, would be worth sixty privates. Instead of being held in prisoner-of-war camps, captured soldiers would be "paroled." That is, the soldier would be allowed to return home on his word of honor that he would not take up arms again until he had been notified that he had been "exchanged" for an equivalent soldier from the other side.

Needless to say, the system was ripe for abuse. Disputes broke out almost immediately about the correct ratios between soldiers of different ranks. The North's practice of dispatching paroled soldiers to the West to fight Indians or perform noncombatant duties behind the lines while awaiting exchange was denounced by the South as a violation of the agreement.

But that was nothing compared to the imbroglio that broke out over the issue of captured black Union soldiers. The whole idea of armed blacks literally made many Southerners mad with fury, and in May 1863, the Confederate Congress passed legislation providing for the enslavement of captured black Union troops, regardless of whether they were fugitive slaves. And that was if they were lucky. The legislation also provided for the execution of captured fugitive slaves and their white officers. This action outraged the Northern public, which demanded that blacks be treated as captured soldiers on a par with whites. The system of exchange ultimately broke down over this issue, and Northern and Southern prison camp populations swelled.

Later in 1863, following the losses at Chancellorsville and Gettysburg, an increasingly desperate South sought to restart the exchanges by declaring that only known runaway slaves would be returned to their masters. The North, however, refused anything short of equal treatment for all.

Still, political pressure on the Lincoln administration to relax its stance was acute. The South could barely supply its soldiers in the field and was not about to expend resources feeding and housing captured enemy troops. Pathetic petitions to resume prisoner exchanges were addressed to President Lincoln from the Union soldiers languishing in the notorious prison camp at Andersonville, Georgia, and elsewhere.

The issue landed on Ulysses S. Grant's desk soon after he became general in chief of the Union armies in March 1864. Although sympathetic to the plight of the captured soldiers, he decided that a policy of no exchanges would ultimately benefit the North far more than the South and so shorten the war. "Every man we hold," he wrote, "when released on parole or otherwise, becomes an active soldier against us. If a system of exchange liberates all prisoners taken, we will have to fight on until the whole South is exterminated."

Perhaps Grant was influenced by his experiences in the West in 1863. He paroled the Vicksburg garrison after the city's surrender because he did not have sufficient transport to send thousands of prisoners northward. Grant was dismayed, however, to find that many of the prisoners his army captured that November at Chattanooga were the same men he had paroled four months earlier, few of whom had been properly exchanged.

Grant's policy, which Lincoln supported in spite of the political cost, was harsh but correct. By the end of the war, the number of Southern prisoners in Northern camps very nearly equaled the size of an entire Southern army. So desperate was the South to liberate this manpower that it hatched a series of harebrained schemes in 1864 to liberate the prisoners via secret agents and the fomenting of pro-Southern uprisings in the North, none of which came to anything.

## SHERMAN'S MEMOIRS

GRANT PROMOTED Sherman to succeed him as full general and general in chief upon Grant's assumption of the presidency in 1869. Sherman published his memoirs in 1875, while still serving as general in chief and while Grant was still president. It was a typically Shermanesque act of bravado. Like any highly opinionated man, Sherman had enemies, and they hoped to profit by perhaps forcing him from his position. "You won't find yourself in the book, General. It seems Sherman doesn't think you were in the war," several people told Grant. Extracts from the book had been published that seemed to confirm the rumors.

"So I sent for the book and resolved to read it over, with paper and pencil, and make careful notes, and prepare a reply. I do not think I ever ventured upon a more painful duty," Grant later told John Russell Young, the correspondent who accompanied him around the world.

It took Grant, who was a slow but careful reader, three weeks to finish the book, during which time he did not see Sherman. "I am glad I did not. My mind was so set by the extracts that I should certainly have been cold to him."

When he finished the book, however, Grant pronounced himself more than pleased. "I found that I approved every word; that, apart from a few mistakes that any writer would make in so voluminous a work, it was a true book, an honorable book, creditable to Sherman, just to his companions—to myself particularly so—just such a book as I expected Sherman to write," Grant said. "You cannot imagine how pleased I was, for my respect and affection for Sherman were so great that I look upon those three weeks as among the most painful in my remembrance. Sherman is not only a great soldier, but a great man. He is one of the very great men in our country's history."

Although Grant had initially listened to those who wanted to create dissension between him and Sherman, he did not take their word without corroboration and insisted on seeing for himself if the rumors were true.

## GRANT'S LESSONS

- "Duty" means putting your personal wants and desires aside for the greater good of the organization. A position of leadership almost by definition imposes acts of duty.

- Accomplishing the ultimate goal may mean hardship for your subordinates. Don't let your feelings for them divert you from the larger task.

- You have a duty to your loyal subordinates. Don't allow gossip or unfounded rumors to undermine your confidence in them.

CHAPTER 13

# SELF-MANAGEMENT

*Stay in Shape, Care
for Your Family*

———————

*There wasn't a lazy bone in his body, he was a little giant physically.*
—JOHN SAPPINGTON, WHO KNEW GRANT
IN ST. LOUIS BEFORE THE WAR

*My father possessed an iron constitution.*
—FREDERICK DENT GRANT, GRANT'S ELDEST SON

GRANT'S SPARE FRAME was one of the elements that people noticed most frequently about him. He stood five feet eight inches tall and weighed about 135 pounds during the Civil War. "Hell, he's no general!" said one startled private who saw him for the first time. But appearances can be deceiving. Grant was far from physically weak. Melancthon T. Burke, a friend who knew Grant in Galena, Illinois, before the war, painted a memorable word portrait of Grant at work there:

> He was favored mostly because he was able to weigh and handle the hides, some of which were in excess of 250 pounds. Grant was of great physical strength and I have seen him many times lift a hide that no ordinary man could manage. After tossing and weighing the hides, he would calmly walk over and wash his hands.

Grant was aware of his physical strength and, according to the testimony of his son Fred, his occasional allusions to it were among the few instances of egotism that he permitted himself. Fred Grant also thought this the source of his father's ability to tolerate tremendous pain during his final illness:

> I have seen him lift heavy objects with no special effort, when three others could not budge it with effort. Knowing of his great physical strength, my father's fortitude and patience during his last long illness impressed me deeply. He would prefer to suffer intense pain than distress those around him. Had he been a weaker man, he could never have lasted as long as he did.

Grant's power—and his pugnacious use of it—was noticed by Colonel James E. Pitman, who served with Grant in Detroit after the Mexican War:

> In those days he was a very sturdy young fellow, well built. Small, but extremely active and strong and he would whip a man who crossed him or who sold him short cords of wood or who was in any way derogatory towards him.

Physical exercise regimens, as we know them today, were little practiced in the mid–nineteenth century, and there was certainly no such thing as weight-training or running for health. Grant, however, was very much aware of the connection between a sound body and a sound mind and success on the battlefield. During their round-the-world trip, correspondent John Russell Young asked Grant what attributes a successful general ought to possess. Rather than citing learning or personal courage, Grant responded:

> A successful general needs health and youth and energy. I should not like to put a general in the field over 50. When I was in the army I had a physique that could stand anything. Whether I

slept on the ground or in a tent, whether I slept one hour or ten in the 24, whether I had one meal or three, or none, made no difference. I could lie down and sleep in the rain without caring.

That seems a bit of an exaggeration. Grant's life in the field might have been less than luxurious, but he doesn't appear to have slept on the ground in the rain very often. (Indeed, on campaign, he, like many generals on both sides, had a taste for staying in commandeered houses.) Nevertheless, life in the field was strenuous enough; and Grant, who was thirty-eight at the time of Fort Sumter and just shy of his forty-third birthday at Appomattox, was young enough to cope. Sherman wasn't much older, and Sheridan was much younger. All enjoyed good health during the war, and it must have played a considerable role in their success.

Grant's insight on the need for physical stamina in a commanding general was an important one. An executive needs physical strength in order to cope with the enormous mental strain that great responsibility brings. President Franklin D. Roosevelt's infantile paralysis may have strengthened him spiritually, as some biographers have suggested, but it manifestly weakened him physically. The enormous burden of carrying the free world's war effort on his shoulders between 1941 and 1945 took a tremendous toll on his body; in his last year, he was plainly living on borrowed time. His deteriorating physical condition probably undermined his ability to successfully guide the sensitive diplomatic negotiations that took place at the end of the war.

Robert E. Lee was in his mid-fifties when the war commenced and nearly sixty when it ended. His health was not robust during the war, and he appears to have suffered several heart attacks, often at critical junctures such as during the campaign and Battle of Gettysburg. It is hard to know whether these ailments adversely affected his battlefield performance, but they certainly could not have helped.

Grant's preferred form of exercise was horseback riding. According to Fred Grant,

> My father was the best horseman in the army, he rode splendidly and always on magnificent and fiery horses when possible to obtain one. He preferred to ride the most unmanageable mount, the largest and the most powerful one. Oftentimes I saw him ride a beast that none had approached. This is another instance of his physical strength.

Colonel Pitman also commented on Grant's strength and prowess in the saddle:

> One impression that obliterated all others was the feeling that Grant was just power and will and resolution and unhesitating action. He was that way even as a young man in Detroit. He had a very fast horse at the time, which he bought from Dave Cicotte, and he was a most excellent horseman.

Indeed, Grant's reputation as a horseman, widely commented on in his lifetime, has been obscured over the years by those who have denigrated his reputation for various reasons. He set a horse-jumping record at West Point that stood for decades, and he wanted a cavalry commission upon his graduation from West Point. He did not get it—some claim because he mistreated a horse, which is hard to believe, given Grant's love of horses. It was more probably because the cavalry arm in the Regular Army was very small, and Grant's class standing meant there were no vacancies when his turn came to choose assignments.

He never lost his ambition to be a cavalryman, however. He once said that early in the war, he aimed no higher than to command a cavalry brigade in the Army of the Potomac.

Grant's taste in food was simple to the point of being Spartan. "He ate less than any man in the army," was the assessment of aide Horace Porter. Grant liked beef, cooked to the point of being burnt. He never ate duck or other fowl ("I never could eat anything that goes on two legs") or lamb or veal. During the Overland Campaign of 1864, Porter claimed the general lived on little besides roast beef and hard bread. On one occasion, however, he greatly enjoyed a meal of oysters, and efforts were made afterward to procure them whenever possible.

He did enjoy fruit and often picked at the fruit bowl between courses. Otherwise, however, Grant's table manners were impeccable. "No matter how great was the hurry, or what were the circumstances of the occasion," Porter wrote, "he never violated the requirements of true politeness."

After the war, Grant was confined to his headquarters in Washington and then the White House and had less occasion for exercise and was eating more. He complained to Rawlins in 1868, "Weigh now 160. Am getting fat." His weight reached its apex in 1883 at 195 pounds, but during his final illness he wasted away. He didn't weigh more than 125 pounds when he died in July 1885.

Although able to go on little sleep if necessary, Grant liked to sleep and thought it necessary for a good leader. "I am a firm believer in the restorative qualities of sleep," he told Porter and his staff on the night of the first day of the Battle of the Wilderness, "and always like to get at least seven hours of it." He didn't take seriously the claims of some of Napoleon's admirers that the French emperor was able to get by on only a few hours of sleep per night. "I for one, never believed those stories," Grant said. "If the truth were known, I have no doubt it would be found that he made up for his short sleep at night by taking short naps during the day."

## STRESS RELIEVERS:
## DRINKING AND SMOKING

NO SUBJECT is so completely and seemingly unalterably associated with U. S. Grant as that of drinking. During his lifetime and afterward, his many enemies, both political and military, sought to play up allegations of his supposed drunkenness. Not insignificant have been the many portrayals in movies and on television of Grant as a hopeless souse. That such a portrait is utterly at odds with reality seems to make little impression. After all, is it really possible that a man could command the troops on the winning side in the greatest war in American history, and then go on to win two terms as president and retire one of the most popular men in America, all the while being unable to control his drinking? To ask the question is to answer it. No one is that lucky.

The truth about Grant and alcohol will likely never be known. Credible eyewitness accounts of Grant drunk are remarkably uncommon, however. Two widely repeated stories, one by journalist Sylvanus Cadwallader and another by Grant's aide Charles Dana, about Grant going on a "spree" during the Vicksburg campaign, have serious flaws. Dana, who was there, claims Cadwallader wasn't; and the colorful details the newspaperman supplied—of Grant heaving empty bottles out a steamship porthole, for example—don't fit with any other accounts of Grant's personality and behavior. Furthermore, both accounts were written years after the fact by men who, by that time, had fallen out with the general.

Most of the tales of Grant's drinking seem to date from the period 1852–1854, when he was assigned to the distant West Coast without his family, with little to occupy his restless mind and with no prospect of an end in sight. Even today, Fort Humboldt is an isolated place that takes considerable effort to reach. What it must have been like to live there 150 years ago can only be imagined. Grant had no radios, television, telephones, or cinemas to divert him. The telegraph was in its infancy. Newspapers were rare and usually well out of date by the time they reached the fort. Books were few, and the lack of electric lights made reading after dark difficult. The mail service was slow and infrequent. As one of Grant's friends later put it, "What could he do but drink whiskey and play pool?"

Some accounts say Grant was run out of the army in 1854 because of drunkenness. Grant, however, had spoken often of resignation as the only means he could see to reunite his family. Also, the army wasn't exactly a hotbed of temperance in 1854. Accusing a mid-nineteenth-century army officer of drinking heavily would be on the order of noting that it often snows in Maine in January. Promoting an officer to captain just as he was about to be cashiered is odd, to say the least. And if Grant really was booted out of the army for alcoholism, then his commanding officer got a bad trade. As Brooks D. Simpson points out, Henry Judah, the officer who succeeded Grant, also drank heavily.

Still, the rumors of drunkenness dogged Grant. During the war, Grant's early successes aroused the jealousy and enmity of many other army officers. "General McClernand was very bitter against Grant from the start and he tried to destroy him," recalled Colonel J. P. Riordan. "He had Grant drunk at Belmont, drunk at Donelson, drunk at Shiloh. He had spies in every regiment. He gave rise to a good many tales concerning Grant's use of liquor."

Some of the tales of Grant's supposed drinking are, quite literally, beyond belief. One widely repeated story told by the British Lord Lytton has a drunken former President Grant pinching and ravishing women and even having sex with Mrs. Grant in front of eyewitnesses while simultaneously vomiting! Even William McFeely, Grant's most hostile biographer, does not credit the tale.

Still, if Grant had an exceptional fondness for alcohol — and the evidence is not clear that he did—one is tempted to ask, So what? The mere fact that a man drinks, sometimes to excess, does not mean, ipso facto, that he is unfit for high command or office. British army and naval officers were sometimes alarmed at President Franklin D. Roosevelt's habit of discussing grand strategy while knocking back a succession of highballs. They needn't have been, since their own chief, Winston S. Churchill, was scarcely more abstemious when it came to alcohol.

Grant was never drunk when his sobriety was demanded, on the battlefield or when planning a campaign. Were it not for the persistent efforts by many to denigrate his reputation, Grant's drinking might be little more than a historical footnote, an escape valve for the tremendous burden of responsibility he bore. Whatever he did, it worked. Lincoln probably never actually spoke the line "Tell me what brand of whiskey Grant drinks and I will send a barrel of it to every general in the army," but it pretty well sums up all that need be said on the subject.

Grant's smoking is remarked upon less frequently than his drinking is, though its ultimate effect upon him was far more dire. Like drinking, smoking was endemic in the army and in society at large in the nineteenth century. Grant smoked a pipe before the war and in its opening phases. After the taking of Fort Donelson in February 1862, however, a newspaperman wrote that Grant liked cigars. A grateful nation deluged him with cigars, and he began smoking them regularly instead of his pipe.

Grant smoked twenty cigars in one day on only one recorded occasion: the first day of the Battle of the Wilderness. (This gives some idea of the strain that was hidden behind his impassive features.) Most days, he smoked seven to ten cigars; and, much of the time, the cigar was unlit. Grant quit smoking cold turkey in November 1884 and claimed to suffer no withdrawal symptoms. Unfortunately, it wasn't soon enough to save him from the throat cancer that would kill him a year later.

## GRANT'S FAMILY

THE MARRIAGE OF Ulysses S. Grant and Julia Dent is one of the great love stories of American history. Gore Vidal, never known for cutting anyone a break, admitted in his review of Julia Dent Grant's memoirs that this couple shared a rare and touching intimacy. Quite simply, the two fell in love and remained romantically attached to each other for the rest of their lives.

They met in the spring of 1844 at White Haven, the home of "Colonel" Frederick Dent in St. Louis, where young Lieutenant Grant was stationed after his graduation from West Point. The family felt they already knew Grant, who had roomed with young Fred Dent in their last year at the military academy. Dent had frequently written home extolling the virtues of the young Ohioan. "I want you to know him," Fred wrote in one of his letters home; "he is pure gold."

Grant was young and handsome and must have seemed a good catch. Julia, however, in spite of her privileged upbringing, could generously be described as plain (her contemporaries were often far more cruel). She suffered from a disease that caused her right eye to wander, and she sometimes appeared cross-eyed. But her personality was lively, and she had a keen wit; indeed, the eighteen-year-old girl was taken with twenty-one-year-old Lieutenant Grant.

Their love endured the long separation engendered by the Mexican War, when they saw each other only once in four years. It also survived the opposition of Colonel Dent, who didn't think army life would be good for his daughter. The two weren't finally married until August 22, 1848.

The marriage survived the difficult separation that followed the war when Grant was posted to the newly won territories on the West Coast. In those days, the only ways to reach California were overland across territory populated with hostile Indians, by sea around treacherous Cape Horn, and across the yellow fever–infested Isthmus of Panama. None was appealing, and Grant loved his family too much to ask them to risk the trip. It was to see them again that he left the army in 1854 and returned to St. Louis.

He had two sons by then: Fred, born in 1850, and Ulysses Jr., born two years later. Ellen, the Grants' only daughter, was born almost exactly nine months after Grant returned from the Pacific coast. A third son, Jesse Root Grant, would follow in 1858.

By all accounts, Grant was an extremely indulgent father who could rarely bring himself to discipline his children and never used corporal punishment. His attitude was highly unusual for the era. He spoiled the children completely, particularly the two youngest. During the war, they were frequent guests in camp. Fred Grant accompanied his father during the Vicksburg campaign and was actually hit by a stray shot, though not seriously. Horace Porter, one of Grant's staff officers, recalled, "the children often romped with him and he joined in their frolics as if they were all playmates together. The younger ones would hang around his neck while he was writing, make a terrible mess of the papers, and turn everything in his tent into a toy."

Like many children of a famous parent, Grant's often struggled at the edge of the spotlight. Fred spent his entire life wondering if he was living up to his father's reputation. He attended West Point, where he accumulated a remarkably large collection of demerits and took five years to graduate. He later served with Theodore Roosevelt as one of New York

City's four police commissioners, where his performance did not impress the future president.

Ulysses Jr., or "Buck," as he was known, probably physically resembled his father most closely. During his life, he spent the least actual time with the general, though there was no estrangement between them. Like all the Grant children, he displayed little of his father's intellectual facility. Buck helped get his father involved with Ferdinand Ward, the Wall Street sharpie who was responsible for the greatest financial disaster of Grant's life, discussed later in this chapter. Eventually, Buck found his calling and became a successful hotel owner, running the opulent U. S. Grant Hotel in San Diego, which is still in business.

Ellen "Nellie" Grant was, as might be expected, her father's favorite; he spoiled her even more shamelessly than he did her brothers. She was outgoing, loved parties and dances, and played the role of the most eligible young woman in Washington, D.C., to the hilt. Unfortunately, the suitor she chose, an Englishman named Algernon Sartoris, was a shallow, vain man, and Grant opposed their union. After their 1874 White House wedding, servants found the president weeping in her bedroom. Alas, Grant's worst fears were realized and the marriage was not a success. The couple divorced soon after Grant's death.

As is often the case, the youngest son, Jesse, fit the profile of family cut-up. His personality was utterly unlike that of his reserved father and, perhaps for this reason, Ulysses Grant showed him special attention, playing "horsie" frequently and wrestling with him on the floor. Jesse, however, grew up to be an irreverent adult and actually sought, without success, the 1908 Democratic presidential nomination.

The Grant home was serene and happy. "The love of my parents for each other and their devotion to us children made no impression on me then," Jesse Root Grant wrote later in life. "I had never known anything different. Appreciation and understanding come to me now, filling me with content. Whatever the storm and stress, the anxieties and the disappointments, they knew happiness. In all my life I never saw one instance of misunderstanding or friction between them; nothing but abiding faith and love in full content in each other."

In point of fact, they did have at least one serious disagreement. Julia desperately wanted Grant to seek a third term as president, both in 1876 and again in 1880. Few women enjoyed the role of First Lady more than she did, and she admitted that she wished her time in the White House would never end. Each time, however, Grant refused utterly. His last day as president, he said later, made him feel "like a boy let out of school." He had no wish to resume the burdens of office.

There is no evidence that either of the Grants ever had an extramarital affair or even considered one, despite their long periods of separation. Rumors that Grant fathered an illegitimate child during his time in California were probably started by his political enemies and have no foundation in fact.

"He was always perfection, a cheerful, self-reliant, earnest gentleman," Julia Grant wrote of her husband in her memoirs. "His beautiful eyes, windows to his great soul, his mouth, so tender, yet so firm. One must not deem me partial to say that General Grant was the very nicest and handsomest man I ever saw."

"Since I have loved Julia, I have loved no one else," he wrote.

Grant's solid marriage was the rock upon which he rested during the most difficult times of his life. Julia seems never to have lost faith in her husband, even during the dark days of the 1850s. To doubters, she would insist that her "Ulys" would make something of himself. With her help, he did just that.

## GRANT'S LAST BATTLE

WHEN GENERAL H. Norman Schwarzkopf was asked by a publisher to write his memoirs after leading the allied coalition to victory in the Gulf War, he knew immediately the model he wanted to use: the *Personal Memoirs* of General Ulysses S. Grant.

As it turned out, that wasn't possible. Grant's autobiography is of its own time and place, though in its own way timeless. But Schwarzkopf's model was very apt. Grant's book is a remarkable one, an achievement that not even his severest critics have sought to take away from him. Unfortunately, it was written under the worst possible circumstances.

After returning from a round-the-world journey following his presidency, Grant faced the problem he knew he would have to wrestle with upon leaving office: making a living. He had no salary or pension and, unlike George Washington and Thomas Jefferson, had no plantation to which he could retire. He owned 800 acres outside St. Louis, which he held on to year after year, hoping the land's value would increase as the city grew. But somehow it just never seemed to happen. Grant and Julia were reduced to living once again in Galena, the one-horse Illinois river town where Grant had worked in his father's leather store before the war. The man who had won the Civil War, served as president, and traveled around the world to wide acclaim was back where he started.

Grant had accumulated wealthy friends while in the White House, and they came to his rescue, raising money to buy him a New York town house and securing for him a position as president of the Mexican Southern Railroad. Grant's role was mostly that of a door-opener in securing business, and it rarely consumed more than a few hours a day of his time. Although the pay was good, maintaining a New York town house in the style that he thought appropriate to a man of his position proved beyond him. He needed another source of income.

Ulysses S. "Buck" Grant, Jr., thought he had a solution. A friend of his in New York named Ferdinand Ward seemed to be making a fortune on Wall Street. For $100,000, Grant could be a partner.

Selling his property in St. Louis, Grant got the money together. In exchange, he would draw a salary of $3,000 a month, plus a share of the profits. The money soon began flooding in, and Grant appeared to everyone a wealthy man.

It was a mirage. Ward was a con man who was running what would become known later as a Ponzi scheme, whereby the money of new investors was paid out to previous investors. For those who got in early, it was a tremendous windfall. For those who came in later, many of whom were former Union soldiers investing on the strength of Grant's name, it meant disaster. As the pool of new investors gradually dried up—as it inevitably had to—the firm could not meet its obligations to the initial investors. Bankruptcy then became unavoidable.

The collapse came in early May 1884. On Sunday, May 4, Grant went to William H. Vanderbilt to ask for his help. Vanderbilt wrote Grant a personal check for $150,000, a huge sum in those days. Ward absconded with Vanderbilt's money and left Grant holding the bag. It didn't matter that many Wall Street hands far wiser in the ways of finance got taken in by Ward as well. Eventually, the con man went to prison. Grant got poverty and public humiliation.

Biographer Geoffrey Perret says that Vanderbilt was willing to forgive the $150,000 debt, but the Grants were too proud to accept the offer. They gave him all of Grant's collection of military memorabilia and keepsakes, most of which Vanderbilt donated to the federal and New York state governments. The Grants sold their house in Galena and most of their other assets, which hardly made a dent in the $500,000 they were estimated to owe. At one point, Ulysses and Julia had scarcely $1,800 to their name.

It was hard to believe the situation could grow worse, but it did, and in very short order. Grant bit into a peach a few months later and felt a stabbing pain. All those cigars had finally caught up with him.

For a time, he ignored the pain, hoping it would subside by itself. In the fall of 1884, however, he finally consulted a doctor, who referred him to a throat specialist. The tests confirmed the worst: The cancer was out of control. Grant had only a short time to live.

What would he do? More important, what would his family do? Now that he had been diagnosed as terminally ill, life insurance was out of the question.

The answer was provided by Mark Twain, who had become fascinated with Grant several years earlier. Grant liked the author, in part because he didn't seem interested in using Grant for some ulterior purpose. Twain had urged the general to write his memoirs. Sherman had already done so; and other Civil War generals, on both sides, were putting their views on the historical record.

Initially, Grant demurred. But by 1884, he was financially strapped, and *Century* magazine had commissioned him to write four articles about the war for $500 each. To Grant, it seemed like a good deal. To Twain, it smacked of outright theft. He offered the dying man terms unheard-of in their generosity if Grant would write and allow Twain to publish the general's memoirs. The copyright was given to Julia, so any profits could not be attached by Grant's remaining creditors.

Grant began writing, in pencil, in longhand, on sheet after sheet of notepaper. He had written many things in the past: memoranda, army reports, and the like, but he had never attempted a book before. Son Fred and onetime aide Adam Badeau moved in with him to serve as fact-checkers and provide general assistance. (Badeau's later claim that he had virtually ghostwritten the book would earn him a deathbed rebuke from Grant.) When Grant's pain made writing difficult, a stenographer was called in to take his dictation. But Grant's cancer-tortured throat soon made his voice so weak that he had no choice but to resume writing.

His once bold hand now reduced to little more than a spidery scrawl, Grant called on the last reserves of his formidable will to keep death at bay until the book could be finished. He was a physical shadow of his former self; and his doctor at least once gave up hope, but still Grant rallied. His family needed him. Wracked with pain, his mind dulled by morphine, he somehow found the strength to keep going.

Mark Twain visited him shortly before the end. Advance orders for 150,000 copies had been received, and tens of thousands more were expected. Success was assured, his family's financial future secure. The dying man completed the last revisions just a few days before his death on July 23, 1885.

And what a book he wrote. Most nineteenth-century memoirs are heavy going, reading like an extended obituary. Not Grant's. His memoir is eminently readable and lively, full of incisive and insightful pen portraits of the men Grant encountered. It is drolly funny in places and eerily prescient in others, such as his prediction in the last paragraphs that the unresolved issue of racial equality would one day return to haunt the nation.

The book was indeed a roaring commercial success, selling hundreds of thousands of copies and making Julia a wealthy woman. Grant accomplished his final mission.

## GRANT'S LESSONS

• Fashion isn't the only reason that so many ranking executives spend a lot of time in the gym. Physical strength is essential to the mental strength required to rise in and lead virtually any organization.

• "Behind every great man is a woman" is more than just an old saying. A supportive spouse and children are tremendous assets to anyone who aspires to success.

• Activities such as drinking and smoking can be helpful in achieving success, both in relieving stress and bonding with others. Engaged in to excess, however, they can saddle you with a bad reputation and even kill you.

# PART V

# THE WHITE HOUSE YEARS AND BEYOND

# CHAPTER 14

# GRANT IN THE WHITE HOUSE

## An Underrated Chief Executive

*A great president, who after Washington and Lincoln, was Chief Magistrate during the most difficult period in our Nation's history.*
—JAMES D. RICHARDSON, EDITOR OF
*A COMPILATION OF THE MESSAGES AND PAPERS OF THE PRESIDENTS, 1789–1897*

IN ALMOST ALL POLLS of U.S. historians, Ulysses S. Grant is ranked as one of the worst presidents, usually sharing the "failure" distinction with Warren G. Harding. Even Richard M. Nixon, the only president to resign his office, is frequently treated with more understanding than the man who, upon his death, was hailed by many as the "Second Father of his Country."

Even those who have otherwise been laudatory of Grant—such as Al Kaltman, author of *Cigars, Whiskey and Winning: Leadership Lessons from General Ulysses S. Grant*—accept the "Grant Was a Failed President" verdict of the historians. For historical purposes, there seem to be two Grants: the successful general and the disappointing president.

"Failure," however, is a loaded word. It tends to imply that success was achievable but did not occur thanks to some misjudgment or character flaw on the part of the leader under examination. A more dispassionate view of Grant's presidency reveals an energetic, honorable, and, in many respects, strong chief executive.

The task Grant faced upon entering the White House would have been formidable for anyone. Few nations had survived a cataclysm approaching the scale of the Civil War, with its 500,000 dead on both sides and hundreds of thousands more wounded and maimed for life. There was plenty of unfinished business left over. Fighting the war had piled up a then-staggering national debt of $2.5 billion. And outgoing President Andrew Johnson's refusal to enforce the Civil Rights Acts passed by Congress over his veto had signaled the worst elements among the former Confederates that they could violently resist black political equality with impunity. Abroad, war with Great Britain threatened over that country's refusal to compensate American shipowners for losses incurred by Britain's decision to allow Confederate warships to operate from British ports.

In tackling these and other issues, the general employed the same character, vision, tenacity, and determination to do the right thing—regardless of consequences—that he displayed at other points in his life. As president, he accumulated significant accomplishments.

The national debt was widely perceived as a major threat to the nation's prosperity. Grant made it clear he favored "hard" money (backed by gold) and would not move to pay off the war debts in the inflated paper currency ("greenbacks") issued during the war. Just two weeks after assuming office, the new president signed the Public Credit Act, which moved the government to redeem the greenbacks in coin as quickly as practicable. Five years later, in the midst of a deep recession, he resisted enormous public pressure to sign a bill that would have undone all this work by inflating the currency. He vetoed the bill instead and backed the 1875 Specie Resumption Act, which four years later put the country back on the gold standard.

That remained the bedrock of U.S. economic policy for more than half a century. Altogether, according to his final message to Congress, he reduced the national debt by over $435 million during his term in office while at the same time reducing taxes by $300 million.

In the realm of international affairs, the major problem confronting Grant was the so-called *Alabama* claims. During the war, Great Britain had allowed the Confederacy to buy, build, and outfit warships in her ports from which they took to the high seas to raid U.S. shipping. The most notorious of these was the C.S.S. *Alabama*, which was finally sunk in a duel with the U.S.S. *Kearsarge* off the coast of France in 1864. The North's shipowners and insurers wanted compensation for their losses.

Hamilton Fish, Grant's capable secretary of state, worked out an arrangement with Britain to submit the dispute to neutral arbitration in Geneva, Switzerland. The arbitrators eventually found in favor of the United States and awarded it $15.5 million in damages. The danger of war with Great Britain was averted, and the principle of international arbitration, which would later be embodied in the Hague Tribunal, the League of Nations, the World Court, and the United Nations, was established.

Also worthy of mention was Grant's humane and forward-looking policy with regard to the American Indian. Grant, recall, had taken the remarkable step during the war of appointing a full-blooded Seneca, Ely Parker, to a post on his staff. After becoming president (in another example of thinking outside the box), Grant named Parker Commissioner of Indian Affairs with an increased budget and a mandate to take "any course toward [the Indians] which tends to their civilization and ultimate citizenship." To this end, Parker fired most of the political officials, known as Indian agents, who were assigned to reservations and who generally used the opportunity simply to steal from and take advantage of the tribes within their jurisdiction. They were replaced with Quaker missionaries, army officers, Catholic priests, and even a religious Jew.

Unfortunately, the new policy aroused opposition in Congress and did not bring conflict between the whites and the Indians to an end. But it was an honest effort to improve the Indians' lot and avoided the path of outright genocide, which would have been just fine with many white Americans of the time. "No president could have done more," writes Grant biographer Geoffrey Perret. "None had done as much."

Reconstruction, however, was far and away the largest issue Grant had to grapple with as president. Some historians have accused Grant of having a narrow view of the presidency, saying that he saw his task as simply enforcing the law. Few stop to consider the laws that he had to enforce: the right of blacks to vote (Grant enthusiastically backed the Fifteenth Amendment, ratified early in his administration); to hold office; to make and enforce contracts; to serve on juries; and to hold all the other rights enjoyed by white male Americans. No U.S. government, indeed, no government *anywhere*, had ever even attempted such a project.

Grant approached it with determination. In his first inaugural address, he made it clear that one of his priorities would be the security of person, property, and free religious and political opinion in every part of our common country, without regard to local prejudice. And, he said, "All laws to secure these ends will receive my best efforts for their enforcement."

Throughout his eight years in office, Grant never wavered from this vision, even though many in his own party urged him to abandon the former slaves to the mercy of their former masters. To enforce civil rights laws, Grant supported the creation of the Department of Justice early in his tenure, and he used it to indict and convict thousands of Ku Klux Klansmen. He took the unprecedented step of declaring martial law in peacetime in nine South Carolina counties to suppress a Klan outbreak in 1871 and to protect black voters in the same state in 1876. In 1875, the White League—a Klan auxiliary—violently rose up against the Republican government of Louisiana and was suppressed by Lieutenant General Phil Sheridan, acting on Grant's orders.

Grant's vigorous support of Reconstruction aroused opposition in the North as well as the South. Many Northerners wanted simply to forget the war and get on with making money in the booming postwar economy. By 1872, Reconstruction had engendered so much opposition within Grant's own party that a faction of it, dubbing themselves the "Liberal Republicans," split off and nominated newspaper editor Horace Greeley for president. Grant still won the election handily, but the Republican Party was clearly beginning its retreat from the idea of enforcing the Constitution's guarantees of rights for all.

Ultimately, of course, Grant's vision would have to wait some nine decades to reach fulfillment. But his devotion to civil rights made him a president with whom, as historian Richard Currant has pointed out, "only Lyndon B. Johnson can even be compared." Frederick Douglass, undoubtedly the greatest African American of his time, was grateful for Grant's efforts:

> To [Grant] more than to any other man the Negro owes his enfranchisement and the Indian a humane policy. In the matter of the protection of the freedman from violence his moral courage surpassed that of his party; hence his place at its head was given to timid men and the country was allowed to drift, instead of stemming the current with stalwart arms.

The Republican split over Reconstruction provides a window on the issue that clings most tenaciously to Grant's presidential reputation—namely, corruption. As Frank J. Scaturro, a New York attorney and author of *President Grant Reconsidered* has pointed out, once Grant drubbed the Liberal Republicans in 1872, they began looking for another focus for their anger against his Reconstruction policies. They settled on corruption.

"Unlike other cases of presidents charged with allowing corruption," Scaturro writes, "the 'corruption' that reformers condemned during Grant's two terms, for the most part, was merely the practice of making appointments through the spoils system. . . . scholars have tended to accept the judgment of the anti-Grant reformers that this (patronage) system was inherently corrupt, but that is a very questionable conclusion, and reformers had ulterior, political motives for making the charge."

Corruption charges against Grant, then, were often a proxy for more serious policy differences, notably over Reconstruction. A not dissimilar phenomenon occurred during the 1980s, when President Reagan's opponents—frustrated by the popularity of many of his domestic and foreign policies—sought to discredit him with charges of ethical laxity or criminal conduct by his appointees. Many of these charges were unfounded or greatly exaggerated, just as in Grant's time.

Indeed, it is difficult to find a scandal during the Grant administration that could be directly attributable to Grant's policies or his administration of the government. Indeed, a close look usually reveals a president who could not have acted more honestly or responsibly. Scaturro gives as an example the so-called Black Friday attempt to corner the gold market by Wall Street manipulators Jim Fisk and Jay Gould on September 24, 1869.

These two men had conspired with Abel R. Corbin, Grant's brother-in-law, to influence the president to keep government gold off the market, thus allowing them to gain control. On several occasions, Grant received invitations to his sister's house only to discover that Fisk or Gould just happened to be visiting at the same time and was eager to talk about gold. Grant was not taken in, coldly refused to discuss government business with the two men, and rebuked Corbin for admitting them to his house. In a letter to Treasury Secretary Boutwell two weeks before Black Friday, Grant bluntly warned his appointee to be on his guard against the "bulls and bears of Wall Street," whom the chief executive rightly suspected of being up to something.

When the storm broke on September 24, 1869, and the price of gold soared, Grant acted immediately to flood the gold markets with government reserves, bringing the price back down and ending the panic. Grant had done the right thing. Yet the involvement of Grant's brother-in-law and the president's alleged failure not to act more quickly against Fisk and Gould are marked down against him. The incident is often cited as proof of Grant's "naivete." His upbraiding of Corbin and his letter to Boutwell, demonstrating that Grant knew perfectly well something was afoot, are downplayed or sometimes ignored completely.

The Crédit Mobilier scandal, which involved members of Congress being given stock in the company that built the transcontinental railroad, is a major entry on the charge sheet against Grant. Blaming Grant is bizarre, however, given that the accused were members of Congress, not Grant appointees, and that the scandal began years earlier, when Grant was still a soldier and had nothing to do with elective politics. Grant's first-term vice president, Schuyler Colfax, was implicated, but for actions committed before he became Grant's running mate.

The Whiskey Ring scandal of Grant's second term, in which Republican officials—prominently including Grant's longtime aide Orville Babcock—were accused of siphoning off government liquor tax revenue, had its roots in the Lincoln and Johnson administrations. It was Grant's own treasury secretary who uncovered the scam, and Grant urged that no guilty man be allowed to escape. Babcock was tried and acquitted, with Grant submitting testimony on his aide's behalf; but even without Grant's testimony, the evidence against him was weak.

Although Grant employed the spoils system much as previous presidents had done, he was the first to show serious interest in civil service reform. The New York Customs House, for years the most lucrative patronage job in the country, operated more honestly under Grant than under any previous president.

Grant's final service as president was the strong, steadying hand he provided during the electoral crisis of 1876–1877, when disputed votes from the Southern states would decide the election between Republican Rutherford B. Hayes and Democrat Samuel Tilden. In a nation still recovering from civil war, there was serious concern over whether a peaceful inauguration would be possible in March 1877. Grant pushed through a bill establishing an electoral commission to award the disputed ballots and studiously avoided taking any action that publicly favored Hayes. When violence was threatened, Grant strengthened military forces in the Washington area. "No greater proof of General Grant's power to command was given, even on the battlefield, than the quieting effect of his measures upon the . . . dangerous elements that would have been glad to disturb the public peace," wrote Democrat James G. Blaine afterward.

Grant's greatest asset, his character, caused him to own up to his shortcomings and take responsibility for them while at the same time making clear that he thought others had mischaracterized his mistakes. This cannot be said of many people who have held high office.

In his final message to Congress, he said:

It was my fortune, or misfortune, to be called to the office of Chief Executive without any previous political training. . . . Under such circumstances it is but reasonable to suppose that errors of judgment must have occurred. Even had they not, differences of opinion between the Executive, bound by an oath to the strict performance of his duties, and writers and debates must have arisen. *It is not necessarily evidence of blunder on the part of the Executive because there are these differences of views* [emphasis added]. Mistakes have been made, as all can see and I admit, but it seems to me oftener in the selections made of the assistants appointed to aid in carrying out the various duties of administering the Government—in nearly every case selected without a personal acquaintance with the appointee, but upon recommendations of the representatives chosen directly by the people. It is impossible, where so many trusts are to be allotted, that the right parties should be chosen in every instance. History shows that no Administration from the time of Washington to the present has been free from these mistakes. But I leave comparisons to history, claiming only that I have acted in every instance from a conscientious desire to do what was right, constitutional, within the law, and for the very best interests of the whole people. Failures have been errors of judgment, not of intent.

There were not "two Grants." His public career followed a continuum. From a man who had tolerated slavery—though without enthusiasm—in his very household, Grant moved toward the view that the war could not end without the abolition of slavery and, finally, that blacks had to be treated on an equal footing with whites. For some odd reason, history books are far more likely to discuss Robert E. Lee's supposed opposition to slavery and secession (highly debatable in any case) than Grant's record on the race issue.

Grant's vision was clear and uncompromising in this regard. Unfortunately for his historical reputation, winning the peace proved to be far more difficult than winning the war had been. In the end, however, Grant's vision triumphed. And that counts as success in any leader's book.

## GRANT'S LESSONS

- Just because you change jobs doesn't mean you should change your basic principles. If they served you well before, they will continue to do so in the future.

- Check carefully the background and employment history of anyone who wants to work for you. Any sign of dishonesty should be the reddest of red flags.

- Don't expect to have good work immediately noticed or lauded. Sometimes, it isn't recognized until much later, if ever.

# GRANT, LEE, AND THE FALLACY OF GENERAL ORDER NO. 9

———◆———

*General Grant's truly great qualities—his innate modesty, his freedom from every trace of vain-glory or ostentation, his magnanimity in victory, his genuine sympathy for his brave and sensitive foemen . . . will give him a place in history no less renowned and more to be envied than any other man.*
—JOHN B. GORDON, THE FIRST CONFEDERATE GENERAL TO SURRENDER AT APPOMATTOX

*[Grant's] concentration of energies, inflexible purpose, imperturbable long-suffering, his masterly reticence, ignoring either advice or criticism, his magnanimity in all relations, but more than all his infinite trust in the final triumph of his cause, set him apart and alone above all others. With these attributes we could not call him less than great.*
—JOSHUA LAWRENCE CHAMBERLAIN, WHO COMMANDED THE UNION HONOR GUARD AT APPOMATTOX AND ORDERED THAT IT SALUTE GORDON AND HIS MEN

AT ABOUT 1:30 P.M. on the afternoon of April 9, 1865, Lieutenant General Ulysses S. Grant, commanding general of all the armies of the United States, strode into Wilmer

McLean's parlor in the crossroads town of Appomattox Courthouse in southside Virginia. Awaiting him was the man he had been directly opposing for the past eleven months, Confederate general Robert E. Lee. In an effort at small talk, Grant observed that they had met once before, during the Mexican War. Lee, for his part, stated that he did not recall the occasion.

That would hardly have been surprising. In Mexico, Lee was one of the army's stars. Second in his class at West Point, he had built a reputation as one of the army's foremost engineering officers. His feats of daring in the war—once lying concealed behind a fallen log on which Mexican soldiers sat conversing, just inches away—had only added to the luster of his reputation. Grant, by contrast, was a freshly minted second lieutenant with an average West Point record. There was little reason for Lee to remember meeting him.

Thus, Grant would have been entitled to a moment of supreme self-satisfaction at Appomattox. There can be no question of how Napoleon would have behaved in a similar situation: strutting about the room, barking harsh terms at his defeated foe. But such behavior simply was not in Grant. What Lee felt at this supreme moment, he never recorded. But Grant's emotions were in conflict. He had attained a great triumph yet felt no elation. "I felt anything rather than rejoicing at the downfall of a foe who had fought so long and valiantly," Grant wrote in his memoirs, "and had suffered so much for a cause, though that cause was, I believe, one of the worst for which a people ever fought, and one for which there was the least excuse."

Although his nickname was "Unconditional Surrender" Grant, the commanding general did not demand these terms from Lee. (Phil Sheridan, however, grumbled that "we should have banged right on and settled all questions without asking them.") Grant had his mind on the postwar country and knew that Lee's unmatched prestige among Southerners would be key in heading off the kind of ongoing guerrilla warfare that so many feared would result if Confederate armies were simply dispersed by armed force. So Grant's terms were generous. Officers could keep their side arms and men their horses. The men, including General Lee, would be allowed to go home and live unmolested—provided they observed the laws in force in their locality.

Historians have generally overlooked the extraordinary nature of this last item. Many in the North wished to try the former Confederate leaders, including Lee, as traitors. The Appomattox terms made this impossible, a fact that enraged President Andrew Johnson when he belatedly realized its import. When Johnson threatened to disregard the terms and try Lee anyway, Grant threatened to resign in protest. Only then did Johnson and the "ultras" back down.

The meeting consumed about an hour and a half all told. Grant dictated orders and dispatches to his own and other armies, making clear what had happened. Almost as an afterthought, it seems, Grant dispatched a telegram to Washington, D.C., informing President Lincoln of Lee's surrender. Grant seems to have given no thought to making any grandiloquent statement to his troops. He had never done so before. He wouldn't start now. He also discouraged any celebrating among his own men.

For Lee, the situation was different. His decision to surrender had to be explained, not merely to his own men, but to the Southern nation and to posterity itself. Never comfortable putting his emotions on paper, he asked his aide, Charles Marshall, to draft something appropriate. With a few edits by Lee, it was issued on April 10 and is known in history simply as "General Order No. 9":

Hd Qurs Army Northern Virginia
10th April 1865

General Order
No 9

After four years of arduous service, marked by unsurpassed courage and fortitude, the Army of Northern Virginia has been compelled to yield to overwhelming numbers and resources.

I need not tell the brave survivors of so many hard fought battles who have remained steadfast to the last, that I have consented to this result from no distrust of them.

But feeling that valor and devotion could accomplish nothing that could compensate for the loss that would have attended the continuance of the contest, I determined to avoid the useless sacrifice of those whose past services have endeared them to their countrymen.

By the terms of the agreement, Officers and men can return to their homes and remain until exchanged. You will take with you the satisfaction that proceeds from the consciousness of duty faithfully performed and I earnestly pray that a merciful God will extend to you His blessing and protection.

With an unceasing admiration of your constancy and devotion to your country, and a grateful remembrance of your kind and generous consideration of myself, I bid you all an affectionate farewell.

R E Lee
Genl

The eloquence of the words is what strikes most people, and given that Marshall composed them in the back of a wagon with a sentry standing guard outside to ensure he was not disturbed makes it all the more amazing. But what about its central point, contained in the first sentence? Namely, that the Army of Northern Virginia was not outfought and out-generaled, but merely the victim of "overwhelming numbers and resources."

If Lee really believed this—and since he put his name to it and never said anything different, it is reasonable to suppose that he did—then it does not put him in a terribly flattering light. After all, the overwhelming numbers and resources were there even before the first round was fired at Fort Sumter. The North's population in 1861 was almost four times that of the South, one-third of which was slaves. At the time, few failed to note that the North was possessed of far more of the industries, money, and infrastructure that were needed to wage a modern war. If Lee believed that overwhelming numbers and resources were decisive in war, then his decision to fight the war for four long years is close to incomprehensible.

It is certainly true that bluecoats in the Civil War enjoyed luxuries of which the graybacks could only dream, especially in the war's last year. During the siege of Petersburg, when the wind was right, Union troops especially enjoyed allowing the aroma of boiling coffee to waft over to the Confederate trenches. At Cedar Creek and several other battlefields, ravenous Confederates actually lost the military advantage they had gained when they stopped to loot the incredibly well stocked Union camps.

But ample supplies alone do not a victory make, as Lee knew—or should have known—from personal experience. In the Mexican War, American forces were usually outnumbered by their Mexican foes, who were operating much closer to their bases of supply and had the "home field" advantage of marching through friendly country. The Americans, far from home, were mostly untrained volunteers, fighting on behalf of a divided country. (Most Northerners, including Representative Abraham Lincoln, tended to oppose the war.)

The Mexicans' advantages were shared to a remarkable degree by the Confederacy, a fact that the North's obvious material bounty tended to obscure. Like the Mexicans, the Confederates enjoyed interior lines of communication. This made it easier to shift troops and supplies from one threatened front to another, thus nullifying to some extent the North's weight of numbers. Moreover, the South had merely to fend off the North's blows in order to achieve her independence, while the North faced the far more formidable task of actually conquering a hostile people. And it had to accomplish this goal while a large and articulate "peace" faction in its own camp hindered its efforts, a feature that had no counterpart in the South.

A veritable mountain of supplies and an army that outnumbered that of his foe did nothing to help George B. McClellan take Richmond in the spring of 1862. The same general outnumbered Lee nearly two to one at the Battle of Antietam, while simultaneously enjoying the inestimable advantage of knowing his opponent's plans and dispositions, and *still* could manage only a tactical draw. At Chancellorsville in May 1863, Lee was down by *more* than two to one and still scored a smashing victory that forced the retreat of the Army of the Potomac.

Even so, the "overwhelming numbers and resources" argument for the North's triumph became current so quickly that Grant himself was confronted by it while he was president. Someone actually suggested to his face that "any man of ordinary capacity" could have easily forced Lee to surrender and that the culminating victory at Appomattox was "not a particularly noteworthy event."

Grant's response to this provocation was characteristically understated. Slowly rolling his cigar from one side of his mouth to the other, he quietly replied, "I have heard of these criticisms before, and there is only one answer that I wish to make. General Lee surrendered to me. He did not surrender to any other Union general, although I believe there were several efforts made in that direction before I assumed command of the armies in Virginia."

Indeed, the idea that Grant couldn't help blundering his way to victory requires overlooking a great deal. At Fort Donelson, the first of his great victories, Grant possessed about 27,000 men to 21,000 Confederates. An advantage, to be sure, but hardly overwhelming or decisive. On the first day at Shiloh, Grant was evenly matched with the Confederates, with about 40,000 men on either side. For the most critical parts of the Vicksburg campaign, Grant had about 29,000 effectives to 23,000 Confederates. As at Fort Donelson, it was an advantage, but hardly an irresistible one.

That Grant "butchered" his way to victory remains a popular charge, with Exhibit A being the Overland Campaign of May–June 1864. Those forty-three days were indeed bloody, but, as other scholars have pointed out, Grant's losses were actually proportionately fewer than Lee's. And Grant himself, in his memoirs, noted that his losses were no greater than had been incurred by the unsuccessful campaigns of the previous three years. It's not as though other generals were achieving stunning successes with little loss of life.

The "butcher" tag also fails to take note of the campaigns where Grant achieved tremendous results at relatively small cost. The capture of Vicksburg cost fewer than 10,000 Union casualties, while inflicting nearly 40,000 on the Confederates. Lifting the siege of Chattanooga was accomplished at a cost of just 761 men killed. The Appomattox Campaign, often overlooked, is a similarly brilliant feat of arms bought at fewer than 200 Union soldiers killed.

Nor is the Overland Campaign merely an example of bull-headed brawling. Rather, as J. F. C. Fuller has pointed out, it reflects an aggressive commander who in forty-three days moved his men over one hundred miles of difficult terrain, avoided all supply problems, changed his supply base four times, made nine flanking movements, and crossed four rivers in the face of the enemy. He transported four thousand wagons and massive reserve artillery without losing a single gun, wagon, or animal to enemy capture and ended up south of the James River, just as he had projected before starting. It affirms rather than disproves Grant's flexibility, ability to maneuver, and understanding of the interdependence of campaigns.

Always the most clear-eyed general in either army, Grant articulated to his White House detractor a simple truth: Leadership and management were required to marshal those "overwhelming numbers and resources" into a form that could produce victory. No general who had gone before him had managed that feat, though many had tried.

Above all else in the Civil War stands this central fact: Every decisive Union victory on land—with the sole exception of Gettysburg—was won either by Ulysses S. Grant himself or under his overall direction. That this was the work of a drunken bumbler with an inordinate lucky streak, as Grant has been portrayed so unfairly and for so long, is simply impossible to credit. Anyone can be lucky enough to win the lottery once; but no one could be so consistently lucky as to produce a record the likes of the one Ulysses S. Grant holds.

# BIBLIOGRAPHY

## BOOKS

Arnold, James R. *The Armies of Ulysses S. Grant*. London: Arms and Armour Press, 1995.

Cadwallader, Sylvanus. *Three Years with Grant, As Recalled by War Correspondent Sylvanus Cadwallader*. Edited, with an introduction and notes, by Benjamin P. Thomas. Introduction by Brooks D. Simpson (reprint edition). Lincoln: University of Nebraska Press, 1996.

Catton, Bruce. *Grant Moves South*. Boston: Little, Brown, 1960.

Clancy, Tom, with General Chuck Horner. *Every Man a Tiger*. New York: G. P. Putnam, 1999.

————. *Grant Takes Command*. Boston: Little, Brown, 1969.

————. *Never Call Retreat*. Garden City, N.Y.: Doubleday, 1965.

————. *Terrible Swift Sword*. Garden City, N.Y.: Doubleday, 1963.

Daniel, Larry J. *Shiloh: The Battle That Changed the Civil War*. New York: Simon & Schuster, 1997.

Fleming, Thomas. *Band of Brothers: West Point in the Civil War*. New York: Walker and Co., 1988.

Fuller, J. F. C. *The Generalship of Ulysses S. Grant*. New York: Da Capo Press, 1929.

————. *Grant and Lee, A Study in Personality and Generalship*. Bloomington: Indiana University Press, 1957.

Garland, Hamlin. *Ulysses S. Grant: His Life and Character*. New York: Doubleday & McClure, 1898.

Glatthaar, Joseph T. *Partners in Command: The Relationships Between Leaders in the Civil War*. New York: Free Press, 1994.

Grant, Julia Dent. *The Personal Memoirs of Julia Dent Grant (Mrs. Ulysses S. Grant)*. Edited, with notes and foreword by John Y. Simon. New York: Putnam, 1975.

Grant, Ulysses S. *Personal Memoirs of U. S. Grant*. New York: Charles Webster, 1885.

Hattaway, Herman. *Shades of Blue and Gray: An Introductory Military History of the Civil War*. Columbia: University of Missouri Press, 1997.

Jones, R. Steven. *The Right Hand of Command: Use and Disuse of Personal Staffs in the Civil War*. Mechanicsburg, Pa.: Stackpole Books, 2000.

Kaltman, Al. *Cigars, Whiskey, and Winning: Leadership Lessons from General Ulysses S. Grant*. Paramus, N.J.: Prentice-Hall, 1998.

Keegan, John. *The Mask of Command*. New York: Penguin, 1988.

Lewis, Lloyd. *Captain Sam Grant*. Boston: Little, Brown, 1950.

Macartney, Clarence Edward. *Grant and His Generals*. Freeport, N.Y.: Books for Libraries Press, 1953.

Marshall-Cornwall, James. *Grant as Military Commander*. New York: Van Nostrand Reinhold, 1970.

McFeely, William S. *Grant: A Biography*. New York: Norton, 1981.

Miers, Earl S. *The Web of Victory: Grant at Vicksburg*. Baton Rouge: Louisiana State University Press, 1955.

Mitchell, Joseph B. *Military Leaders in the Civil War*. New York: G. P. Putnam, 1972.

Perret, Geoffrey. *Ulysses S. Grant: Soldier and President*. New York: Random House, 1997.

Porter, Horace. *Campaigning with Grant*. New York: Putnam, 1897.

Puryear, Edgar F., Jr. *American Generalship: Character Is Everything: The Art of Command*. Novato, Calif.: Presidio Press, 2000.

Richardson, Albert D. *A Personal History of Ulysses S. Grant*. Hartford, Conn.: American Publishing, 1868.

Scaturro, Frank J. *President Grant Reconsidered*. Lanham, Md.: Madison Books, 1999.

Sears, Stephen W. *Controversies and Commanders: Dispatches from the Army of the Potomac.* Boston: Houghton Mifflin, 1999.

———. *George McClellan: The Young Napoleon.* New York: Ticknor & Fields, 1988.

———. *To the Gates of Richmond: The Peninsular Campaign.* New York: Ticknor & Fields, 1992.

Sherman, William T. *Memoirs of W. T. Sherman.* New York: Library of America, 1990.

Simpson, Brooks D. *Let Us Have Peace: Ulysses S. Grant and the Politics of War and Reconstruction, 1861–1868.* Chapel Hill: University of North Carolina Press, 1991.

———. *Ulysses S. Grant: Triumph over Adversity, 1822–1865.* New York: Houghton Mifflin, 2000.

Trudeau, Noah Andre. *Bloody Roads South: The Wilderness to Cold Harbor, May–June 1864.* New York: Fawcett Columbine, 1989.

———. *Out of the Storm: The End of the Civil War, April–June 1865.* Boston: Little, Brown, 1994.

Waugh, John C. *The Class of 1846: From West Point to Appomattox—Stonewall Jackson, George McClellan, and Their Brothers.* New York: Warner Books, 1994.

Weigley, Russell F. *The American Way of War: A History of United States Military Strategy and Policy.* Bloomington: Indiana University Press, 1973.

Williams, T. Harry. *Lincoln and His Generals.* New York: Alfred A. Knopf, 1952.

———. *McClellan, Sherman, and Grant: How the Temperaments and Moral Courage of the Three Great Union Generals Affected Their Military Leadership.* Chicago: Ivan R. Dee, 1962.

Winschel, Terrence J. *Triumph and Defeat: The Vicksburg Campaign.* Mason City, Iowa: Savas, 1999.

Woodward, Bob. *The Commanders.* New York: Simon & Schuster, 1991.

Young, John Russell. *Around the World with General Grant: A Narrative of the Visit of General U. S. Grant, Ex-President of the United States.* New York: Subscription Book Department, American News, 1879.

## ARTICLES AND ESSAYS

Allen, Christopher J. "Devil's Own Day." *America's Civil War*, January 2000.

Allen, Stacy. "Shiloh: 2nd Day Battle and Aftermath." *Blue & Gray*, Spring 1997.

Anderson, Kevin. "Grant's Lifelong Struggle with Alcohol." *Columbiad*, Winter 1999.

Burden, Jeffry C. "Bloody Fight in Vain." *America's Civil War*, May 2000.

Epperson, James F. "The Chance Battle in the Wilderness." *Columbiad*, Spring 1998.

Fleming, Thomas. "Band of Brothers." *MHQ: The Quarterly Journal of Military History*, Special Issue: The Civil War, 1994.

Kaltman, Alvin. "Bill Clinton Is No Ulysses Grant." The *Washington Times*, September 28, 1998.

Lutz, Stephen D. "Grant's Ignoble Act: General Orders No. 11." *America's Civil War*, March 2000.

Mitchell, Brian. "Leaders and Success: Ulysses S. Grant." *Investors Business Daily*, August 10, 1998.

Morris, Roy, Jr. "Titans Clash in the Wilderness." *Military History*, April 1997.

————. "Ulysses S. Grant Could Thank Assistant Secretary of War Charles A. Dana for His New Command at Chattanooga." *America's Civil War*, March 2000.

Riggs, Derald T. "Commander in Chief Abe Lincoln." *America's Civil War*, July 2000.

Sears, Stephen W. "Lincoln and McClellan." In *Lincoln's Generals*, ed. Gabor Boritt. New York: Oxford University Press, 1995.

Simon, John Y. "Grant, Lincoln and Unconditional Surrender." In *Lincoln's Generals*, ed. Gabor Boritt. New York: Oxford University Press, 1995.

Smith, David M. "Too Little Too Late at Vicksburg." *America's Civil War*, May 2000.

## WEB SITES

The Ulysses S. Grant Association: http://www.lib.siu.edu/projects/usgrant
The Ulysses S. Grant Home Page: http://www.mscomm.com/~ulysses
The Ulysses S. Grant Network: http://saints.css.edu/mkelsey/gppg.html

# ACKNOWLEDGMENTS

FIRST OF ALL, I would like to thank Steven Martin of Prima Publishing, who first proposed this book to me after I had approached him about another. The entire staff at Prima, especially my editor, Andi Reese Brady, could not have been more courteous and helpful.

Frank J. Scaturro, a New York attorney, author of *President Grant Reconsidered* and chairman of the Ulysses S. Grant Monument Association, was an inexhaustible source of fact and opinion about Grant. Frank generously took time out from his busy schedule at his law firm to read the manuscript and saved me from many foolish errors.

Thanks to Elsa Lohman of the National Park Service, who guided me around the battlefields at the Wilderness and Spotsylvania. Ditto for Terry Winschel and Lieutenant Colonel Parker Hills at Vicksburg National Battlefield Park, as well as the staff at the Grant Monument in New York City. Also, Len Reidel and Becky Cumins at the Blue & Gray Education Society.

My friends at the Civil War Round Tables of New York, Nassau County, and the North Shore of Long Island—especially Patrick and Joan McDonough Falci, E. A. "Bud" Livingston, Paul Windels, Cass and Patty Baker, and Leonard Kornblum—fanned the flame of my Civil War enthusiasm and kept it burning bright throughout this project.

The Lehrmans, Lewis and his son Thomas, were great sources of inspiration and friendship and kindly arranged a grant for me to see this book through to completion.

Thanks also go to my colleagues at Pfizer Inc., Tom Sanford, Ray Jordan, Cathy Windels, Lou Clemente, and Hank McKinnell.

Thanks also to Lucianne Goldberg, who had acted as my literary agent on an earlier project. Even though she had gotten out of that business when fame was unexpectedly thrust upon her in another realm, she nevertheless graciously agreed to review the contract for this book and offer her advice.

My mother, Mary McAuliffe Barnes, my sister Joan, my brother Thomas, their spouses and children, along with Uncle Jerry McAuliffe, always enquired after my progress and urged me on. My late father, Thomas Desmond Barnes, remains in all our prayers. He will always be my personal "leadership model." My mother-in-law and father-in-law, Marilee and Jack Reiner, have been my "second parents" and among my most ardent fans. Jack, an attorney, also did me the favor of reviewing the business aspects of this book. My brother-in-law, Clark Reiner, offered support from his home in Los Angeles.

Finally, my wonderful wife, Mary, mother of our beloved daughter, Mary Elisabeth. Both offered me incomparable support while at the same time no doubt feeling like the last widow and orphan of the Civil War. I could not have done it without them.

# INDEX